Understanding
The Bible
In The
End Time

Understanding
The Bible
In The
End Time

Expanded Commentaries
On Age-Old Bible Questions

2nd Edition

Felix Jegede, Ph.D.

Copyright © 2022 by Felix Jegede, Ph.D.

All rights reserved. No part of this publication may be reproduced, distributed, or transmitted in any form or by any means, including photocopying, recording, or other electronic or mechanical methods without the prior written permission of the publisher. For permission requests, solicit the publisher via the address below through mail or email with the subject line "Attention: Publication Permission".

This publication contains the opinions and ideas of its author. It is intended to provide helpful and informative material on the subjects addressed in the publication. The author and publisher specifically disclaim all responsibility for any liability, loss, or risk, personal or otherwise, which is incurred as a consequence, directly or indirectly, of the use and application of any of the contents of this book.

Ordering Information:
You may search this book in Amazon, Barnes & Nobles and other online retailers by searching using the ISBN below.

This book was first published in 2020.

ISBN (eBook): 978-1-956135-54-1
ISBN (Paperback): 978-1-956135-55-8

Dedication

This book, *"Understanding The Bible In The End Time"*, is dedicated to Yehovah *(Jehovah)*, The Almighty God, My Father and Creator, The Owner, Possessor, Faithful Provider, and Sustainer of the heavens and earth with all in them, The Most High, The I AM That I AM, The Lord of Hosts, the God of love, mercy and grace, One who alone deserves all thanksgiving, glory, honor, praise, worship, adoration, majesty, and power, through Yehoshua *(Yeshua, Jesus)* of Nazareth, The Word, The Lamb, The BRANCH, The Messiah, Anointed King and Priest, Son of the Most High, the I AM Salvation From The I AM That I AM, in The Power of His Holy Spirit, *(Ruach Hakodesh)*, Amen!

Acknowledgements

All glory and thanksgiving to The Holy Three-In-One, who are the same, and who have at diverse times appeared to me, to assign and equip me for the writings:

To The Father, God Almighty, and Creator in Heaven, the One and only True God, and

To The Begotten Son Of The Father, Yeshua, The Messiah, the Redeemer and Giver of eternal life, The Lamb, The Wisdom, and Righteousness, and Sanctification, and Ransom for deliverance, The Branch, Anointed King and Priest over the coming Kingdom of God on Earth, (John 3:16, Zechariah 6:12-13, Isaiah 11:1, Jeremiah 23:5-6, 1 Corinthians 1:30), and

To The Holy Spirit my Helper, Comforter, Advocate, Intercessor, Sustainer, Companion, Guardian, Teacher, Instructor and Revealer of the deep things, even the very mind of The Father and of The Son unto me, (John 14:16-17, John 14:26, John 15:26, John 16:7-11, Revelation 5:6).

I also want to sincerely thank my wife and children for their love, patience and encouragements, whilst The LORD has been working with me on the writing of this and other end time books, as well as the End Time Bible, ETB and other assignments.

Acknowledgements

As before, I cannot acknowledge enough, all those, too many to list here, who have each been a source of great encouragement to me. The LORD God knows you all by name in His Book of Life, where the names of those who are His for eternal life are written, (Revelation 20:15).

The LORD does nothing, such as will affect humankind or the earth, until He first reveals it to His servants, (Amos 3:7). God is righteous, merciful and warns ahead to allow people to change their ways.

He revealed to Noah, towards the end of the first generation, and repeatedly warned them before the flood, (Genesis 6:13-14). God also first revealed the impending end of Sodom and Gomorrah to Abraham before their destruction in the days of Lot, (Genesis 18:17-19).

God is now also revealing to us in this generation, to know of what is soon to happen. The end of this world as we know it, and the destruction coming to the wicked.

God is the sovereign Creator who knew us all before we were created, (Jeremiah 1:5). Little did I know that God would assign me to deliver His end time messages to this generation. And neither did I know until The LORD Himself appeared to assign me to write the End Time Bible, ETB, for this generation. Now we have His Word in today's language to understand. We also have the end time books on events to come. And this book, *"Understanding The Bible In The End Time"*, provides expanded commentaries on selected verses or areas of the Bible, and age-old questions, that have been difficult for people to understand.

God The Father, as well as the Son and the Holy Spirit, have appeared to me face to face in bodily form together and separately at various times. I have thus become a living witness of the existence of All The Three in One, and also to hear and receive the messages directly from them, and at other times through His angels, for the world in this end time. It is for His glory, His Name, His Kingdom and for the salvation of souls to populate His Kingdom.

I bear no title except that am only a servant and messenger of God by His divine assignment for this generation, to alert all awaiting His trumpet call. I have no message of my own, similar to a loud speaker, assigned to echo what the Master, the Speaker, is saying to us for the end time. The loud speaker cannot add to or remove from what it is receiving. The loud speaker cannot of its own move from where it is kept until the owner, the Master, repositions it, if necessary. And for this, I have my own little thorn placed in me as a reminder, like He did to Apostle Paul, so that I would remain who He wants me to be in Him for His glory.

End Time Bible or ETB:

God speaks to us through His word, the Bible, which is empowered by His Holy Spirit. When God speaks, He does so with simplicity of language for us to know and to understand Him. While language may evolve with people over generations, the original meaning of God's message remains the same. It must not be changed, but preserved. This is why The *End Time Bible or ETB*, has been written in today's language that is clear and simple to understand.

The *End Time Bible or ETB*, is complete with both the Old and New Testament, in which no verses have been removed, altered, or corrupted, but all preserved. It also comes with helpful commentaries for greater understanding. It provides Cross referencing between verses, and makes End Time Events easy to identify, follow, and understand.

The *End Time Bible or ETB*, is written for both the Jews and the Gentiles alike and is also suitable for all: for personal use, family use, or group study. One main purpose of this Bible is to equip readers in the end time, waiting for The LORD to return. It also retains the original and modern measuring units and uses color schemes to know what is said and by whom.

Not written out of human will or desire, but solely from the instruction of The LORD Himself, *The End Time Bible* is about the Kingdom of God and His glory.

The End of Time Mysteries Unveiled:

The end time had been shrouded in mysteries for centuries. Then at the right time, God chose to unveil it to this generation, in our time. It started with the first book: *"The End of Time Mysteries Unveiled"*.

Finishing Strong In The End Time:

Consistent with His nature, as the loving and righteous God, He did not stop there. He followed through to show us how to get help from Him in the end times, to stand firm and finish strong. This is contained in the second book: *"Finishing Strong In The End Time"*.

End Time Countdown Messages:

The third book, *"End Time Countdown Messages"*, contains the undiluted truth of His word for the end time as the countdown starts. It provides clarity of truth, removing any ignorance, confusion, heresies, deception, and doubt about His plan. It also reveals how to identify deceivers, their workings and avoid being deceived. For in the end time, the Adversary will empower his agents with power and oratory to show great signs and wonders, with the purpose to deceive many. It will be such that if it were possible, they shall deceive the very elect, (Matthew 24:24).

Celebrating God's Faithfulness In The End Time:

The fourth book, *"Celebrating God's Faithfulness In The End Time"*, is about the coming fulfillment of The Feasts of the Lord. It is about God's coming harvests celebrations of His household, the body of the

Lord, Jews and Gentiles together for the End Time. God will harvest and fulfill in the End Time each of the Feasts, and in the order He originally commanded the Israelites of Old to celebrate. The Lord's Sabbath, Passover, FirstFruits, Pentecost, Trumpets, Atonement, Tabernacle & Ingathering, will be given their full meaning in the End Time. The book also provides understanding to the Church, pulpit and believers alike, about God's true desire and purposes for Offerings, Thanksgiving, Tithing, and Generous Free-will Giving and how do it God's way, the way that pleases and is acceptable to Him.

The Mirror Of The Timeline Of The End Time:

Being the same yesterday, today and forever, God has not changed in His methods and desires. This Fifth book, *"The Mirror Of The Timeline Of The End Time"*, reveals God's farming process with identical patterns for the past, present and future seasons. The book reveals God's objectives, plans and timeline for the coming harvest of His crops (God's people) for this generation, the number of those to be saved and God's plan for them, and the establishment of His Kingdom on earth, with His Son as the King and Priest, just as this second season ends and The Millennium, the third farming season starts. The book removes the fogs, like from a misty mirror, concerning the end time revelations and prophecies to provide clarity, connecting them clearly. This includes those of Zechariah which are as profound as those of Daniel for the end time, previously covered as in a mist or fog until the right time, and are now fully unveiled with clarity.

Understanding The Bible In The End Time:

The sixth book, *"Understanding The Bible In The End Time"* is about getting clarity to verses or sections of the Bible and some age-old questions that are difficult. For example, many want to know the beginning, What is the True Name of God?, why God has left the Devil to still be around? Why do believers still experience trials,

Acknowledgements

some so severe with anguish? Is it because of sin, or the Devil or some other reasons? How long are we expected to live? Why do some people die so early in life, how does God see death of a person, how should believers handle such? Why are unbelievers rich? Does God not want believers to be rich? What is The Day Of The LORD? Who will be the two end time prophets of God in Jerusalem? Are Elijah And John The Baptist the same or different? What does the Bible say about sexual immorality and unnatural relationships? What is the difference between the Antichrist and Gog of Magog? Does God have a seal or number for His own, just like the Antichrist will have for his followers to buy and sell? How many will be saved in the end time? What are the eight kingdoms ruling the world? What or where is Babylon the Great that the Bible talks about? What does the Bible say about the great tribulations in the end time?

This sixth book, *"Understanding The Bible In The End Time"* provides clarity on these and many other difficult verses or sections of the Bible, and age old questions.

Finally, I pray and commit to God Almighty, all who are eagerly awaiting the trumpet blast of the return of the Messiah, the King of kings and Lord of lords. I pray He will strengthen our hearts by His Spirit and preserve all who are His, in Him, and also all He has given unto each of us. I pray He will continue to empower us to daily bring glory to Him and to finish strong like the Master, (John 17:2-4). To strengthen and empower us to be faithful and effective co-laborers in this end time, as well as to be among His harvest when the trumpet sounds. His return will be sudden, like a thief in the night, (1 Thessalonians 5:2). May the love, mercy and grace of God the Father through His Son, the Messiah and Lamb, and the power of His Holy Spirit be with each and every one in Him. Amen!

End Time Books By Same Author

The End Time Books:

Book#1: "The End of Time Mysteries Unveiled", FelixJegede, Ph.D (2017)

Book#2: "Finishing Strong In The End Time", Felix Jegede, Ph.D (2017)

Book#3: "End Time Count Down Messages", Felix Jegede, Ph.D (2017)

Book#4: "Celebrating God's Faithfulness In The End Time", Felix Jegede, Ph.D (2018)

Book#5: "The Mirror Of The Timeline Of The End Time", Felix Jegede, Ph.D (2018)

Book#6: "Understanding The Bible In The End Time ", Felix Jegede, Ph.D (2020)

The Bible By Same Author

End Time Bible (ETB), Old & New Testaments, (2020).

Contents

Dedication v
Acknowledgements vii

Chapter 1: Introduction..1
Chapter 2: About The Beginnings..9
Chapter 3: About Why The Devil Is Still Around Not
 Yet Bound 15
Chapter 4: About Why Believers Are Severely Tested 20
Chapter 5: About The Name And Other Titles of God 55
Chapter 6: About The Jealous God And Consuming Fire 64
Chapter 7: About Past Sins And Generational Curses 68
Chapter 8: About Long Life And How Long 72
Chapter 9: About The Death Of Loved Ones 76
Chapter 10: About Statutes, Judgments, Testimonies of God 80
Chapter 11: About 'idols, gods, and God of gods' 82
Chapter 12: About Offering, Tithes & Giving 86
Chapter 13: About "Baal, Bel, Molech And National
 gods, idols, deities" 92
Chapter 14: About To Bless The LORD and The Blessed Person 96
Chapter 15: About The Revenge Of The Gibeonites...................98
Chapter 16: About Wisdom, Proverbs and Parables 100
Chapter 17: About King Solomon And Shulamite 103
Chapter 18: About Appearances Of God 105
Chapter 19: About The Three Groups in Zion in End Time......109
Chapter 20: About When Righteousness Is or Not Filthy Rags ..111

Chapter 21: About Asherah, Queen Of Heaven, Easter
And Passover 115
Chapter 22: About 70years of Captivity And the Three
Kings Of Babylon 120
Chapter 23: About The Thirtieth Year In Ezekiel 1:1 122
Chapter 24: About Three Righteous Men Noah, Daniel
and Job In Their Time 124
Chapter 25: About Gog of Magog And The Anti Christ
In Two End Times 126
Chapter 26: About King Jehoiakim And Daniel 132
Chapter 27: About The Little Horn And Hanukkah At
End Of The Greek Kingdom 135
Chapter 28: About The Kings Of The North And South
From Greece Kingdom 139
Chapter 29: About The Day Of The LORD In End Time 142
Chapter 30: About The Scribes, Pharisees, Sadducees,
Essenes and Herodians In Israel 147
Chapter 31: About Family Division, Love And Hate 151
Chapter 32: About Matthew, Mark And Luke Minor
Differential Emphasis of Details 156
Chapter 33: About A Hundred Fold Return For Losses
ForThe Kingdom Of God 162
Chapter 34: About Stars Falling From Heaven 169
Chapter 35: About Resurrected Saints Seen In Jerusalem 172
Chapter 36: About Elijah And John The Baptist Identical
Ministry 175
Chapter 37: About The Roman Empire, Syria And Jerusalem 179
Chapter 38: About The First Disciples First Meeting
With Yeshua 182
Chapter 39: About The Only Begotten Son Of God 185
Chapter 40: About The Resurrection And Early
Appearances Of The LORD 187
Chapter 41: About Sexual Immorality And Unnatural
Relationships 195
Chapter 42: About Grace And Being Dead To Sin 199
Chapter 43: About Spiritual Warfare And Authority 203

Chapter 44: About End Time Apostasy And Troublesome Times 207
Chapter 45: About The Two Veils—The Temple Veil And Tabernacle Veil 211
Chapter 46: About The Nicolaitans 215
Chapter 47: About The Two Witnesses In The End Time 217
Chapter 48: About The War In Heaven And The Great Persecution 223
Chapter 49: About The Seal Of God And Number Of The Beast 226
Chapter 50: About The Eight World Super Kingdoms 231
Chapter 51: About The Great City, Babylon The Prostitute 234
Chapter 52: About Trials And Temptations 237
Chapter 53: About The Coming Severe Tribulations In End Time 243
Chapter 54: About Believers Not Made Poor And Unbelievers Rich 247
Chapter 55: About The Blood Of The LAMB For Protection 255
Chapter 56: About The Believer, 5G, Coronavirus, Microchip In The End Time 266
Chapter 57: About The Future Glory of The Temple In End Time 291
Chapter 58: About The Eight Main Stages Of The End Time 296

Chapter 1

Introduction

There are many verses or sections of the Bible, as well as some age-old questions that are still difficult for readers and believers to fully understand. When they are not understood, it creates ignorance. For example, the Scripture encourages us to bless, call, confess, declare, glorify, magnify, praise, remember, sing, and trust the Name of GOD. But what is the True Name of God? If the Name is not The LORD, then what is it? Why is the Devil still around and God has not removed him away or put him in hell? Also why do believers still experience trials, some so severe, with much anguish? Are they not the beloved holy people of God or Is it because of sin? Or How long are we expected to live? Why do people die early? How does God feel and what should be our attitude? How is the promise of hundred fold return for losses for Kingdom Of God fulfilled? Why are unbelievers rich? Does God not want believers to be rich? What are the three godly ways for believers to be rich?

The Scripture mentions The Day Of The LORD. What is that Day? Is it just one day or more than one, and what will happen? Will stars actually fall from heaven in the end time? Will there be war in heaven in end time? What does the Bible say about the great tribulations in the end time? The Antichrist will have a number for his followers to buy and sell. Will God have a seal or number for His own? Some sects go around saying only a small number of people will be saved in the end time. Is it not heresy? Does the Bible actually give the

Introduction

number people that will be saved in the end time? Or Who will be the two end time prophets of God in Jerusalem? Are Elijah And John The Baptist the same or different? The Bible mentions the man of sin, the Beast, the Antichrist, and Gog of Magog. What is the difference between them or are they the same? Or What are the eight kingdoms ruling the world? Or What or where is Babylon the Great?, Or What does the Bible say about sexual immorality and unnatural relationships? and several other questions.

This sixth book, *"Understanding The Bible In The End Time"* is about getting clarity on these and many other difficult verses or sections of the Bible, and age old questions. The book provides expanded commentaries for people to understand these for the end time.

We start in Chapter 2 with discussing from the Scriptures of all the three beginnings, including of the universe, earth, mankind, the beginning of the angels and of the beginning of beginnings, that relate to God and the Trinity. We also discuss, the ending of everything, including the earth, universe, and the start of a new a beginning with a new earth and new heaven.

The Devil, was bad before the creation of Adam and Eve. But why did God or Yeshua not bind the Devil and send him to hell. Why does God allow Satan to have so much power to continue to roam around. We discuss these in Chapter 3.

The Bible says Yeshua The Messiah came that we may have life and have it more abundantly. But why do believers experience severe trials and afflictions. These are explained in Chapter 4 along with the cycles.

The Scripture encourages us as the Children of God to Bless, Call, Confess, Declare, Glorify, Magnify, Praise, Remember, Sing, and Trust the Name of GOD. The question is, what is the Name of God? The True Name of God, as well as the other known Titles of God are discussed in Chapter 5.

The Bible says God is a Jealous God and a consuming fire. What does this really mean? These are discussed in Chapter 6.

In Chapter 7, we discuss about past sins and general curses. How has Yeshua taken care of these and how can we be free from them?

How long does the Scripture say we are expected to live, if it does say so? Is it 120years, or 70years or neither? These are discussed in Chapter 8.

Let us see what the Scripture says about death? How does God feel or see the death of people? What should be the attitude of believers when someone they love or know dies?. These and more are discussed in Chapter 9.

The Old Testament talks a lot about Statutes, Judgments, Testimonies of God. We see what they are in Chapter 10.

God hates idols. And when the Bible says God is the 'God of gods' what does it mean. Chapter 11 discusses about idols, 'gods', etc.

In Chapter 12, we discuss about Offering, Tithes & Giving. We also discuss that the New Testament says about them.

And what are Baal, Bel, Molech and National gods, Idols, Deities? These are discussed in Chapter 13.

Who is a blessed person and how do we bless The LORD? These are discussed in Chapter 14.

Chapter 15 discusses The Revenge of The Gibeonites, while Chapter 16 discusses Wisdom, Proverbs And Parables.

King Solomon had 700 wives and 300 concubines. But who was the Shulamite and why did King Solomon singled her out to show so much love and affection? These are discussed in Chapter 17.

Introduction

Chapter 18 discusses about the various Appearances Of God and Chapter 19 discusses about The Three Groups that will be with The LORD in Zion.

The Scripture says all our righteousness is like filthy rags. But when is a righteous act not filthy. These are discussed in Chapter 20.

Chapter 21 discusses about Asherah, the Queen Of Heaven. It also discusses why Easter popularly celebrated with eggs, bunny, rabbits, etc is not Scriptural. It is very different from Passover which is what believers should be celebrating.

Chapter 22 discusses about 70years of captivity of Israel and the Three Kings Of Babylon.

Chapter 23 explains what is meant by the Thirtieth Year In Ezekiel 1:1.

Chapter 24 discusses about three righteous men of their times, Noah, Daniel and Job.

What is the difference between the Antichrist and Gog of Magog? Will they appear together or at different end times. These are discussed in Chapter 25.

Chapter 26 discusses about the times and exile of King Jehoiakim And Daniel.

What is the origin of Hanukkah and who was the Little Horn And Hanukkah of the Greek Kingdom. These are all explained in Chapter 27.

Chapter 28 discusses the Kings Of The North and of the South from the Greece Kingdom.

What does the Scripture mean by The Day Of The LORD? Is it just one day, and when will it be? These are discussed in Chapter 29.

Who were the Scribes, Pharisees, Sadducees, Essenes and Herodians in Israel at the time of Yeshua? These are discussed in Chapter 30.

Yeshua the Messiah said His coming was not peace to earth, but war. It will bring family conflict and whoever loves his father or mother more than Him is not worthy of Him. What these mean are discussed in Chapter 31.

In Chapter 32, we will compare and discuss the Gospels according to Matthew, Mark and Luke. We will see how there is little or no differences in their accounts.

Yeshua The Messiah said that anyone who has left houses or brothers or sisters or father or mother or wife or children or lands, for the sake of His Name, will receive a hundred times over, and will obtain eternal life. What this means and how it is fulfilled is discussed in Chapter 33.

Yeshua The Messiah said in the end time, just before He returns, stars will fall from heaven to earth. What does this mean? Is it literal falling of stars or a metaphor, a figure of speech, and how will this be in the end time? These are discussed in Chapter 34.

In Chapter 35 we discuss about Resurrected Saints seen in Jerusalem when Yeshua died on the cross.

Are Elijah And John The Baptist the same or different? Why are they mentioned so much in connection with the coming of The Messiah? These are discussed in Chapter 36.

Chapter 37 discusses about the Roman Empire, Syria and Jerusalem during the time of Yeshua on earth.

Who were the first Disciples of Yeshua The Messiah? When did they meet and what happened afterwards? These are discussed in Chapter 38.

Introduction

The Scripture refers to angels, and even humans as sons of God. So what does it mean that about the only Begotten Son Of God? This is discussed in Chapter 39.

Chapter 40 discusses about the resurrection of The LORD and those He had appeared to, as witnesses. Why were the disciples not the first to see Him?

What does the Bible say about sexual immorality and unnatural relationships? Today many countries all over the world have same gender sexual relation, sodomy, homosexuality lesbian, gay, bisexual, transgender, queer, intersex, asexual, lesbigay, bestiality, zoophilia and others. And some of them identify themselves with those who go to Church. What does God or the Scripture say? What should be the believers attitude? These are all discussed in Chapter 41.

The Scripture says salvation is by grace, a free gift from God. Does a believer still have any responsibility? Are the past, present and future sins wiped out? What does it mean that those in The Messiah (Christ) are dead to sin? These are all discussed in Chapter 42.

How does the believer fight the enemy and win? Chapter 43 discusses about the Spiritual warfare, the authority, and weapons of the believer.

Chapter 44 discusses about the End Time Apostasy of believers, the man of sin and the troublesome times ahead that believers should know about.

What is the implication of the Temple veil being torn, and about the Tabernacle Veil that was not torn for the believer? These are discussed in Chapter 45.

Who are the Nicolaitans that Yeshua was referring to in the Revelation to Apostle John, and are they still around? These are discussed in Chapter 46.

The Book of Revelation says there will be two witnesses or prophets in the end time. Who will they be? Will they be Moses and Elijah, or Enoch and Elijah, or Elijah and John The Baptist, or Elijah and Apostle John, or some others mentioned in the Bible? If they are, then why? And if they would not be, why? These are discussed in Chapter 47.

Chapter 48 discusses about the coming end time war in Heaven and the great persecution on earth.

The Antichrist and false prophets will provide special identification numbers '666' for their followers. And anyone who does not have it cannot buy or sell on earth in the end time. What about the believers of Yeshua The Messiah? Does God have His own number or seal for them? These are discussed in Chapter 49.

The Book of Revelation mentions eight world rulers. It says 'Five of them have fallen. One is presently ruling (the world) as we speak. But the seventh one is yet to come. And when he comes, he must continue to rule over the world for a short time (till the eight kingdom comes). The Beast that was once alive, but is not alive on earth at the present, is himself also the eighth king'. (Revelation 17:10-11). What are these world rulers? What is the current number? The Eight World Super Kingdoms and their effect on Israel are discussed in Chapter 50.

Chapter 51 discusses where is the Great City, Babylon the prostitute? Does the city exists today or is it in the future?

Chapter 52 discusses the sufferings of Job, as well as about trials and temptations in general.

Chapter 53 discusses the great tribulations in the end time.

Introduction

Until Yeshua comes, believers will continue to live on this earth and God will continue to provide the best things for them. In Chapter 54 we discuss why unbelievers get rich. We also discuss why God wants believers to be blessed and rich. We discuss the ungodly, satanic ways to get rich, and the godly, God's way for believers to get rich.

There will be deadly pestilences or plagues and arrows of the enemy as the world moves into the end time. Anointing Oil has its place. But more powerful protection for the believer from death is through the blood of The LAMB of God. Chapter 55 discusses this as well as the promises of God.

Chapter 56 enlightens the Believers in The LORD about 5G, Coronovirus, MicroChips and their end time implications.

The Future Glorious Temple of The LORD In End Time is discussed in Chapter 57

Finally, Chapter 58 summarizes the events of the end time in Eight main stages.

Chapter 2

About The Beginnings

Scriptural Verses:

Genesis 1:1 (ETB)*: In the beginning of the creation of the universe, God (Elohim) created the heavens and the earth, [ref John 1:3, Hebrews 1:2, Colossians 1:16].*

John 1:1-3 (ETB)*:1 In the beginning was The WORD! The WORD was with God, and The WORD was God,[ref Psalm 90:2, John 1:1-2, John 17:5, Revelation 19:13].*

2 He was existing with God from the very beginning. 3 Everything was created (brought into existence) by Him. There was nothing created, except through Him, [ref Genesis 1:1, John 1:3, Hebrews 1:2]

Explanation:

There are three separate types of beginnings referred to in the Scriptures. The first relates to God and the Trinity from eternity past. The second is the Beginning of Angels. The third is the Beginning of the creation of everything else including the earth.

The Beginning Of Beginnings:

There is the beginning of beginnings, which goes back to Eternity. It is of God, Elohim, The Creator. No other existed before or bequeathed to God, but He created everything, (Job 41:11). He is the eternal God. He always was, He always is, and He always will be. He has been the God of all from everlasting past. He is now, and will continue to be forever and ever, (Psalm 90:2).

In this beginning of beginnings, God The Father, God The Son, referred to as The Word, and God The Holy Spirit had always existed, (Psalm 90:2, John 1:1-2, John 17:5 and Revelation 19:13). They are One and were not created. But from them came everything else. The Father is like the Architect or Designer of everything. The Son is like the Creator or Builder. The Holy Spirit is the Finisher, the Beautifier of what has been created.

The Son shared the same identity and glory with the Father from the beginning, (John 17:5). The Son is the Creator of everything else, (John 1:3, Colossians 1:16). It is through The Son that all things were created, in heaven and on earth, visible and invisible, whether thrones, or dominions, or principalities, or powers: All things were created by Him and for Him, (John 1:3, 1 Corinthians 8:6, Colossians 1:16).

It is impossible for a mere object such as a paper car or a paper aeroplane or any toy to try to know or fathom the origin of the person who made or designed it. The created object does not have such a capacity. And that is who we are! We are like the mere object and in fact the Scripture describes us as mere empty breath, (Psalm 144:3-4, James 4:14). It would be impossible for us to understand or fathom the origin of our Creator. This is regardless of how smart we may think we are or what extraordinary abilities we may possess, which The Creator has kindly bestowed on us. A person who is really smart, will know the smart thing to do is to stop wasting time on what is totally impossible or unfathomable. He has created us for His own pleasure, (Revelation 4:11, Ephesians 2:10, Ecclesiastes 12:13). And with this understanding, the best course of action is to focus on knowing the purpose for which each of us has been created. It is to focus on knowing and fulfilling that purpose for the pleasure of the Creator. It is to fear Him and obey His commandments. This is the conclusion of the wisest man who ever lived on earth, (Ecclesiastes 12:13).

The Beginning Of The Angels:

The Angels have their own beginning because they were created by God. We do not know how or when they were created. Angels worship and serve God day and night, (though no nights in heaven). Angels are also ministering spirits sent out to minister, caring for the needs of those who will inherit salvation of God, (Psalm 104:4, John 3:5-8, Revelation 14:6-7).

The earth is not where they live, but they have their own abode assigned to them in the heavenly by God. It is in the heavens above the earth, but below God's highest of heavens.

The Angels, had been created and were existing before the creation of the earth. They witnessed the creation of the earth. The Scripture tells us that the morning stars (Angels) sang together, and all the sons of God shouted for joy when the earth was created, (Job 38:7). If the earth is billions of years old, then The Angels are much older than that.

The angels possess the ability to pass through any material objects, and not be seen by the human eye. So they are called spirits. But from time to time, they make themselves visible, as may be necessary in their assignments. There are angels around us at anytime. They record in the Book of Records the words or actions of each person, (Revelation 20:13).

Just like we have good and bad human beings, there are also good and bad angels or spirits. Angels also had the freedom to make their own choices after their creation, (just like humans were given freedom to do the same). At some point in the past, perhaps billions of years ago, some of them sinned due to sinful choice through pride and disobedience. They became corrupted, and were separated from God and the good angels, (Isaiah 14:12-17, Ezekiel 28:12-19). The good Angels love God and are devoted to serving Him. They cannot be corrupted again and live forever. The bad ones are disobedient, opposing God, and wanting to do things their own way as they want. Some of the bad angels are in hell, and would all end up in the lake of fire, with Satan and the human beings who are also disobedient to God, (Revelation 12:7-10, Revelation 20:10, Isaiah 66:24).

The Beginning Of The Earth And Material Universe:

We know little or nothing about the world of the angels. The beginning of angels and their world do not concern us. What really concerns us is about our own world, our own beginning, how God loves and relates to us, and how we can please Him. And the Scripture has revealed these to us. In addition, the Scripture tells us of the earth and creation of things in it by God.

The beginning spoken of in Genesis 1:1 is of the creation of the Universe, the heavenly bodies, the galaxies, the stars, the earth, the moon and the things in them. This is the beginning also referred to in John 1:3 and Hebrew 1:2. It is within this that the earth has its own beginning.

When the earth was first created, it was disorderly like a mass of dust and gas, before it became a solid. Then it was empty for a while, covered in darkness, before The Holy Spirit moved over the surface, (Genesis 1:2).

After this, came the creation of the things we see today on the earth. This includes human beings, animals (on earth, seas and in the sky,) the plants and vegetations we see.

Adam and Eve had Cain first, and then Abel who was murdered by Cain, (Genesis 4:1-12). They also had Seth and other male and female children. It was from these women that Cain, Seth and other male children of Adam took wives for themselves.

From Adam to Noah were ten generations, (Genesis 5:1-32). And from the time Adam was created, to when the flood came was about 1,656 years. Noah's father, Lamech died about four years before the flood. And Methuselah, the grandfather of Noah, died the same year that the flood came.

The entire ten generations of humans, from Adam to Noah's time, either died before or were destroyed by the flood, due to extreme wickedness, (Genesis 6:1-7, Genesis 7:11-24). But Noah found favor with God. So Noah and his wife, their three sons, Japheth, Shem and Ham and their wives, a total of eight of people, were saved, (Genesis 6:8-10, Genesis 7:7). Every human being from after the flood till now, is descended from one of the three sons of Noah.

The End of This Generation, The Earth And Universe

In Noah's time, the peopled turned away from God and went their own wicked ways. The same is happening in this generation, where more and more have turned away from God, and gone their own wicked ways. The end for this generation is fast approaching. But the wicked will not die by flood. Instead it would be by a series of various trumpet warnings and woes in the end time. It will start from when the seals start to be opened, (Genesis 6:1). It will continue through to the seventh seal, (Revelation 16). And the last of the wicked, along with the antichrist and false prophet will be eliminated when The LORD physically returns to the earth, (Revelation 19:19-21). This will lead to the millennium reign, and then the second rebellion of

Satan with the people on earth. Then will come the final judgment of all human race on earth, of the fallen angelic beings, of Satan and the universe, (Revelation 20:7-15).

A New Earth And Universe In The End:

The earth as it currently is, has been polluted with sin and evil of all kinds by human beings. The heavenly (expanse of the sky) is also polluted by Satan and his evil angels who will be expelled down to earth, (Revelation 12:7-9). Then they will stay in hell, and then finally be thrown in hell fire, (Revelation 20:3, Revelation 20:10).

The created have polluted their abodes through their choice of disobedience to God. Due to these pollutions, there will be the creation of a new earth and a new heaven, expanse of the sky, (Revelation 21:1).

However, this new heaven does not include the highest of the heavens where God is, in purity and holiness. God's highest of heavens has never and can never be polluted. It would not need to be recreated.

CHAPTER 3

About Why The Devil Is Still Around Not Yet Bound

Luke 10:18-20 (ETB): *Yeshua said to them: "Yes, I saw Satan fall like lightning from heaven! 19 Look, (know this), that I have given you the authority to trample on serpents and scorpions, and over all the power of the enemy. Nothing will be able to hurt you!, [ref Matthew 16:19, Matthew 18:18, Mark 16:15-18, Luke 10:19, Philippians 2:9-11]. 20 However, do not rejoice just because the unclean (evil, demonic) spirits submit to you. But instead, rejoice because your names are written in the Book of Life in Heaven!",[ref Matthew 7:21-23, Revelation 20:11-15].*

Revelation 20:1-3 (ETB): *1 Then I saw an angel coming down from heaven. He was holding the key to the bottomless pit. He also had great chain in his hand, [ref Revelation 9:1, Revelation 20:1]. 2 He took hold of the Dragon, that Serpent of old, who is the Devil and Satan. The angel bound Satan for a thousand years (1,000 years), [ref Revelation 16:13-16]. 3 Then the angel threw the Dragon into the bottomless pit. He locked him up and placed a seal on him. This is so that the Devil would not deceive the nations any more, until the thousand years were finished. But after that, it would be necessary to release the Devil for a little while (a short period of time). [ref Isaiah 24:21-22].*

Revelation 20:10 (ETB): *10 Then the Devil, who deceived them, was thrown into the lake of fire and brimstone where the beast and the false* *prophet are. And they will be tormented there, day and night forever and ever, [ref Isaiah 24:21-22, Revelation 13:11-17, Revelation 19:20, Revelation 20:10].*

Believers Have Authority As Children Of God

A believer should not be focused on binding the Devil, but on doing what pleases The LORD.

The Devil is known or called by several names, such as Lucifer, Dragon, Serpent of old, Devil, Accuser, Adversary, Deceiver, Satan, prince of power of the air, the god of this present world, etc, who deceives the entire world, (Genesis 3:1-7, Matthew 4:3-11, Luke 4:3-13, Revelation 12:7-9, Revelation 20:7-8).

All believers are workers for God to build His kingdom on earth. They have been sent out on assignments for the Kingdom of God, to preach the gospel of Good News of Salvation and to win souls. To do this, the LORD Yeshua has given believers authority, (Matthew 28:18-20, Mark 16:15-18, Matthew 10:1, Matthew 24:14, Mark 13:10, Matthew 16:19, Matthew 18:18, Philippians 2:9-11, Luke 10:19-20).

So believers have authority from Yeshua The Messiah over the kingdom of darkness. However, many do not know what that means and when they are allowed to apply it or cannot apply it.

Do Not Look For A Fight or To Bind The Devil

Some say they have bound or are binding the Devil. Some say they have or are sending him to hell. Binding the Devil or sending the Devil to hell are both unscriptural. If they have been able to pray to bind Satan, how come he is still very much around on earth, and even near the believer, causing much havocs.

Some others say they are not fighting the Devil. And that is wise. Indeed no one should go looking for the Devil for a fight with him, no matter how spiritually strong they think they are. For this is not how God does things. And God has not called, assigned or sent anyone to go looking for the Devil to fight him. It is a waste of time and a misplaced purpose.

We do not initiate or set the fight with Satan. He does and will bring the fight or try to challenge the believer or interfere with the assignment God has for us. And when this happens, the Scripture says we should resist the Devil and he will flee, (James 4:7). He will do so because we are living and working for God in total obedience to His will, desire and assignment to the praise and glory of His Name! As long as the believer is living or working in obedience to God, the Devil will flee. If the believer is living a life of disobedience or acting in disobedience, the believer is not much better than the Devil. So the Devil may refuse to flee!

So everyone should be focused on doing what pleases The LORD, what has been assigned to the person, leading to the salvation of souls. This is what God wants. This was the focus of Yeshua The Messiah. And if Yeshua came across a soul that was being oppressed, needing or wanting to be rescued and set free, then He exercised the authority to deliver the person. That is the spiritual order of things.

Many times before Yeshua did anything for the oppressed, He will ask the person, 'What do you want me to do for you?'. Other times, He will say to the person, 'Your faith has made you whole', (Mark 5:34, Mark 10:51-52, Luke 17:19, Luke 18:41). When He ask 'what do you want me to do for you?' He wanted them to make a declaration by themselves for the salvation available from God through Him. Yeshua was also spiritually discerning. He knows when people have by themselves chosen the kingdom of God over that of darkness. So when He says 'your faith has made you whole', He is simply confirming the choice the people have made. They have chosen to place their faith in God and not in the Devil. They have chosen salvation or deliverance from God over the oppression of the kingdom of darkness.

The LORD Yeshua did not go out looking to fight the Devil or to arrest him. It was not like He did not know where the Devil was or had not seen or met the Devil. He knew where the Devil was and they met several times. He met the Devil face to face during His temptation, saw him all the time He was preaching, and even fought and defeated him on the cross. He won the victory. He did not bind the Devil and kept him in hell or lake of fire. He could have done this very easily. God Himself could have done this before we were born or Adam was created. But both God the Father and Yeshua The Son and Messiah did not do so. What He told the Devil during the temptation was "'Be gone from Me, you Satan!', (Luke 4:8). He said the same thing when Peter was being influenced by the Devil to speak against the purpose of God for Yeshua that He would not die on the cross, (Matthew 16:22-23). He did not bind Satan. Not even the angels of God went fighting or to bind the Devil yet. They did not even rail insults against him, (Jude 1:9). What they all did was to rebuke him.

This was because Yeshua and the angels also knew that God has His planned time for everything. The time to bind and throw Satan into hell or lake of fire had not yet come. He knew God's plan and desire. And the Scripture tells us that the Devil will continue to roam around like a roaring lion looking for who to devour (1 Peter 5:8). There is a set time by God, as The LORD returns, when the Devil will be arrested and imprisoned, (Revelation 20:1-10). But the time is not now. God still has a purpose to leave Satan unbound as he is for now.

And here are two of such purposes: For the Devil serves as agent to test the faith and total love of believers for God. For God Himself does not test or tempt or afflict, but it is the Devil and his agents that do it. Secondly the Devil also serves as the leader and father of those who are disobedient to God, who reject God and are heading to hell. They belong to the Devil who is their father, (John 8:44). They will together go to hell or lake of fire in the end with the Devil, the Antichrist, and the false prophet, (Revelation 19:19-20, Revelation 20:10, Revelation 20:11-15).

So for now, the Devil cannot be bound. But he can be rebuked and told to move away, when he tries to interfere with God's assignment given to us. He may try to challenge us, but He cannot violate the will of God. No one can or should waste time thinking or trying to fight or bind him. We should focus on doing the will and assignment of God, to preach the good news of salvation from God through Yeshua to people. Preach the word of God to people, like spreading seed on the soil, not knowing which will receive it or not.

The spiritual order of things is for people by themselves to make the choice to follow God or to follow Satan. They cannot be forced. People who are tired of their oppression and wanting deliverance is an indication they have willingly chosen to be delivered and saved by God. The authority is there to save them and the Devil cannot do anything about it. But those that have chosen to remain with him, there is nothing anyone can do. No one can convert anyone, for conviction and repentance is of the Holy Spirit.

Lesson: God has not assigned anyone to go looking for the Devil to fight the Devil for Him. Also, no one has been given the authority to bind the Devil. For this is not how God does things. For if God wanted, the Devil could have been bound and taken away by now, even before we were born. Yeshua could have easily done that. However, believers have the authority to rebuke the Devil in the Name of Yeshua if or when Satan tries to challenge us as we go doing the assignment of God. God's assignment to the believer is to preach, spread the gospel of good news for all lost souls to hear. Those who hear the message and are tired of the oppression of the kingdom of darkness, can be then saved and delivered from the hold of the kingdom of darkness.

CHAPTER 4

About Why Believers Are Severely Tested

Scriptural Verses:

John 15:1-2 (ETB): 1 "I am the True Vine, and My Father is the Vinedresser (Farmer). 2 He cuts away every branch in Me that does not produce fruit. But He prunes (cleanses away filth from) every branch that produces fruit, for it to produce more fruit.

Psalm 34:19(ETB): Many are the troubles that beset the righteous person. But The LORD delivers him out of them all. 20 He protects all his bones. Not one of them gets broken.

Job 13:15(ETB): Though He slays me, yet will I trust Him. I will defend (keep, maintain) my own ways before Him.

Introduction

When a believe remains focused on doing what pleases The LORD, loving and obedient to Him, even the enemy becomes frustrated in his battle and gives up. For within or out of trials, God is looking to see our commitment, obedience and love for Him. He cannot turn His back on the believer who is committed, faithful, loves and is obedient to Him. He is jealous over such a person and goes all out to help the person.

This chapter has been written based on what I have learnt directly from The LORD from my experience with Him. For as I was writing this chapter, on why believers get severely tested to the point of despair, I myself was also in the middle of a major storm, trial of faith, which got even worse and seemed like no way out. I had been working on something for about five years, and had staked everything on it. But it seemed like nothing was left. It was like a do or die scenario. I had applied all manners of faith, and quoted all kinds of Scriptures to remind God why it must never fail. It took a long time coming, and like I had reached the end. Then I decided to hand it over completely to God. I told Him that even in the midst of impending failure, all I want was for Him to take every iota of glory that may be left or may come from it, all for Himself. Then I began to praise Him like never before.

From that point on, God began to use it to unfold things about trials to me, step by step to the end. Then I began to understand, daily writing things, as The Spirit was teaching me, and finished at the same time as at end of the storm. On the day it reached a climax, I had reached a decision that whatever happened, whether He rescued it or not, I will not flinch in my dedication, love or obedience to God. So my love and commitment to God and the assignment He gave me never wavered. It became clear that God was using the whole thing to teach me the lessons, for me to write them down, not just from the Scriptures alone, but from personal experience. Then I realized it fits in completely with the Scripture and what others had gone through, though different. This has made it richer and more meaningful. God used it to teach me things, and from which this chapter has been written to be more helpful to all believers.

Many believers daily go through various tests in life. Though the wind of the signs of the end is starting to blow all over the world, but the end itself has not yet taken place. The Antichrist and False prophets are approaching the stage, but have not yet taken their positions of power. And The LORD has not appeared yet. But as we wait for His return, we still daily continue to live our lives here on earth. As a result, we constantly see, encounter or experience challenges or trials of varying degrees.

Many believers out there are going through one storm or the other. And it is not because of any sin. Some of the challenges can be quite perplexing and take people to the point of extreme despair. This chapter provides deeper understand on why believers face trials and challenges. It also helps believers to understand the godly way to handle the storms of life and remain standing.

And all the glory be to Him who never fails to give victory to those who trust in Him, Amen.

The Unbelievers Seem At Ease Without Disturbance

Those who are not of God belong to the Devil. They are already under the Devil as their ruler. They do not need to be tested or afflicted to fall or be brought in subjection to him. What he does in their case is to maintain them in their imprisoned state. He gives them what keeps them there. So, they seem to go on enjoying the things of the world untouched or disturbed.

They are boastful, at ease, prosper with much abundance and increase in riches. But they are on a slippery slope, heading to their destruction with no hope of eternal life with God, (Psalm 73:1-28). As such the believer in The LORD must however never be envious of them.

Unlike the unbelievers under him as his slaves, the Devil sees the believer as an opponent. Therefore he does take advantage of every opportunity he has to attack them.

Lesson#1: The first lesson is that a believer must never be jealous of an unbeliever. The unbeliever may seem prosperous and untroubled, but has no relationship with God or hope of eternal life with Him. The unbeliever is held a prisoner, a slave under Satan and on a slippery slope to destruction.

Who Is The Believer

But who is the believer? The Scripture says: 'For God so loved the world that He gave His only begotten Son, that whosoever believes in Him will not perish but have everlasting life', (John 3:16). The Scripture further says: 'If you confess with your mouth that Yeshua is The LORD and believe in your heart that God has raised Him from the dead, you will be saved. 10 For it is by believing in your heart that you are made righteous with God. And it is by confessing with your mouth that you are saved', (Romans 10:9-10).So the believer is anyone who has confessed their sins with their mouth, believes in the heart, accepting Yeshua The Messiah as LORD and savior. When the person does that, the sins of the person are forgiven. From that moment on, the person is a new creature in Him, and the old nature is gone, (2 Corinthians 5:17). The person is regarded as a believer and a follower of The LORD Yeshua. The believer is covered by the righteousness of God through Yeshua The Messiah, (1 Corinthians 1:30). The believer has also spiritually become a part of the body of The LORD, and is seated with Him in the heavenly places far above powers and principalities, (Ephesians 1:20-21).

Lesson#2: The second lesson is that a believer has been saved, has relationship with God and has hope of eternal life through Yeshua The Messiah. The believer has the righteousness of God, and is spiritually seated with Yeshua in the heavenly places far above powers and principalities.

Oppression Versus Trial of Faith By Affliction

To be oppressed is to be under the power of another. It is to be a slave and servant to the rulership or dominion of another. Many people are being oppressed, enslaved, under the dominion of the Kingdom of darkness. When they hear the message of God, they have to by themselves make a choice as to what they want. They choose whether they want to be set free or not. When they choose to be set free, then the authority and power is released through the Name of Yeshua The Messiah for them to be free. The believer exercises this authority to set the oppressed freed. The Devil cannot contest this and will fail if he tries to. Those that have thus been set free, become like a new creature and are free in Yeshua The Messiah. If however they decide to remain with the Devil, then nothing can be done for them and the Devil will contest it. Any authority exercised by the believer or minister will be like using trying to use a physical authority over a spiritual authority. It will be meaningless, resisted and unfruitful or at best the result will be temporary. For God does not use force for anyone to accept His love and salvation. Accepting the love and salvation of God must first be a personal decision by the individual and then the person can be helped.

On the other hand, the trial of faith by affliction is not suffering in slavery or imprisonment under the kingdom of darkness led by the Devil. It is a state of temporary discomfort brought on through a contention or resistance against the opposing power. It comes to a believer through the test or trial to confirm the believer's choice, love and obedience to God. This is what believers go through when they are under trial of faith, through a struggle or affliction with the enemy. It is a state of not allowing the enemy to win or take control but to resist it, regardless of the sacrifice or what it takes. The believer resists the Devil, and in so doing show total love and obedience to God.

Lesson#3: The believer cannot be oppressed or enslaved by the Devil or agents of the kingdom of darkness. But the believer can experience trial of faith with affliction to prove or confirm their choice, total love and obedience to God.

From The Old Covenant To The New Covenant And Today

No one is immune from being tested, regardless of whether they were of the old covenant or of the new covenant in Yeshua The Messiah.

Some do not believe the Devil exists. But the Scripture tells us the Devil exists and we see the manifestation of evil day after day in this world. Some who believe the Devil exists add that those of the old covenant like Abraham, Job, etc did not have the benefit of the new covenant. They conclude that was the reason why they suffered from all kinds of attacks from the Devil.

And they further argue that anyone who is a believer in The LORD Yeshua, is above and should never have any attack from the Devil. Then they say Yeshua defeated the Devil on the cross and imprisoned him forever. It is true Yeshua by His victory has placed the believer far above the Devil, principalities, powers and demonic agents of the kingdom of darkness. However, the Devil has not been imprisoned yet. He was freely roaming around in the days of Job before Yeshua came to defeat him. He is still free today to roam about and will continue to do so until the second coming of Yeshua, when he will be imprison for 1000 years, (Revelation 20:1-3). And just because he is spiritually defeated and below (weaker than) believers does not mean he has been stopped from continuing to try and attack believers, who physically live on earth. The Scripture says, be sober, be vigilant, be alert, for your adversary, the Devil is roaming around like a roaring lion, looking for who do devour, (1 Peter 5:8).

They confuse demonic oppression with a believer's affliction, suffering or trial of faith. Believers should not suffer from demonic oppression or dominion. They are in the Kingdom of God and not of the darkness. The kingdom of darkness has no dominion or authority over them. However, both kingdoms are in constant contention. And the believer can experience trial of faith as permitted by God through affliction or suffering.

They also add that the believer in Yeshua under the new covenant is much more than those of the old, including even John The Baptist. That is true. Indeed, the Scripture says, among those born of women there is not a greater prophet than John the Baptist and he who is least in the kingdom of God is greater than he, (Luke 7:28). However, this does not answer why believers in the new covenant go through trial of faith, by affliction or suffering.

Let us go back to Job and the old covenant: Was Job attacked so viciously simply because he was of the old covenant? Did God not declare Job as righteous by the standard of God. Was Job not targeted by the Devil because of his righteousness? And just as Job's friends blamed him, so are some today who still argue that Job was ignorant and made a 'mistake'. They forget Job was righteous and for that reason, God had a hedge of protection around Job. Job could not have been attacked, if God Himself, who knows everything, did not temporarily remove His hedge of protection around Job, and released him into the battle field to be tested and afflicted by the Devil, (Job 1:8-12, Job 2:1-6).

These same people extend their argument to other believers in the new covenant that they afflicted or suffer trial of faith because of their ignorance or mistake. But God released Job into the battlefield of the Devil for a purpose. To prove to the Devil that Job was not faithful to Him for the reason of material blessings. And also that Job would still make the choice to remain faithful to Him even if there were no material blessings. He also wanted to further prove to the Devil, beyond any doubt, that Job would remain faithful to Him even under severe personal suffering, to the point of death. This was the purpose of the second affliction of Job.

God through the trials of Job showed the kind of faithfulness He expects of His children, including those in the new covenant. He expects each of them to remain faithful, regardless of their condition, whether in blessing, lack or adverse suffering. Apart from Job, we also have examples of Noah, Abraham, David, Daniel, Shadrach,

Meshach, and Abednego who all demonstrated the same kind of faithfulness God expects from His children. God is looking for people who are willing, if required, to forego their personal comfort to serve and remain faithful to Him.

Let us further look at the wrong argument of some people that Job and others of old were attacked because they were not of the new covenant. If that were the case, then what of the Apostles, such as James, John, Peter, Paul, etc? Were they not the bearers of the new covenant and handed down to us what they knew from The LORD? Were they not mightily filled with the power of The Holy Spirit, on that day of Pentecost? And did not speak in tongues even more than the believers of today (Acts 2:1-4)? Did they not have the power to perform diverse miracles? Did not even their mere shadows or handkerchiefs heal the sick because of the power of the Holy Spirit flowing in through them, (Acts 5;15, Acts 19:12)? Did some of them like Peter and Paul not also raised the dead, (Acts 9:36-42, Acts 20:7-12)? Was it not these same Apostles or disciples that also wrote the New Testament Scriptures which we all read today?

Despite all these, did the Apostles or disciples have any rest from the constant attacks of the enemy, the Devil or his agents or other means? Were they not continually attacked in diverse ways? Did they not hold to their faith to the very end of their lives. Did some of them not die as martyrs in the process, instead of denying The LORD? Did the LORD not also forewarn them and indeed all those who will be His followers of attacks, persecutions and tribulations? Did this not happen to the Apostles, (Matthew 10:16-23, Matthew 24:9-13, Mark 13:9-13, Luke 21:12-19, Acts 4:1-22, Acts 5:17-42, Acts 6:8-15, Acts 7:54-60, Acts 8:1-3, Acts 9:1-2, Acts 9:23-24, Acts 23:12-14, Acts 12:1-5, Acts 13:44-51, Acts 14:5-6, Acts 14:19-20, Acts 16:16-24, Acts 17:5-15, Acts 18:12-17, Acts 19:23-41, Acts 19:27-41, Acts 21:26-36, Acts 22:22-25, Acts 23:1-25, Acts 24:1-21, Acts 27:1-8, 28:16-31, 1 Thessalonians 2:18).

These things happened to them despite who they were in The LORD and the mighty power of the Holy Spirit working in them. Many of them including James, Peter, Paul, etc resisted the Devil to the end and died in the hands of the enemy. Are we therefore to say we know better than the Apostles and cannot be attacked by the enemy? Were they ignorant or under the same covenant like Job? Are there a special selected few these days, who are reading a different kind of gospel and not the one from the Apostles? Do they as a result today know better than the Apostles of old or other believers on how to live holy and not be attacked! Are they spiritually higher than the Apostles and other believers or better at mastering how to keep the Devil far away? Or has God changed? Or rather, is God not using the challenges His children face to train and teach them something they need to know, such as to help to grow in Him, or to stay in their place with Christ in the heavenly realm. The LORD said: He who endures to the end will be saved, (Matthew 24:13). What is the endurance He is referring to? Is it the endurance of luxury or of the attacks that come with following Him. The Scripture says: 'He who overcomes will inherit these things, and I will be his God and he will be my son', (Revelation 21:7-9). What are they to overcome? Is it not the test of their faith?

Lesson#4: The third lesson is that no one, no believer, is immune from trial of faith by suffering or affliction. This is regardless of whether they were of the old covenant or of the new covenant in Yeshua The Messiah. God has a purpose in allowing every test or trial of faith, and ultimately He wants every of His children to remain faithful to Him regardless of their circumstances.

Attacks Are Not If But When Until The Devil Is Restrained

The dead are inactive, posing no threat to their enemies and as such they are never attacked. In the same way, those who are spiritually dead, or inactive, or lukewarm pose no threat to the camp of the enemy. As such they do not appear in the radar or plans of the enemy as threats to be attacked. If we carefully look around, we will notice that those believers who are active and being used by the LORD even in our own time also come under severe attacks of one kind or another. Those that do not face any opposition or attacks, are in all probability idle, doing nothing of worth for the Kingdom of God. They may be doing nothing of significance to trouble the camp of the enemy or catch the attention of the Devil. In spiritual terms, they are dead, lukewarm or sleeping spiritually. And the Devil wants to leave them that way, lest they rise and create more trouble for his camp through active evangelism to bring others from his camp to the Kingdom of God.

It is true the believer is seated high above in the spirit and stronger than the Devil. But nonetheless the believer, both spirit and flesh. The believer is alive, and still living in the physical body of clay on the earth. Whether one is spiritually stronger above than the Devil or one goes out fighting the Devil or not, that does not stop the Devil. He roams around and would try to find the opportunity to bring the fight to the believer's door. It is not if, but a matter of when and how. What every believer should do is to be constantly alert to resist him.

The faith of the believer is therefore being constantly challenged through various trials, requiring constant renewal of the mind and strength from God. For As long as a believer remains active and effective for God, the Devil will try to come and attack. Some of the attacks may not be through the physical affliction of the body, but of the mind. The attack may come from any source, even including the social media.

I had received many visions and revelations from The LORD by His grace. They are for our benefit and to understand things better as written in the Scriptures. Some of these I shared as necessary in the first five end time books. Since we are discussing the attacks of the Devil, and is relevant here, let me share with you another visions.

The Devil and his agents passionately, intensely and naturally hate those building the Kingdom of God. They are always attacking and would quickly pounce viciously without mercy when they have such an opportunity to do so. It is like food to them or what truly delights them.

In one of such visions and revelations, I was an observer. Not only did I see the Devil, but also some of his spiritual agents in their natural, vicious and hateful operations of the kingdom of darkness towards believers. The LORD allowed me in this vision to see the intense hate by the enemy and of their permanent or constant motivation to attack God's children. I was also very surprised how the Devil knows those going to heaven and those going to hell with him. He was pointing or separating out those on his side from those on the other side, going to heaven. This is how his agents know who to attack or not to attack. And they are always ready, hungry like lions, looking for every opportunity to attack.

In this same vision, I saw angels of God at hand ready to help. However, they only take instructions from God and not from anyone else or human. They only moved into action when the believer makes request to God, and then they act based on the instruction of God.

We know that God hates sin and the agents of the kingdom of darkness are ready to attack. This is why believers should not play with sin in their lives. They become too vulnerable, like a lonely chick that has strayed out of the protection of the mother. Any believer who has sinned, should therefore immediately repent and ask for forgiveness. And God will forgive, (1John 1:8-10). The repentance should be done immediately, before the Devil or his agents can take any opportunity to attack. While righteousness or the forgiveness of sins will not stop the Devil from trying to attack, it however ensures God's will answer and help, if and when a believer is being attacked and calls on Him.

So from the angle of the Devil, he and his agents are of the darkness. They naturally hate light, hate the kingdom of God and those involved in it. They are jealous of believers and cannot understand why God continues to show them love. This is why the Devil sets out to target and attack, with the intention to destroy or cripple those actively involved in building God's Kingdom.

But from the angle of God, and in His wisdom, He turns the Devil's plans or attacks into His advantage to advance God's Kingdom, to train, buildup and equip His children.

God still has a purpose to leave Satan unbound as he is for now. And here are two of such purposes: For the Devil serves as agent to test the faith and total love of believers for God. For God Himself does not test or tempt or afflict, but it is the Devil and his agents that do it. Secondly the Devil also serves as the leader and father of those who are disobedient to God, who reject God and are heading to hell. They belong to the Devil who is their father, (John 8:44). They will together go to hell or lake of fire in the end with the Devil, the Antichrist, and the false prophet, (Revelation 19:19-20, Revelation 20:10, Revelation 20:11-15).

So God has allowed and continues to allow the Devil to roam freely around the earth, (Job 1:7, Job 2:2, 1 Peter 5:8). And so, the Devil cannot be bound by anyone as of now. He will continue to freely roam about, until The LORD comes. Then he will be imprisoned initially for 1,000 years. After being released again for a short while, he will be thrown permanently into the lake of fire, never to come back again, (Revelation 20:1-3, Revelation 20:7-10). But until then, we must continue to work with The LORD to help us resist and overcome the Devil every time he tries to attack.

Attacks of various nature, means or magnitude come against believers. The question therefore still remains why are the believers in The Messiah not completely shielded by God from these challenges? Or why do believers still suffer daily, and some like lambs are being led to the slaughter! Does God not have a purpose in all these, to turn them into a means to training His children?

Every believer needs to know the reasons why God allows the attacks from the enemy. Knowing that attacks will come and why God allows them is key to ensuring victory. It moves the believer past the bewildering or questioning stage to the cooperation phase with God for success. They also need to know about the protection God has in place. They need to know how the protections can be re-enforced so they can remain standing to continue to fulfill God's purpose for their lives. When we understand these, we have a better perspective on the attacks of the enemy, we are more encouraged to stand and fight with the weapons God has given us and not succumbed to the enemy.

Lesson#5: The Adversary, the Devil is still freely roaming around. He takes the fight or attack to the door of the believer. One who is spiritually active in doing something to build the kingdom of God will be noticed by the enemy and marked for attack. But the idle, lukewarm believer is not affecting the kingdom of darkness, and as such does not appear on the radar view for attack.

The Cycle Of Training, Testing and Graduation

Every parent expects a child to grow up, mature in character, well skilled and equipped to fulfill the demands of life. To do this, the child goes through various kinds of training and at different levels of their development.

The child first goes through training. Then comes the testing of the child on the acquired skills. When this is successfully achieved, then comes graduation, from that level unto the next level.

So the child starts in grade 1, goes through with the training, then with examination or testing appropriate for that grade level. After successfully going through the test, the child graduates from that level. That grade ends with a time of celebration and joy. The confidence level also becomes high.

A holiday, a period of rest or respite may even come with the graduation from that level before the child enters to start the next grade. Then the child moves to grade 2, the next higher grade. The child goes through the same cycle of training, testing and graduation. As the child advances through higher grades, the type of training and testing are always more challenging than the previous lower grades. This cycle continues until the final graduation, until completing all stages of the training required.

God does the same with all His children, and testing or trials are not always pleasant.

Lesson#6: Training and testing, examination or review of progress are essential parts of the development of a child. Just as parents take their children through these, so does God with His children for many reasons.

Reasons Why Believers Go Through Trials

The believers will each be tested, and it is not because of sin. It is for them to grow in their relationship with God. They go through the cycles of training, testing and graduation, as they move to the next level.

God allows the testing for many reasons:

God does it to examine the content of the heart, (Jeremiah 17:10). He does so to know the state, the motive, to show or confirm the firmness of the faith of the person in Him. He is checking the integrity of our heart, along with our faithfulness, and commitment to Him. The believer being tested also gets to know the true state of the heart and of his/her faith in God. The one who denies Him at the slightest sight of trouble, knows where he/she stands in faith. The one who continues to hang on despite adverse conditions also will know. So God allows the training and testing of His children.

God does it to get His children to be fully conformed to His standard, and not to the standards of this world. God does not want the mind of the believer to be conformed to the standards of this world. God wants to get the mind of the believer away from loving the world or the things that the world has to offer. For friendship with the world means enmity with God. Those who set their minds on the things of the flesh, live according to the sinful carnal nature. He wants the believers to set their minds on the things of The Spirit. For all the things that the world has to offer are: the lust (sinful carnal desires, cravings) of the flesh, the lust of the eyes, and the pride (boasting, self-confidence) of life. They are not of The Father but of this world, (Romans 8:5-6, Romans 12:2, James 4:4, 1 John 2:15-17). So God allows the training and testing of His children.

God wants His children to remain as His chosen people, a royal priesthood, a people of God's own special possession, chosen to declare the excellence (praises) of the wondrous deeds of Him, who called them out of darkness into His marvelous light!, (1 Peter 2:9-10, Revelation 1:5-6, 2 Corinthians 6:14, Ephesians 5:7, Ephesians 5:11). So God allows the training and testing of His children.

God wants total and complete obedience of His children to Him, lacking in no area. Obedience is how God measures our love for Him, (1 Samuel 15:22-23, John 14:15). No form of disobedience can attain eternal life. God wants His children to be fully ripe and ready, to attain eternal life with Him. So God allows the testing of His children.

God is looking to see our love for Him, if He is first priority. He wants to see the believer is prepared to leave, lose, forego, turn the back to what is most important to the person within or through that test, to demonstrate or for the sake of our love, commitment and obedience to Him. It typically represents a major sacrifice or a huge loss that would seem impossible to replace in the condition or situation of the person. It is like God has made a huge bet on our love for Him, against our love for the thing in question. At that point, the question would be are we prepared to forego it all, endure the suffering or loss and still continue to praise, worship, obey God, and also without blaming Him, despite the actual or impending loss. What is most important within or through the test to the person may vary from another: It may be potential loss of comfort, it may be something very pleasurable, it may be material or wealth like Job did, it may be position, it may be a loved one such as a child like Abraham or even Job, it may be money, it may even be life itself, like Shadrach, Meshach and Abednego. It is not really that God wants the person to lose any of them, but He wants to see if the person has gotten to the point of being prepared to forego it for the sake of love, commitment or obedience to God. In the end, God turns around to make alternative provisions and/or blesses the person back.

God does allow the testing of His children as a means to prune them to be more productive. He does this for His children to mature, become well equipped, fruitful and able to fulfill their assigned purposes. For He has a purpose assigned for each of His children. He wants all of them to grow and attain in Him. The believer needs to continue to learn, be pruned and grow in their relationship and faith in God. This is for them to be more fruitful for God. So God allows the testing of His children. He puts them through the battle field with the enemy. They mature and gain confidence in their victory over the enemy.

God has created us for His own purpose, to bring pleasure and glory to Him. God is building His Kingdom on earth. Our basic purpose is to be part of that building, to win others to Him, (Matthew 28:18-20, Mark 16:15-18). The manner and how we do that is the specific assigned purpose. A shovel, hammer, nail, brick or a tile each have their unique purpose when they are used in building a house. They have been made for their unique purposes and used for such. There may be many shovels, but not all will be shovels. There may be many nails, but not all will be nails. So is the same with the children of God, who are building His Kingdom. Each have their unique assignment.

Some of His children know Him and start fulfilling their purposes early in life. Examples include Yeshua The Messiah, John the Baptist, Prophet Samuel or Jeremiah. Some know Him and start later in life such as Moses, Aaron. If you want to know more about your specific purpose and how to discover it, please refer to the Book on *End Time CountDown Message*.

Lesson#7: God trains and allows His children to be tested for many reasons including to examine the content, motives of their hearts and firmness of their faith in Him; to bring them to be fully conformed to His own standard and not to the standards of this world; for them to remain as His special possession, chosen to declare the excellence (praises) of God; to bring them to the level of total and complete obedience to Him; to prune them to be more mature, well equipped, fruitful and able to fulfill their assigned purposes in His Kingdom.

The Four Active Components In Spiritual Test

For better understanding, here is another way to look at it. In the spiritual test of faith, temptation or affliction to taking place, there are four active components or parts involved.

Component#1: The Evil component. On one extreme, the bad or wicked side is the Devil. First the Devil is involved because of his jealousy and wicked intentions. He is jealous of the relationship between that person and God. Second, his desire is to destroy or ruin that relation. To get the person away from God, for the person to fall into sin, or to deny, reject or turn away from God. He goes about this by trying to inflict the maximum possible damage he can to the person, to crush the person, to destroy or even kill the person. He may first start by trying to destroy or take away what the person loves so much, that gives comfort to the person. This is to get the person to the point of despair. Then he may follow through with suggestions or enticement of sinful alternatives through temptations. The desire of the Devil to try to destroy or cause pain through loss or discomfort to the person or cause the person to choose or value something else in place of God.

Component#2: The second active component is the Believer. In the middle is the believer, who claims to love God and wants to remain committed or obedient to God no matter what happens. We discuss later about the helps and armor of God available to the believer to overcome the enemy.

Component#3: The third active component is anything the person dearly loves, desires or is holding unto: It is next to the believer, or in the life of the believer. It is something the believer deeply loves, desires or cherishes. This is anything in the physical that is of very high value, that means so much to the believer. The person's entire life or physical wellbeing may be tied to that thing. Before the test, it is not sinful or idolatry. But it is valued highly, almost taking the place or next in line to God. The person is vulnerable in his love or attachment for that thing. It typically represents a major sacrifice or a huge loss and would seem impossible to replace in the condition or situation of the person. It may be something that brings great pleasure to the person, such as the love a child has for candy, the love an adult has for food, or comfort or wealth, or a loved person in the life of such a person, such as towards a child or spouse, etc. In some others it may be the relationship with an opposite gender. They may become the source of potential temptation. Would what brings pleasure to the person become more important than the love for God? This component varies from person to person, and the kind of trial.

Component#4: The fourth active component is God, the godly or righteous side. This is on the opposite side to the evil one. Unlike Satan that wants to destroy, the purpose of God in the test is not to destroy the person. But God wants to see the demonstration or show of greater love, commitment, or obedience to God. To see if the believer is prepared to willingly leave, give up, lose, forego, turn the back to what is so important or may bring pleasure to the person within or through that test. It is not God's desire to take away or deny the person what adds joy to the person's life, as long as it does not lead to sin. But if during the test, it is taken away, what will the person do? Would the person start to harbor any blame towards God or be resentful or be doubtful of God's love, righteousness and faithfulness? God wants to see if the person has gotten to the point of being prepared to forego it for the sake of love, commitment or obedience to God. In the end, God usually makes alternative provision or turns around to bless or even restore what has been lost.

In Abraham's life it was Isaac at the time of his trial. God provided the ram as the alternative to sacrifice of Isaac, (Genesis 22:10-14). In Job's life during the first affliction, it was his wealth and love for his children. In the second affliction, it was his health he had left that was of value to him. God blessed Job with children and double of what he had before, including length of life, (Job 42:10-13). In the case of Shadrach, Meshach, and Abednego it was their life. God protected them in the fire and they did not die, (Daniel 3:25-27). In the case of Yeshua, it was His life, He willingly sacrificed in obedience to God. And God greatly exalted Him and given Him a Name above all others, (Philippians 2:9-11).

Therefore, the best attitude or way to live is to love God and hold very tightly unto Him. He is the creator and the only that is permanent. Then gratefully appreciate everything else, the valuable component, which God has graciously given or blessed the person with. However, also hold them with love and care as entrusted to you by God. Not hold them to yourself so selfishly, with tightfist, but 'loosely' enough without carelessness. That is, it should be with the mindset, as if they belong to God, and can be taken away with or without forewarning. This is just like the person also belongs to God.

Lesson#8: There are four components that are involved in every trial of faith. The person that overcomes is the one who is willing to leave, give up, lose, forego, turn the back to what is most important to the person within or through that test, and through it demonstrates greater love, commitment, or obedience to God.

The Believer Goes Through Cycles Of Growth

God is continuously building and pruning His children to make them more productive and to fulfill His purposes in their lives, (John 15:1-2). He prunes to remove the dead or the weak areas to create room for greater growth.

There are several cycles in growth and maturity. Within a cycle, the child of God goes through building up and pruning. Then comes the testing and examination, during which God releases every believer, every faithful child of His, for the examination or testing. The child of God successfully defeats the enemy in the spiritual battlefield of that cycle. Each successful cycle ends with graduation, joy and celebration from that level of training. Then a new and higher one starts.

God does not allow anyone to be tested beyond their grade level, that is their level of ability, (1 Corinthians 10:13). A grade 1 will not be tested with a grade 2. And God is always available, ready to help, providing a way of escape, when the one being tested cries for His help.

God Himself does not do the testing. The Devil and or his agents in the spiritual or in the physical are used for the testing, temptation and affliction. For it was the Devil that went to tempt Yeshua The Messiah. It was also the Devil that afflicted Job. The Devil and his agents try to take advantage of God's presumed quietness as He watches.

During the process of testing, God may become quiet as He watches how well we will perform in the spiritual battle field against the enemy. He watches to see how well we have received His training, and how well we are using it in faith. For Yeshua, after 40days of being in the presence of God, He was released for testing. God was watching as He was being tested.

Lesson#9: God's training and testing of His children come in phases, from one cycle to a higher cycle. God does not do the testing. Instead, He releases them, at the appropriate time, into the battlefield to be tested against the Devil and his agents. God watches how each will perform, ready to help, and does not allow them to be tested beyond their ability or level of faith. A believer is expected to show total love to God in obedience and faith in Him.

How Believers Get Tested:

All believers continue to go through the cycle of training or development in relationship and faith with God. They also go through testing or examination of faith to see how they would hold. Then they graduate with some celebration or respite, before the next level.

The deeper and more devoted they are, the more severe the enemy will try to afflict to test them. For the testing is done in proportion to the individual's level of faith and relationship with God. So no one gets tested below or beyond their level.

The enemy has an array of tools he brings to the battle field. The enemy deploys the one he feels will be most effective against the opponent.

In some cases, the testing of a believer may be through temptation by the evil one(s). This is in an attempt to attract or entice the believer to sinful pleasure of the flesh or things of the world. The aim to bring about sin and a spiritual fall of the believer.

It may also be through making sinful suggestions to the mind of the carnal flesh, and so create a conflict between the flesh and the Spirit, (Galatians 5:17). For this reason, we must continue to renew our minds and be transformed by the word of God, (Romans 12:1-2, John 15:3, John 17:16-17, Psalm 119:11, Jeremiah 29:11).

It may be through nature such as wind, storm rain, or something to create an adverse environment or condition that discourages the believer from continuing in faith in the work of God. Many times, I pray to stop rain from falling for the period am out on something for God. The rain obeys and stops. After am done, I release the rain to continue falling.

In some other cases, the weapon used by the enemy may be by affliction or a combination of affliction and temptation.

Sometimes, when the enemy cannot directly reach the believer, he may go indirectly through the loved one or those under the care of the believer. Initially, the Devil could not reach Job because of God's hedge of protection around him. But he attacked Job's possessions, children and servants through various means, (Job 1:11-20).

Regardless of the form and nature the testing takes, some believers will stand well and some will be shaky. For some believers who are weak, it may take only a little temptation or a little discomfort and affliction for them to give up.

For others who are much deeper in their relationship with The LORD, temptations alone would have no impact. The enemy would therefore try to apply a combination of greater affliction and denial. His desire is to get the believer to the point of despair or desperation. Then the Devil may follow through with presentation of some propositions, enticement or inducement to the believer at his/her weakest moment. For example, The LORD Yeshua was not tempted until after the extreme affliction of the body. This was when He had become weak and hungry from the fasting, (Matthew 4:2-3).

In the case of Job, the Devil did not start with tempting Job. Job had consistently proved to fear God, to be righteous. The Scripture says, in his days, there was no one else like Job on the earth, a blameless and upright man, (Job 1:8). In other words, he had a very deep relationship with God. And he was also well blessed in wealth. So the initial condition was not right for Job to be tempted to fall. So the Devil resorted first to personal losses, affliction and persecution. His desire was for Job to be afflicted to the point of despair, when Job may become vulnerable to temptation and so fall into sin. For it was at his point of despair for life, that Job's wife was used to tempt him to see if he would curse God, sin and die. But Job refused, (Job 2:9-10).

Even at the point of weakness, the believer with a deep relationship with God would prefer physical death to denying The LORD because of affliction. Some of the Apostles were killed for not denying their faith in The LORD. And today, some believers in The LORD are killed in some parts of the world for not denying Him.

So the believer who is spiritually weak in faith, in whom the word of God has not really taken root may easily fall from God through temptation or the enticement of pleasure. It could be with food, money, sexual immorality, or whatever pleasure they cannot resist. They love God but are still easily enticed by the sinful canal desires of the flesh. They are engaged in the battle between the Spirit in the believer, and the carnal flesh taking sinful suggestions and enticements from the enemy, (Galatians 5:17). So they go back to their old ways or continue to compromise.

The testing of the believer's faith in God may not come through temptation. It may come through afflictions. Some believers at the sight of some discomfort, a little discomfort, or delay in answer to prayer, may give up. They abandon and take flight away from their faith in The LORD.

But for the believer who is stronger in The LORD, it would take much more. The affliction of some may come through severe suffering, including the loss of the material things or wealth of this present world or what they dearly love or value. This was what happened to Job. The losses do not indicate that God has abandoned them. For He is always watching and would provide for their needs. But they would need to have faith in Him, to become rich in the things of the Kingdom of God.

Therefore, when the believer has grown deeper in their relationship with The LORD, the person may not easily fall to temptation, or ungodly offer of enticement or inducement to sin. The things or pleasures of the world would not easily entice the person. For they are rich in the things of the kingdom of God. They do not measure their success through the pleasure or material things offered by this world. They derive their joy from obeying God. So the enemy may try to apply a stronger level of affliction than before.

So in the trial of the believer, the person may first be severely afflicted. This is brought against the believer by the Devil, his high-level agents, principalities and powers. Due to the believer's high level of resistance through faith and armor of God, the enemy will try to unleash the worst of their weapons and attacks against the believer from every angle possible. This is in an attempt for the believer to be weakened during the trial to the point of despair or desperation. The enemy wants the believer to cave in, deny God and fall. This is how or why those that are very deep in their relationship with The LORD or have higher calling experience more severe and protracted affliction or trial than others. This is in the same way that the level of testing for grade 3 will be much more difficult than for grade 1.

Lesson#10: The enemy has an array of tools he brings to the battle field, and deploys the one he feels will be most effective against the opponent. It may be temptation, discomfort or severe affliction. The Devil sees the believer as an adversary and does not go to simply test. Rather he aims to completely defeat, crust or destroy the believer. However, God does not allow anyone to be tested beyond their ability. He is always watching and ready to help the believer, to provide a way of escape.

The Test Through Miracles And Unanswered Prayers

For many, the test may be through temptations or afflictions. Yet for some other, the challenge may be the issue of 'no miracles and no answer to prayers'. Some people trust God only because they are seeing miracles and all the prayers they pray answered. These are called miracle chasing believers or evangelists. So, when miracles stop or prayers take long to be answered or not answered, they begin to doubt God and slack behind.

In the days of Yeshua, some followed Him because of food, (John 6:26-27). While some others followed Him looking for miraculous signs (John 6:30). He often rebuked them for this. And for those rejoicing because of the evil spirits are subject to them, He said they should rather rejoice because their names are in the book of life in heaven, (Luke 10:20).

The greatest miracle is not the miracles such as of healing the body, food, provisions for the physical bodies or of casting out demons, etc. The biggest miracle is salvation of the souls of the unsaved. This is what makes angels in heaven to celebrate, (Luke 15:10). Yeshua further warned that there will arise false christs, and false prophets, who will perform great miraculous signs and wonders, so that, if it were possible, they will deceive the very elect, (Matthew 24:24).

Yeshua's focus is doing the will of God and whatever pleased God. He said 'not my will but your will be done', (Luke 22:42). Also Shadrach, Meshach, and Abednego, said whether God saved (answered) them or not, it would not matter, (Daniel 3:17-18). They would not be shaken in their faith in Him. We must all get to the point to surrendering to the total will of God.

We must stop doing a 'tit and tat' with God, only following or trusting Him if He answered a prayer or performs a miracle. God is sovereign, and omnipotent and does as He pleases. And who is the mere mortal to dictate to Him what He should do and how He should do it.

Miracles are good. Prayers answered immediately are good. But in some cases, God may withhold performance of some miraculous signs or delay answer to some prayers, as test, to see what is the person's motivation for believing in Him. Ultimately God shows through when He sees the commitment, obedience and love for Him.

Lesson#11: Trusting in God must not be motivated by just miracles or immediate answer to prayers. It must be of total surrender to His will and purpose and of salvation to souls.

The Believer Must Deploy The Full Armor of God

During the trial, there will be times of extreme loneliness and despair where it feels like God is very far away and nowhere to be seen. But He is always near.

No matter how intense a battle may be, we must never be so engaged in the battle, and forget to go back to God to ask for His help. We cannot win it on our own. For it is not by might or power, but by The Spirit of God, (Zechariah 4:6).

Secondly, we must always remember we are already victorious through Yeshua the Messiah. We must constantly renew our minds with the word and promises of God.

Thirdly, though and because we know victory has been won for us, we must release everything to God. That is for God to do what He desires, for His will to prevail. We should release and be prepared to accept what His will may be. We must get to the point of no longer questioning or wrestling with God on what we want.

Fourthly, all through the testing, we must remain and not waver in our love for God and faith in Him. For those are the things being tested and God is watching. God is looking to see if we will place our love for Him above everything else. We must love Him enough to be prepared to lose what is so important to us, if that is His desire. Even if we are being poured out in totality, as an offering before Him, holding unto nothing for ourselves. Abraham released his hold away from Isaac, to prove his love for God.

Now, the Scripture warns us that the enemy the believer is fighting is not flesh and blood. Rather, it is against principalities, against powers, against the rulers of the dark world, and against a host of wicked spirits in the heavenly realms, (2 Corinthians 10:3-6, Ephesians 6:12-18, Daniel 10:12-13, Ephesians 2:2, Revelation 12:7-9).

While Yeshua was being tested by the Devil, God and the angels in heaven watched on. Yeshua left by Himself had to choose to follow God or bow to the Devil. He chose to follow God.

So while this trial of faith is ongoing for the believer, God is taking notice of the strength of faith of the believer towards Him. The believer cries in prayers to God for help. The believer fights back against the enemy with the full armor of God with which the believer is clothed, (Ephesians 6:12-18). And after the battle is over, the believer will still be standing firm, having won the trial.

During the trial, the believer has to take his/her battle position and fight back with the full armor of God. This is done with the help of the Holy Spirit. The armor includes the belt of truth (faithfulness) of the word of God and of the believer, the breastplate of righteousness from God through Yeshua The Messiah who is our righteousness, the believer's continued focus and preparedness that comes as a messenger of the gospel of Good News of peace to win souls, the shield of faith with which to quench all the fiery arrows, spears, or missiles of the Evil One, the helmet of salvation and the word of God, which is sword of The Holy Spirit. The word, the appropriate promise of God or what His word says are used to renew the mind or the faith of the believer and then turned to attack the enemy.

Read more on the Armor of God in the second end time book, *'Finishing Strong In The End Time'*.

God is our shelter and strength, a Mighty Help ever present in trouble, (Psalm 46:1). He says 'Call on Me in the day of trouble. I will deliver you, and you will glorify Me", (Psalm 50:15). Therefore, the believer must keep on praying always, presenting every prayer and request to God with the help of The Holy Spirit. The believer must stay alert, be watchful and be persistent, (Isaiah 11:5, Isaiah 54:17, Isaiah 59:17, Isaiah 52:7, Nahum 1:15, Romans 10:15, 1 Corinthians 1:30, Ephesians 6:12-18, 1 Thessalonians 5:17).Read more on the chapter in this book on Spiritual Warfare And Authority.

The Devil gains inroad in his attacks through creating doubts by false suggestions into the spiritual ears and minds of people. Renewing the mind with the word of God, the sword of the Spirit is a weapon against the Devil. It is not to stop the Devil from coming to attack, but a weapon to gain victory over him, to send him back when he comes. So as a start the believer should know the word of God and constantly renew his/her mind or spirit with the truth of the word of God.

Also the believer while praying should ask for wisdom on what to do. For prayers in faith may have to be followed through with real action or work. Faith without work is dead. Someone just praying for work without taking steps of going out to look for the work is incomplete.

Regardless of the form that trials and persecutions take, they are never pleasant. No one looks forward to it and no one enjoys it when it comes. Trials and persecutions are like missiles thrown by the Devil to try to break the outer shell(s) of resolve or resistance first. The purpose is to destroy or to try to weaken the person to the point of vulnerability to temptation.

And at the appropriate point of the affliction, at the point of deep anguish, despair or desperation, then temptation may be included as an inducement. The Devil is looking to the believer to desperately accept any option to ease the anguish, including ungodly suggestions. The objective of the evil one is to breakdown the resistance, or to weaken the person to see if the person will submit to the enticement of sin, loss of faith or denial of God.

Lesson#12: We must always be alert and be clothed in the full armor of God. The shield of faith is very important, along with the true word of God to renew, refresh our minds and strengthen our faith in God. We must pray always, and never waiver in our love and obedience to God, and faith in Him. We must also release or give everything to God, to do what He desires, for His will to prevail about the situation, and be ready to accept what that may be. Abraham had to release his hold unto Isaac, to prove his love for God.

The Attitude Of Those Totally Devoted To God:

Those who are totally devoted to God are totally devoted to Him regardless of what happens. Regardless of miracles, or abundance of material things or wealth in their lives.

Those devoted may look physically or materially poor, weak or wretched. That is what the physical eye is seeing. The spiritually minded will see much more.

Those totally devoted to God are rich, very rich in the things of the Spirit and very strong like pillars in the LORD.

They have total contentment all the time, and are untroubled whether they have or do not have. Whether in want or surplus they have contentment. They have learnt how to live humbly when there is scarcity and to live in abundance when there is prosperity. They can do this and more, and indeed all things, through The Messiah who strengthens them, (Philippians 4:12-13).

Their faith is in God, and focused on pleasing Him who supplies all their needs. For them, being in this world is The Messiah and to die is gain, (Philippians 1:21). They love The LORD and are devoted to serving Him with all their heart, soul and mind, (Matthew 22:37). They love not their lives but God, even when faced with death, (Revelation 12:11). They are focused on completing their assignments for God.

They use all opportunity and everything they have to serve the LORD. By putting God first in everything, He adds everything they need for them, (Matthew 6:33). For the silver, the gold, on earth, everything on earth or in heaven, and indeed life itself belong to Him, (Haggai 2:8, Psalms 24:1, Psalms 115:16). It does not belong to the Devil. For God created all, including the Devil!

But God is looking to see if we will place our love for Him above everything else. Even our love for Him above our lives. This is where God wants to get every believer, every true child of His. And God never fails to show through when He is needed, and all the time!

Lesson#13: Put God first, by releasing everything, including yourself to God. Then He will show through for you.

God Gives The Victory In Each Cycle Of Trial

The Scripture also tells us that God will not allow us to be tempted more than we can withstand. And with every temptation, God will also make away out for us to escape. This is so we are able to endure it, (Matthew 6:13, Luke 11:4, Matthew 4:3-11, Luke 4:3-13, 1 Corinthians 10:12-13, Hebrews 4:15, James 1:2-4, James 1:12-15, James 4:7).

After the believer has successfully completed the testing phase, then comes the graduation from that level. This comes with a period of joy and celebration before the next level. For example, after the testing of The LORD Yeshua, the Scripture says the Devil left Him, while the holy angels came and ministered unto Him, (Matthew 4:11). In the same way, there will be God's reward at every stage for everyone who successfully endures. The final and ultimate reward at the end is the gift of Eternal Life.

When the Devil or tester has failed, he withdraws and waits for the next opportunity. For example, the Scripture says of the LORD Yeshua, that after the Devil had finished the temptation, he left Yeshua, until another opportunity, (Luke 4:13). The last one came, as He prepared to die on the cross, (Matthew 16:21-24, Mark 8:33).

After one cycle is completed, the believer moves unto the next higher level of the cycle of training, testing, graduation and celebration. This way and with every victory over the enemy, the believer is also moving from glory to glory. This continues until the person reaches the end point of the training, the top level desired by God. That is the point at which the purpose of God as desired in the life of that person is fully fulfilled. At that point, whether at the threat of death or life, the person fully trusts God. The person stops to question God and his obedience become total. It becomes the will of God, and not of the person.

Lesson#14: We have been created to serve God, and are like clay in His hands. He can do what He wants. But nonetheless, God is righteous and never unfair. He is a rewarder of those who diligently seek or serve Him.

Examples Of Holy People Who Attained:

Many holy people of old in the Scriptures attained to where God wanted them. They achieved total obedience to God and dependence on Him.

For example, Abraham got to the point of total trust and obedience to God. He had waited most of his adult life for his special child, Isaac, the seed. When Isaac came, Abraham loved him so much.

Isaac was everything to Him, having waited all his married life for him. It was about a 60years wait, given that men in Abraham's days married around 30 years old, and Isaac came when he was 100 years old, (Genesis 11:12-24, Genesis 21:5). However, Abraham got to the point where he had to demonstrate that his love for God was much higher than his love for Isaac. He went on a three days journey to give up Isaac in a sacrifice. Before he could carry through the sacrifice on Mount Moriah, God showed through by providing him with a ram in place of Isaac, (Genesis 22:10-14).

Job also got to the point of total fear of God and trust in Him. Despite all the afflictions that had happened to him, he refused to fall into the temptation brought through the wife, to curse God and die. Instead, he said he was prepared to accept the will of God, good or bad, (Job 2:9-10). Job never fell into the temptation. Job further said that 'though He slays me, I will continue to trust in Him' (Job 13:15). He continued steadfastly in his fear and love for God. The Scripture says that God makes everything to work together for the good of those who love God, to those who are the called according to His purpose (Romans 8:28). And to give thanks in all circumstances (everything). For this is the will of God for you who belong to The Messiah Yeshua everything, (1 Thessalonians 5:18).

Also Shadrach, Meshach, and Abednego got to the point of total trust and love for God. They said: 'We know the God we serve. If you throw us into the hot burning furnace fire, our God whom we serve is able to save us. He will rescue us from your hands, your majesty, the king! But even if He does not do so, let it be clearly known to you, your majesty, the king, that we will not follow your gods', (Daniel 3:17-18). They were ready to die for their love and faith in God. And God showed through, (Daniel 3:25-27).

Also, in the case of The LORD Yeshua, He prayed to God saying: 'not my will but your will be done', (Luke 22:42). It was his ordained purpose to die as the Lamb for the sins of the whole world, (John 1:29, John 1:36). He did not waver in this. He submitted Himself to

God and continued steadfastly in total obedience to God. And He was gloried, being exalted to the highest place of honor at the right hand of God, with a Name above all names, (Philippians 2:9-11, Ephesians 1:20-22, Matthew 28:18-20, Mark 16:19, Hebrews 8:1-2, Hebrews 12:2, Acts 2:33, Romans 8:34, Colossians 1:16).

Walking with God in His purpose is not always easy. For example, prophet Jeremiah once accused God of deceiving Him, in one of Jeremiah's moments of desperation, (Jeremiah 20:7). Every child of God who is obedient and walking with Him will be refined through trials to the level desired by God. The refinement will feel like going through fire, and it will take many cycles.

There will be times of intense anguish, or extreme despair as God molds each person into who He wants them to be.

Regardless of the intensity of the anguish and despair, those that remain faithful to God cannot die before the end of their assignment or purpose for Him. It is not the same with unbelievers who are not working in His purpose. God has no pleasure in the premature death of any of His faithful children, before an assignment or purpose for someone is completed. So, as long as we are alive, it means we are not finished yet with our assignment(s) or purpose in this present world. And as long as we are not yet through with our purpose, then there is still a higher level to go. And as long as there is still a greater level to go for God, then there will be greater training, as well as testing along the way to fully complete it. Only after doing so does the end come for each faithful child of God in this present world. The person goes to God, the creator, to rest from the assignments and troubles of this present world.

Lesson#15: God is the same, and is no respecter of persons. He trains, equips and releases His children to the battlefield where they get tested according to His purpose. God does not ever abandon or leave His followers in the battlefield on their own. He is always there to help as we cry to Him. Just as God showed up for those tested in the Scripture, in the old and new covenant, who had faith in Him, so will He show up for us in our time of testing.

The World Of Eternity After Leaving The Earth

As the Scripture says, our affliction now is light and is only for a moment while we are on earth And it is working for us, weight of glory that is far greater and is eternal, (2 Corinthians 4:17).

We will soon be joining the myriad of angels who are not of this world, who are heavenly beings with immortality. They are spending eternity with God. In the same way, we will also be transformed into glorious bodies. We will put on immortality, never to die again. The body, soul and spirit of the child of God will together receive immortality from God and spend eternity with God. The limitations of this present world and of the present mortal or perishable body of clay would be removed forever, (1 Corinthians 15:50-55, 1 Thessalonians 4:15-17).

1 Corinthians 15:50-52 (ETB): "Look, let me tell you a mystery (hidden secret): Not everyone of us will fall into the sleep (of dead people). But everyone in The Messiah will be changed. 52 It will happen in a flash of moment, in the twinkling of an eye, at the last sound of the trumpet. For the trumpet will be sounded. Those who are dead (asleep) will be raised up with incorruptible bodies (that cannot decay) forever. And we who are alive (not asleep, not dead) will also be changed".

Then the enemy of death with its sting through sin, the enemy of the carnal nature of the flesh, and the enemy in the form of the agents of the kingdom of darkness would be done away with and gone from us forever and ever. The testing or trials of faith and the momentary afflictions will be no more, gone forever!

Here is also a further understanding. God is always working, (John 5:17). The angels also work for God in their diverse assignments, all to the praise and glory of God. So will it be with every individual who has gone to spend eternity with God. Since God is always working, and His angels have diverse assignments, so will we also be working for Him after being transformed into immortality. The individual will be re-assigned for an eternal purpose. It will all be to the praise and glory of The Father! Amen.

Lesson#16: Every believer will be transferred in the twinkling of the eye into a glorious body, with immortality. They will spend eternity with God, serving Him in the assignment of their eternal purpose, to the praise and glory of God the Father.

Chapter 5

About The Name And Other Titles of God

Scriptural Verses:

Exodus 3:15 (ETB)*: Furthermore, God said to Moses:*

"*Say this to the Israelites:* '**YEHOVAH**' *('YHVH', or 'JEHOVAH'), The God of your forefathers, The God of Abraham, The God of Isaac, and The God of Jacob, has sent me to you. This is My Name forever. And this is how I am to be remembered by all generations', [ref Exodus 3:15, Exodus 6:3, Exodus 34:6-7].*

Exodus 6:3 (ETB)*: I appeared to Abraham, to Isaac, and to Jacob, as God Almighty, (El Shaddai).*

But I did not make Myself known to them by My Name: '**YEHOVAH**' *('YHVH', or 'JEHOVAH'), [ref Exodus 3:15, Exodus 6:3, Exodus 34:6-7].*

([Note: 'YEHOVAH', 'YHVH' in Hebrew or 'JEHOVAH' in English are each pronounced 'Yeh-ho-vaw' with three syllables or substituted with the title 'The LORD, 'ADONAI']).

Explanation:

Hebrew YHVH or YEHOVAH

YEHOVAH, *(or YHVH)* each pronounced 'Yeh-ho-vaw' is The Name of The Most High God in Hebrew. (Exodus 3:15, Exodus 6:3, Exodus 34:6).

In Hebrew language, the Name of The Most High is represented in with four consonants also known as the tetragrammaton, 'YHVH'. It is properly pronounced when the vowels are filled in between the consonants. It is like the abbreviation 'blvd' filled in to have 'boulevard'.

In Hebrew, two vowels cannot stand beside each other for pronunciation. For the actual correct pronunciation, the tetragrammaton, 'YHVH' in Hebrew, has three syllables with three vowels between the four consonants. These vowels in Hebrew are 'sheva' or 'e', and 'cholam' or 'o' and 'kamatz' or 'a'. And when filled in, we have 'YeHoVaH' or 'YEHOVAH'!The name of God starts with 'Yeho' and ends with 'aH'.

This is also consistent with Jewish names that has parts of God's Name in them. They either start with 'Yeho-'or end with '–aH'. And all the Jewish names that begin with the three first consonants of the Tetragrammatonare pronounced'YeHo-'. Examples are Yehohanan, Yehonathan, Yehoshaphat. Examples of some ending with 'aH' include JonAH, YeshayAH (IsaiAH), YirmeyAH (JeremiAH),NechemyAH (NehemiAH), OvadyAH (ObadiAH), ZecharyAH (ZechariAH), etc

Hebrew YHWH or YEHOWAH

There is also another alternative of the tetragrammaton or four consonants of 'YHVH' which is 'YHWH'. Just like the 'YHVH', the 'YHWH' is pronounced with three syllables. The 'YHWH' also has three vowels, ('sheva' or 'e', and 'cholam' or 'o' and 'kamatz' or 'a') in Hebrew. With these vowels, the 'YHWH' is pronounced 'YeHoWaH' or 'YEHOWAH'.

The Name is not 'Yehoweh', but 'Yehowah'. We know this from Hebrew names bearing a part of God's Name, that they end with 'aH' and not 'eH'. We have already seen some examples of these. And there are also some other Hebrew names ending with 'EL' from attributes or titles of God (such as from El Elyon, El Shaddai). Examples of such Hebrew names include IsraEL, SamuEL, DaniEL, JoEL, GabriEL, MichaEL. One special example with both 'El' and 'aH' in the name is Elijah or Eliyahu. Again, they do not commonly have or end with 'eH'. Therefore, the Name is not 'Yehoweh'.

The Name is also not 'Yahweh'. Apart from having an 'eH', the name 'Yahweh' has two syllables instead of three syllables. The Name of The Most High God, whether as YHVH or YHWH has three syllables. It is therefore not 'Yahweh'. If 'Yahweh' is a title, and it could be, but we do not know.

Hebrew YEHOVAH or YEHOWAH

Thus, the Name could be 'Yehovah for YHVH' or 'Yehowah for YHWH'. Both are consistent with all the Jewish names that begin with the three first consonants of the Tetragrammaton pronounced 'YeHo-'. Or end with '-aH'. The 'vah' in 'Yehovah' and 'wah' in 'Yehowah' have more to do with differences in the pronunciation of the last or third syllables of the Name. The correct pronunciation is 'Yeh-ho-vaw'.

The Name YEHOVAH or YHVH in Hebrew is the Name of The Most High God used in the End Time Bible (ETB) and therefore also in this book.

English JEHOVAH:

The transliteration of YEHOVAH to English is JEHOVAH, also pronounced 'Yeh-ho-vaw'. 'Jehovah' conforms to the corresponding English usage with respect to Hebrew names in the Bible. For example, the name 'Yerushalayim' in Hebrew, is pronounced 'Jerusalem' in English. Similarly, 'Yehudah' in Hebrew is pronounced 'Judah' in English. Also Yirmeyah in Hebrew is pronounced Jeremiah in English, and so is Nechemyah in Hebrew pronounced Nehemiah in English.

YAH, Y'AH (or JAH, J'AH):

God Almighty is also referred to as **YAH** (or Y'AH) in Hebrew. The YAH is a contraction of the Name of The Most High! It is a shortened form of YehovAH. The English equivalent is **JAH** or J'AH the shortened form of JehovAh, (Psalm 68:4, Isaiah 12:2, Isaiah 26:4, Isaiah 38:11).

This shortened form Y'AH or J'AH is also used in 'Hallelu-YAH' or 'Hallelu-JAH', meaning 'Praise The LORD', or 'Praise YehoVAH', or 'Praise JehoVAH', (Psalm 104:35, Psalm 105:45, Psalm 106:1, Psalm 106:48, Psalm 111:1, Psalm 112:1, Psalm 148:1, Psalm 149:1, Psalm 150:1, Revelation 19:3-4, etc).

YEHOVAH (JEHOVAH)
The Everlasting Covenant Keeping God

YEHOVAH (or JEHOVAH) is Elohim, God Almighty, The Most High God, The Creator of the heavens and the earth, The One Who was, The One Who Is and The One Who is to come. He is The Self Existing One who is the Covenant keeping God Who delivers! He is the God of Abraham, Isaac and Jacob. And because of His Covenant with them, He came to deliver or save the Israelites, their descendants from slavery in Egypt, (Exodus 2:23-25, Genesis 15:13-

16). YEHOVAH is the Covenant Keeping Deliverer! He is the I AM THAT I AM.

Israelites were His chosen people because of His covenant with Abraham, Isaac and Jacob. The world was to be blessed through Abraham. This was through the Savior of the entire world whocame through Israel, the seed of Abraham. As such, God often defended and fought for them against their enemies, as He worked out His plan for the Savior of the world. He was therefore seen or known by the Egyptians, the Canaanites, the Philistines, and other enemies of His people, as the God who caused disaster, calamity, plagues, destruction or ruin (such as of hailstones, lightning, thunderbolts, fire, etc) to fall from heaven on the enemy!

'ADONAI' or 'LORD'

ADONAI in Hebrew is a very popular title of God Almighty. And God has often referred to Himself as 'ADONAI'. The English equivalent is LORD. It means 'Ruler or Master'.

He is the Creator and Ruler over all, including of divine heavenly beings, principalities, and rulers. Therefore, The Most High God bears as one of His attributes or titles 'LORD', 'The LORD', 'LORD of lords', 'God of gods', (Deuteronomy 10:17, Psalm 136:2-3, Daniel 2:47). This does not mean He is the God of idols. He said: "I am The LORD (YEHOVAH, JEHOVAH), that is My Name. And I will not give My glory to another, Or My praise to carved idol images", (Isaiah 42:8, ETB).

For more understanding, please refer to the Chapter About 'idols, gods, and God of gods'.

ADONAI or The LORD is more often conveniently used in the Scriptures in place of the true Name of God, YEHOVAH, YHVH or JEHOVAH, (each pronounced 'Yeh-ho-vaw'). The origin of this practice goes back to the warning given not to blaspheme, disrespect or use in vain the true Name of God, (Exodus 20:7, Leviticus 24:16).

In fear of this potential misuse and also of mis-pronunciation, subsequent Priests and Hebrew writers substituted the true Name of God (YHVH, YEHOVAH or JEHOVAH) with '**ADONAI**' in Hebrew. ADONAI translates to mean '**The LORD**' in English (or Dominus in Latin). This is why there are more than 7,000 uses of 'ADONAI' or 'LORD' in more than 6,000 verses of the Scripture to represent the Name of God in many versions of the Bible.

Some other Hebrew writers have used the word 'Hashem' which means 'The Name' as alternative representation of the true Name of God (YHVH, YEHOVAH or JEHOVAH). But such a representation is not used in the End Time Bible as God's Name, Title or Attribute. Rather, ADONAI or LORD are used in the End Time Bible, since they are proper titles God has used for Himself.

But where ever ADONAI or LORD is used in the End Time Bible, it is written in uppercase letters. This is to differentiate it from other uses of 'lord' for lower lords (master, ruler, or all 'lords' other than The LORD, God Almighty).

YEHOSHUA or YESHUA:

Yehoshua orYĕshua, or Yĕshuw`ah, pronounced Yesh·ü'·ä, in Hebrew, with three syllables. Yehoshua is derived from Yehovah. It meansThe salvation of Yehovah. Yeshua is the shortened Aramaic Hebrew form of Yehoshua. Yeshua became popular among the Hebrew's after the return of the Jews from captivity in Babylon. But both forms, Yehoshua and Yeshua are used.

Yehoshua or Yeshuaisthe Name of the begotten Son of the Father. He is The Messiah or The Anointed One or Savior.

Yehoshua (or Yeshua) means 'Yehovah is Salvation'!.Or 'The Salvation from Yehovah'!. Or The salvation of Yehovah. He is the Yeshua of Nazareth, the Lamb of God, born in Bethlehem of Judea, who was crucified on the cross for the sins of the world.

His Name and date of birth on earth were recorded in heaven at His Birth. And indeed, what this writer saw in a large scroll of the record shown to him by two angels was 'The I AM Salvation from The I AM That I AM'. This was recorded along with His date of birth, which the writer also saw!. The shortened meaning of Yeshua is 'Salvation' and He is also 'I AM', (John 8:58).

Yeshua or JESUS in Other Languages

Yeshua is also known among the Gentiles (non-Jews) as '**Jesus**' in English or '**Iēsous**' in Latin/Greek. In many other languages all over the world, He is known as 'Yasu, Yesu, Jezuz, Jesu, Gesus, Iesu' etc. He is The Messiah. And many languages all over the world use the word 'Mesi, Mesias, Almasih or Messiah' to represent The Messiah. It means The 'Anointed One' of God!.

The Messiah Yeshua is the creator and head of all principalities and powers, (Colossians 2:10). The disciples and followers also fondly referred to Him as 'LORD' or 'Master' (John 13:13, John 11:3, Luke 7:13, Luke 24:34), etc. He is also the King of kings and LORD of lords (Revelation 19:16).

In the End Time Bible, a differentiation is made between the use of the word 'LORD' for God The Father and 'LORD' for The begotten Son. The way this has been done is to add 'Yeshua' to the word LORD such as 'LORD Yeshua' where LORD is used in reference to Him.

Calling The Name Of God The Father:

Finally, and very importantly, the Scripture encourages us as the Children of God to Bless, Call, Confess, Declare, Glorify, Magnify, Praise, Remember, Sing, and Trust the Name of GOD.

We know His Name to be YEHOVAH, YHVH, or JEHOVAH. They are each pronounced

'Yeh-ho-vaw'. Some may prefer YHWH or YEHOWAH pronounced 'Yeh-ho-waw' (but not Yahweh).

Therefore, we should reverently do this as the Scripture says, with our whole heart in Spirit and Truth, (John 4:23-24).

As His children, we should reverently:

Bless His Name: Psalm 145:21;
Call His Name: Psalm 80:18, Psalm 99:6, Isaiah 12:4, Acts 2:21, Romans 10:13;
Confess His Name 1 Kings 8:35-36, 2 Chronicles 6:24-25;
Declare His Name: Exodus 9:16, Psalm 22:22, John 17:26, Romans 9:17, Hebrews 2:12;
Exalt His Name: Psalm 34:3;
Glorify His Name: Psalm 86:9, Psalm 86:12; Honor His Name: Psalm 66:2;
Magnify His Name: 2 Samuel 7:26;
Praise His Name: 2 Samuel 22:50, Psalm 69:30;
Remember His Name Exodus 3:15, Psalm 45:17;
Sing His Name: Psalm 68:4;
Trust His Name: Isaiah 50:10

In these intimate circumstances, it is proper and good to use the True Name of God, YEHOVAH or JEHOVAH !.

Other Titles Of God:

We should do this along with His many other unique Titles in the Scripture, which represents Who He is to us. Some of these include:

Jehovah-Jireh: The LORD will Provide, Genesis 22:14
Jehovah-Nissi: The LORD is my Banner, Exodus 17:15
Jehovah Tzva'ot (Sabaoth): The LORD of Hosts, 1 Samuel 1:3
Jehovah-Rapha: The LORD Who Heals Exodus 15:26
Jehovah-Rofecha: The LORD Your healer, Exodus 15:26
Jehovah-Shalom: The LORD our Peace, Judges 6:24
Jehovah-Shammah: The Lord is There, Ezekiel 48:35
Jehovah-Tsidqenuw (Tsidkenu): The LORD our Righteousness, Jeremiah 23:6
Jehovah-Goel: The LORD Thy Redeemer, Isaiah 47:4
Elohim: God The Creator, Genesis 1:1
El Shaddai : God Almighty, Genesis 17:1, Revelation 1:8
El Gibor: Mighty (Great, Powerful) God, Isaiah 9:6
El Elyon: The Most High God, Genesis 14:19
El HaKavod : The God of Glory, Psalm 29:3
El Kanah: The Jealous God, Exodus 34:14
Elohim Tsedeq (Tzidki): God my Righteousness, Psalm 4:1
Elohim-Kedoshim: The Holy God, Joshua 24:19
El Roi: The God who Sees, Genesis 16:13
El De'ot: The All Knowing God, 1 Samuel 2:3
I AM or I AM THAT I AM, Exodus 3:14-15
The Alpha And The Omega, Revelation 1:8
The Beginning And The End, Revelation 1:8
The One Who Was, Who Is And Is To Come, Revelation 1:8
(And many more in the Scripture).

In addition, some may have their special, unique or personal name for God, based on how He has related or revealed Himself to them. After all, God can reveal Himself to a person in any manner for He is the I AM THAT I AM. And He may also have a special 'petname' for an individual who is very close to Him.

CHAPTER 6

About The Jealous God And Consuming Fire

Scriptural Verses:

Exodus 34:14 (ETB): *14 You must not worship any other god, because The LORD, Whose Name is "Jealous One", is a jealous God.*

Deuteronomy 4:24 (ETB): *24 For The LORD your God is a consuming fire, a jealous God.*

Hebrew 12:29 (ETB): For our God is a consuming fire.

Other Scriptures:

Exodus 20:4-5(ETB): *4 "You must not make for yourself a carved image or any kind of representation of anything that is in heaven above, or that is in the earth below, or that is in the water below the earth. 5 You must not prostrate to them nor worship them. For I, The LORD your God, Am a jealous God. I punish the iniquity, (sin of abomination) of the fathers upon their children, upon the third and fourth generations of those who hate Me.*

Deuteronomy 4:23-24 (ETB): *Watch out for yourselves, so that you will not forget the covenant of The LORD your God which He made* *with you, and make for yourselves a carved image in the form of anything which The LORD your God has forbidden you. 24 For The LORD your God is a consuming fire, a jealous God.*

Deuteronomy 5:9 (ETB): *You must not prostrate, (bow down) to them or worship them. For I, The LORD your God, Am a jealous God. I punish the iniquity, (sin of abomination) of the fathers upon their children, upon the third and fourth generations of those who hate Me.*

Deuteronomy 6:14-15 (ETB): *You must not follow after other gods, the gods of the peoples who are all around you, 15 because The LORD your God is a jealous God among you.*

If you do, the anger (displeasure, indignation) of The LORD your God will be was stirred up against you and destroy you from the face of the earth.

Explanation:

Jealousy could be evil, such as wanting to have what does not belong to one. It could also be a jealous (zealous) protection of someone over what rightly belongs to the person. And it may simply be a loving parental protective jealousy over a loved child.

Jealous God:

Jealous God means God is zealously, passionately loving, possessive, while vigilant, guarding, protective over His own, never tolerating unfaithfulness, and as the Almighty God, the Creator and Giver there is no envious jealousy which is evil. He is protective of His own, His people, His Name and His Glory!

Satanic or Evil Jealousy:

Satanic or Evil jealousy is the envious, evil kind of jealousy for what he does not have. This is the kind of jealousy Satan has against the elect, the saints or holy people of God, for what God has for them and he cannot have. This was the kind of jealousy Cain had against Abel and murdered him, (Genesis 4:1-12).

This kind of jealousy involves contentious rivalry, being negatively apprehensive, vengeful, hateful or insecure out of fear of being replaced by someone else. The sinful carnal nature of the flesh, which came from Satan after the fall of Adam and Eve, exhibits this type of jealousy. Satan did not create or own anything. God Elohim, The Creator of all, has no such fear for He created all and cannot be replaced by any other.

God The Consuming Fire:

God can also show His wrath, fury, fierce anger, indignations or strong displeasure about something or an act of anyone that is sinful in His presence.

We know that God hates all forms of sin. But one sin on the top most list is idolatry!

In the Scriptures, God repeatedly strongly warned against idolatry and acted against those who practiced idolatry. He has not changed!

The LORD summed it up with this statement from Him: "I am The LORD (YEHOVAH, JEHOVAH), that is My Name. And I will not give My glory to another, Or My praise to carved idol images", (Isaiah 42:8, ETB).

God does not tolerate or be patient with anyone when they indulge in idolatry in any form. For He does not share His glory with any others. The Canaanites, the Israelites of old, and any society or people today who indulge in idolatry, God has no pleasure in them. As the Creator, He is the One that must be worshipped. God would not hesitate to consume those associated or involved in idolatry!,(Exodus 20:4-5, Exodus 34:14, Deuteronomy 4:23-24, Deuteronomy 5:9, Deuteronomy 6:14-15, Isaiah 42:8, Hebrews 12:29).

The other kind of grievous sin, is one that tries to frustrate, work against or end His creation. He gave the command to Adam and Eve, and to Noah and their descendants to multiply and replenish the earth, (Genesis 2:27-28, Genesis 9:1-7). Yet the Devil was essentially leading Sodom and Gomorrah against this. It brought the consuming fire action of God!, (Genesis 19:1-29). Societies that engage or promote such kinds of practices are invoking the wrath of God! Yet we see that Lot's family engaged in incest, to have children,(Genesis 19:30-38). Though this was sinful, but they were not immediately punished, like Sodom and Gomorrah or those involved in idolatry. This does not mean incest is acceptable. It is still sin before God.

And of course, there are other forms of previous sins, like deliberate cold blooded murder, without any cause. God will always require the blood of the innocent from the hands of the murderer, (Genesis 4:10, Genesis 9:5-6).

We must always remember that God hates all forms of sin. His patience is shorter for some forms of than for others. He is also a patient God, who delays punishment, to give room for repentance. But ultimately, all kinds of sins will be punished, if the person or people do not repent.

Chapter 7

About Past Sins And Generational Curses

Scriptural Verses:

Exodus 20:5-6(ETB): *5 You must not prostrate to them nor worship them. For I, The LORD your God, Am a jealous God. I punish the iniquity, (sin of abomination) of the fathers upon their children, upon the third and fourth generations of those who hate Me. 6 I show mercy, (acts of loving kindness) for thousands (of generations), to those who love Me and keep My commandments.*

Exodus 34:6-7(ETB): *6 Then The LORD passed before Moses. And He proclaimed:*

"YEHOVAH, YEHOVAH God, Who is compassionate (merciful) and gracious, longsuffering (patient, slow to anger), and abounding, (filled, plentiful) in loving kindness (goodness) and truth, 7 showing loving kindness for thousands (of generations), forgiving iniquity, transgression and sin; yet not justifying, (excusing) the guilty, but visiting, (causing the negative effects of) the iniquity of the fathers to be experienced by their children and their children's children to the third and the fourth generation", [ref Exodus 3:15, Exodus 6:3, Exodus 34:6-7, Exodus 20:5-6, 2 Corinthians 5:17, Ezekiel 18:1-29].

(ETB Note: 'YEHOVAH or YHVH' in Hebrew or 'JEHOVAH', in English are each pronounced Yeh-ho-vaw', or substituted with the title 'The LORD, 'ADONAI').

Explanation:

The First Generational Curse:

The inherited sin from Adam is the first generational curse on everybody conceived of the seed of man on earth. Sin came to each of us when Adam our forefather fell into sin along with Eve in the garden of Eden, (Genesis 3:6). We partook in committing this as seeds in Adam's loins. In Adam, God's righteous nature was exchanged for the sinful carnal nature from the Devil. So we have all been conceived and formed in sin, (Psalm 51:5). So we are brought forth wearing the natural filthy garment of sin, (Zechariah 3:1-5). The only exception of course is LORD Yeshua. He was not conceived of the seed of man, but of the God through the Holy Spirit, (Matthew 1:20, Luke 1:31-35).

Just so that we have no doubt about our sins from birth, the Scripture clearly says that all have sinned and fallen short of the glory of God, (Romans 3:23). And sin, results first in spiritual death, (Genesis 2:16-17, Romans 6:23, James 1:15). And spiritual death brings about a gradual decay of the physical body till it dies. So, we are all born, spiritually dead, and live in a physical body that decays to death as a result.

The Second or Family Generational Curse:

Then, added to this may also be a wicked, abominable sin committed by our own parents or their own parents or great grandparents before we were born. It may be for example idolatry, sexual immorality, murder, etc. This brings a curse on who committed it and is passed down to the seed or descendants that come from that line. For the seeds or descendants were in the loins of the previous generation or father who committed that sin. This results in a generation curse, passed down. It is the second generational sin. This curse is not just of spiritual death and gradual decay of the body that came through Adam. There may be other manifestations that are peculiar to a particular family lineage. It may be inherited sicknesses, premature death at certain age, continuous failure at point of success, or something else.

This is what God is saying when He said He punishes the iniquity of the fathers on their children to the third or fourth generation of that family line, (Exodus 20:5-6, Exodus 34:6-7). As long as a sin has not been repented from, then the curse or punishment decreed by God for it remains in effect.

As long as a child continues in the sinful nature of the father or forefathers, the punishment for the iniquity remains. However, once a sin has been repented of, there is no longer a punishment or curse still attached to it. Each person needs to confess and renounce past sins with their own mouth and receive Yeshua into their heart.

The Deliverance From Generational Curses:

When a person comes to The LORD Yeshua, confesses his or her sins, all the sins committed or previously recorded against such a person are wiped out. The old sinful nature is removed and is replaced with the righteousness of God that comes through Yeshua, (1 Corinthians 1:30). The person becomes a new person, (2 Corinthians 5:17). All old or present sins, including the first generational sin passed down from Adam, and the second generational sins passed down from the family lineage, as well as own sins committed by the person are forgiven. All the curses attached to those sins are also terminated and replaced with the right standing and blessings that comes from God through His Son.

The Scripture assures us that if we confess our sins, including generational sins, God is faithful and just to forgive us and to cleanse us from all unrighteousness, (1 John 1:8-10). Not only this. In fact, once God has forgiven a person, He does not remember the past sins counted against that person, (Isaiah 43:25, Hebrews 8:12).

So a person who has repented and confessed past sins is no longer liable for the past generational sins or curses. He will not bear the sins of the father or past generations. But a person who does not repent, but continues in the same life style of the fathers, such a person will continue to bear the consequences of generational sins and curses.

For more reading, please refer to the following Scriptures: Exodus 34:6-7, Exodus 20:5-6, Ezekiel 18:20-23, Ezekiel 18:1-29, Isaiah 43:25, Hebrews 8:12, Ezekiel 18:21-22, Jeremiah 31:34, Jeremiah 18:7-10, John 3:16-17, 2 Corinthians 5:17, 2 Peter 3:9, 1 John 1:8-10, Ezekiel 33:1-20.

CHAPTER 8

About Long Life And How Long

Scriptural Verses:

Psalm 90:10 *(ETB):10 The active (hot, warm) years of our lives is seventy. And if we are still strong, eighty years. Yet, the years are only full of struggles and pains. The end comes quickly, and we fly away. [ref Genesis 5:1-32, Genesis 11:10-24, Deuteronomy 34:7, Job 42:16, Psalm 91:16].*

Explanation:

God's first thought for us is not about death, but of life. It is of abundant life on earth, followed by eternal life with him, (John 10:10, John 3:16, Revelation 2:7, Revelation 22:1-2, Revelation 22:14-15).

It is God's desire that we live long, (Psalm 91:14-16, Genesis 5:1-32, Genesis 11:10-24, Deuteronomy 34:7, Job 42:16).

But for how long we live depends on how much time is needed to fulfill God's purpose for each person on earth. For example, both John the Baptist and The LORD lived for less than 35years to fulfill His purpose for them on earth. On the other hand, Enoch lived for 365years before being taken away, (Genesis 5:21-24). Methuselah (Enoch's son and grandfather of Noah) lived for 969years to fulfill his purpose, (yes he had one) till the year just before the flood came. Methuselah means 'messenger'. He was the symbol and representation of God's message to the wicked world during his time, that the end was coming for them. He died the year the flood came, not in it but just before the flood. Noah lived for 950 years. He lived to build the ark that saved the eight of them and all the animals that escaped the flood to begin the new world for their kinds after the flood. Noah lived to father and mentor the new generation of the families of Japheth, Shem and Ham after the flood. Moses lived for 120years to fulfill God's purpose to lead Israelites out of Egypt to Canaan and to receive God's Law for them on the righteous way to live as God's holy people. Similarly, Abraham lived for 175years to fulfill God's purpose, to bring forth the seed in God's time, through whom the world would later be blessed. And so did Job. David lived to fulfill God's purpose, despite Goliath, and despite the extreme persecutions from king Saul and all the armies Saul sent to hunt down David. Those are but only a few examples of the holy people from the Scripture.

As for the wicked, God is a merciful and patient God. However, God may also cut short a life if it is completely derailed from His purpose into wickedness or when the allotted time of mercy for the wicked is exhausted, (Numbers 16:16-33, Acts 5:1-11).

The life span of mankind is not set at 120years. Many have confused the statement God made not to strive further with mankind but to allow them to continue for another 120 years before the flood came, (Genesis 6:3). It was an added time of grace for repentance. It was also during this time that the Ark was built. Noah's three sons, Japheth, Shem and Ham were born after this statement (or about 100years before the flood, when Noah was 500years old). God's prophesies are ever firmly established and fulfilled. So, if the desire or command of God was for mankind to live for only 120years, then Shem for example who was born after the statement would not have lived for 620years (Genesis 11:11). The scripture also did not record the other two sons died before Noah, who lived for another 350years after the flood, (Genesis 9:28). They lived long after the flood, and had many children. Also, if God had pegged the lifespan of mankind to 120years, then neither would the generation who were born after the flood, lived for between 200years and 400 years, (Genesis 11:11-22). Similarly, Abraham, Sarah, Job, Isaac, Jacob, Ishmael, etc lived beyond the 120years. However, due to sin, the life span of mankind began to degrade from the time of Adam, and is down to around a tenth of that today.

Neither is 70 years the set life span of mankind on earth! If so, then why do many people in this current generation live beyond this to 90years or 100years? Did God change this without telling us. No! For He did not set it at 70years! Many have confused Moses' statement in Psalm 90:10. It becomes clearer when we look at the original meaning of the word Moses used. It is "active, hot or warm years". So it actually reads: "The active (hot, warm) years of our lives is seventy, and, if we are still strong, eighty years. Yet, the years are only full of struggles and pains. The end comes quickly, and we fly away", (Psalm 90:10). This is in agreement with what we know even in our present days. Many today live beyond 70years, but degradation of strength falls after 70years, and only a few are still very active or agile after 80years.

Length of life degrades with sin, and sin came through Satan. In the end time, just as the LORD returns with the Saints from heaven, Satan will be imprisoned for 1000years (Revelation 20:3). During that time, the LORD, the source of life will reign on earth, initially for 1000years. In the millennium reign, sickness and early death would be a thing of the past (except in the case of sin by an individual). The falling trend of life expectancy will be reversed at the millennium, when the humans on earth will have longer life. It would be at least ten times longer than the present, as long as a millennium. But not immortality.

Prophet Isaiah had also prophesied about this. He said infants would no longer live for just a few years. Anyone who dies at 100years would be considered too young and as a sinner who is accursed. For as the days of a tree, so will be the days of God's people. Their children or offspring will be the descendants of the blessed of God. They will receive instant answers to their prayers, (Isaiah 65:20-24).

Eternity or immortality is God's plan for all. The Saints will receive this either after death or during rapture in the end time. The Saints are the holy people of God. They have the righteousness of God through His Son and also remain obedient to the end.

CHAPTER 9

About The Death Of Loved Ones

Scriptural Verses:

Psalm 116:15 (ETB): 15 In the sight of The LORD, The death of His Saints Is precious (deeply touching, highly valued).

1 Corinthians 15:16-19 (ETB): 16 For if the dead do not rise, then The Messiah is not risen.

17 And if The Messiah is not risen, then your faith will be in vain, being of no purpose. Furthermore, you would still be in your sins! 18 Then also those who have fallen into sleep (of dead people) in The Messiah have perished. 19 If our hope in The Messiah is only in this world, then we are to be pitied the most, among human beings!

1 Thessalonians 4:13-14 (ETB): 13 Brothers and sisters, I do not want you to be ignorant, about what will happen to those you have fallen into sleep (of dead people). Otherwise, you will be in sorrow like those who have no future hope. 14 For we believe that Yeshua died and rose again from the dead. In the same way, God will bring with Yeshua, those in Him, who have fallen into sleep (of dead people), [ref 1 Corinthians 15:12-23].

1 Thessalonians 4:15-17 (ETB): 15 We want to tell you this, as received directly from The LORD:

That those of us who believe in Him, who are still alive and remain in The LORD until His coming back, will not go ahead of those who have fallen into sleep (of dead people).

16 For The LORD Himself will (suddenly) come down from heaven with a loud sound. The loud sound will be the voice of an archangel blowing the trumpet (shofar) of God. Those who have fallen into sleep (of dead people), who are in The Messiah, will rise up first, [ref Acts 1:9, John 14:3, Matthew 24:36, 1 Thessalonians 5:2].

17 Then those of us who believe in Him, who are still alive and remain in The LORD, will be taken up together with them in the clouds. We will meet The LORD in the air (atmosphere). And from that time we will always be with The LORD forever, [ref Acts 1:9, John 14:3].

18 You should therefore, encourage one another with these words.

Explanation

We have all experienced or been affected directly or indirectly when a family member, spouse, child, parent, a sibling or a loved one dies. It is human to grieve for such a loss. As believers and followers of The LORD Yeshua, were to show empathy, love and comfort to those who are grieving, even if we are not related to them. And only The Holy Spirit of God, who knows and understands the situation and each person can fully comfort and give peace to everyone who is openly or silently grieving.

Let us see what the Scripture says about death:

God is deeply touched when any of His Saints (the holy people) dies. The Scripture says in Psalm 116:15 (ETB): "In the sight of The LORD, the death of His Saints is precious (deeply touching, highly valued)". In other words, the death of a Saint or beloved one of God, is a significant event that God deeply cares about and pays attention to. It is the ending of the assignment of the Saint on earth, and the call home by God.

Physical death is like deep sleep, the long deep sleep of the dead. This is because they have only gone to rest from the troubles of this world and will wake up again. This would be either at first the resurrection of the holy people of God or at second resurrection which leads to judgment or permanent death, (Revelation 20:4-6, Revelation 20:11-15). That second death is for the wicked and not for those in The LORD.

The Scripture says we should take courage, and not go on sorrowing like those who have no future. It is not for the lack of care or love for them. It is also to rejoice for them that they have gone to rest in The LIRD. And because Yeshua The Messiah died and rose again, everyone in Him who dies will rise again, (1 Thessalonians 4:13-14). If He had not risen our faith would have been in vain and we will be pitied the most among human beings, (1 Corinthians 15:16-19).

So every believer in The LORD Yeshua should have this confidence that we will see them again. This will be either in paradise, if we ourselves die before The LORD returns, or we will see them if we are still alive and the resurrection of the dead and rapture of the living Saints takes place, (1 Thessalonians 4:15-18).

Our loved ones sleeping now in The LORD will arise again at the trumpet sound of resurrection of the dead or rapture of the living and we will see them again.

At the resurrection or rapture there will be no marriage then or having children. The LORD said, those who will be alive and found worthy to attain the coming age, and those worthy to be resurrected from the dead, will not marry or be given in marriage. But will be like angels in heaven, (Matthew 22:30, Mark 12:18, Luke 20:35). Everyone will be like one big family together enjoying the love of The Father and of each other His children.

With this hope, let us take encouragement in The LORD and encourage each other. Our waiting is not for much longer for the return of The LORD.

But there are many who are alive today who have no such hope if they were to die now. This is because they do not know The LORD. They are not in Him or of Him. It is the duty of everyone who is in Him to tell them the good news of salvation through The LORD in the Kingdom of God.

Chapter 10

About Statutes, Judgments, Testimonies of God

Scriptural Verses:

Leviticus 18:4-5 (ETB): *4 You are to obediently do according to My judgments, (ordinances, rulings, decisions) and to carefully hold unto My laws, (statutes, regulations, instructions). You are to follow them: I AM The LORD your God. 5 You must therefore follow My laws (statutes, regulations, instructions), and My judgments, (ordinances, rulings, decisions), which if any person does, the person will have life through them: I AM The LORD.*

Deuteronomy 4:44-45 (ETB): *44 This is the law, (Torah) which Moses set before the Israelites.*

45 These are the testimonies, the statutes (laws, regulations, instructions), and the judgments, (ordinances, rulings, decisions) which Moses spoke to the Israelites after they came out of Egypt.

Explanation:

Statutes: Are laws, regulations, and instructions.

Judgments: Are ordinances, rulings, and decisions.

Commandments: Are specific orders, commands or mandates given by God, including the Ten Commandments, (Exodus 20:3-17, Matthew 22:34-40, Mark 12:28-34, Luke 10:25-28, John 13:34-35, John 15:12-17).

The Testimonies of God: Are the already verified, established words, revelations, doings or evidence attesting, bearing witness to God such as written in the Law, Torah, of Moses.

The Testimonies of God also include God's divine acts contained in the books of the prophets in the Old Testament. In the New Testament, it includes the acts of God by His Son, The LORD, and of the Holy Spirit through the Apostles as written in the New Testament of the Bible.

Chapter 11

About 'idols, gods, and God of gods'

Scriptural Verses:

Deuteronomy 10:17 (ETB): *17 For The LORD your God is the God of gods and The LORD of lords. He is The Great God, Mighty and Awesome, Who will not show partiality (discriminate) or take a bribe, (be compromised).*

Explanation:

Idols:

In general, idols are products of human origin or imaginations, which they turn around to worship. They are carved images, the works of men, being worshipped by humans as a 'god'. More broadly, anything a person worships, or places their trust or give a higher priority than God Almighty is like an idol or god. It may be carved idol images, animals, human beings such as leaders of some nations, celebrities, wealth, technology, etc.

God Almighty is very much against idols of any kind. Carved images or idols are not supposed to be made or worshipped in any form, (Exodus 20:4-5, Exodus 23:13, Isaiah 42:8). This was the main undoing of the Israelites who constantly went for the idols (or gods) of the Canaanites despite repeated warnings from God.

References to idols or dead gods in the Scripture will state idols, caved images, vanity, worthless, or works of men, wood, or gods of silver or gold, with eyes but cannot see, mouth but cannot speak, etc. They are not gods, but the work of men's hands, wood and stone. They can and are destroyed at will, (2 Kings 19:18). They are dead, and do not count before God. Therefore, God Almighty who is living and did not create them cannot be their 'God of gods', (Deuteronomy 10:17, Psalm 136:2-3, Daniel 2:47). The humans in their depraved minds carve or mold them and the turn round to start worshipping them as their gods or creator!.

Then there are those who take animals as their 'gods' in some parts of the world. Meanwhile, God has given to mankind the dominion over all animals and the animals as food for mankind, not as 'gods', (ref Genesis 1:26, Genesis 9:3). They too can be destroyed at will. Yet through ignorance and the deception of the evil one, mankind worships animals, stones, woods, silver, gold, etc as gods.

'god' or 'gods':

'god' or 'gods' in the scripture, are sometimes confused by readers with idols. However, unlike idols, they are in general not of human origin. They are divine heavenly beings or angelic. They are rulers or 'lords' with power or authority over some other angelic beings under their domains. Hence the scriptures generally refers to them as 'gods', 'lords', or as rulers, princes, principalities and powers, with domains. They were created by God through the LORD (His Son) for some purposes.

These special heavenly beings belong to Him and are alive in spiritual realms. It is for this reason or in this context that God Almighty is not only referred to as the Most High God, but also as the God of gods, and LORD of lords, (Genesis 14:18-22, Deuteronomy 10:17,

Daniel 2:47, Psalm 136:2-3, Mark 5:7). The Scripture further says the LORD (The Son) is the head of all principalities, the King of kings, and LORD of lords (Colossians 2:10, Revelation 19:15, 1 Timothy 6:15, Ephesians 1:21). These special heavenly beings are also referred to as 'gods' or princes (Psalm 82:1, Psalm 138:1, Psalm 97:9, Daniel 10:20-21, Daniel 12:1).

They are all subject to the power and authority of the Creator, the LORD, (Colossians 1:16; Colossians 2:15, Ephesians 3:10, 1 Peter 3:22).

None of them is ever to be worshipped by human beings. They too are to worship God Almighty, as their creator, just like we do to Him.

Most of the special angelic beings, rulers, princes, lords are good. Examples include archangels, such as Michael, and Gabriel, (Daniel 10:20-21, Daniel 12:1, Luke 1:11-28). There are many others in the Scriptures without names. There are the four living beings, and the cherubim. There are also the twenty-four elders or leaders before the throne of God in heaven, (Revelation 4:4).

But some of the angelic lords are bad, very bad and have fallen from their estate, due to disobedience, (Genesis 6:2-4, Jude 1:6, 2 Peter 2:4, Revelation 9:13-16). An example of the bad rulers, lords or 'gods' is the prince of Persia with spiritual kings of Persia under him, (Daniel 10:13). Another example are the 'gods' of Egypt, which God Almighty said He will execute judgment against (Exodus 12:12). The Judgment is not against dead woods, idols or carved images, but against active 'gods' in celestial or angelic realm. Another example is Abaddon or Apollyon (Destroyer), the king of the Abyss, (Revelation 9:11). Another is Lucifer, an anointed Cherubim, (Ezekiel 28:14-28, Isaiah 14:12-14, Luke 10:18). Lucifer who became known as Satan or Adversary is also referred to as the 'god' of this world or prince of the air, (John 14:30, Ephesians 2:2). These bad rulers or 'gods' contend with God to rule over and be worshipped by human beings. They and other bad angels under them therefore organize themselves to oppose everything of God, including the true Saints of God, (Daniel 10:13, Daniel 10:20, Ephesians 6:12, 1 Peter 5:8). They also mislead humans and entice them into rebellion against God Almighty.

Human 'gods'.

There are 'gods' amongst humans, in a manner similar to angelic 'gods'. An example in the human level was Moses. God made Moses like a 'god' to Pharaoh and Aaron as his prophet by giving Moses authority and power over them, (Exodus 7:1).But Moses was not worshipped by Pharaoh, Aaron or by the Israelites.

A person, or an angelic being referred to as 'god' in the scripture does not mean they are to be worshipped. The term 'gods' is more of a designation of the special powers given to them by God.

No human being, regardless of how powerful, is ever to be worshipped. Apart from Moses, Saints are or will also be like 'gods', 'rulers' or 'lords', (Psalm 82:6-7, John 10:34, Revelation 2:26-28). While they may even judge the bad angels and rebuke them, the good angels do not and will come under any judgment and are excluded, (1 Corinthians 6:3).

Chapter 12

About Offering, Tithes & Giving

Scriptural Verses:

Genesis 4:3-5 (ETB): 3 After some time had passed, Cain brought an offering of some of the fruit, (produce), of the ground to The LORD. 4 Abel also brought an offering of the firstborn of his flock, including their fat, (best portions). And The LORD regarded with respect, (favor), Abel and his offering. 5 However, He did not regard with respect Cain and his offering. For this reason, Cain became very angry and his demeanor, (countenance, expression on his face,), was downcast.

Genesis 14:18-20 (ETB): 18 And Melchizedek, the king of Salem and priest of God Most High, brought out bread and wine. 19 Then he blessed him and said:"Blessed be Abram by the Most High God, the Possessor of heaven and earth.20 And blessed be The Most High God, who has delivered your enemies into your hand." And Abram gave him a tithe, (one-tenth), of all.

Deuteronomy 12:4-6 (ETB): 4 You must not worship The LORD your God in their manner.5 "Instead, you must go to the place where The LORD your God will choose from all your tribes, to make His Name abide as His home (where He dwells). Look for that place and only there you should go. 6 There you should bring your burnt offerings and sacrifices, your tithes and heave offerings (personal contribution portions set aside), your vow offerings and freewill (voluntary) offerings, and the firstborn of your herds and flocks.

Deuteronomy 14:22-29 (ETB):22 "You must faithfully tithe all the increase of your grain that the field produces year by year. 23 You are to eat the tithe of your grain, your new wine, your oil, the firstborn of your herds and your flocks, in the presence of The LORD your God, in the place where He will choose to make His Name abide. This is so that you may learn to fear The LORD your God always, (ref Deuteronomy 12:6-12). 24 But if the journey is too long for you, such that you are not able to carry the tithe; Or if the place where The LORD your God will choose to put His Name, is too far from you, when The LORD your God has blessed you: 25 Then you should exchange it for money. Take the money with you and go to the place which The LORD your God will choose. 26 You should exchange (spend) the money for whatever you want: such as oxen, sheep, wine or similar drink, or for whatever you desire. You must eat there in the presence of The LORD your God. And you should rejoice, you and your household, [ref Ephesians 5:8, Leviticus 10:8-11, 1 Corinthians 3:16-17, 1 Corinthians 6:19-20, Proverbs 20:1, Proverbs 31:4-5, 1 Corinthians 10:31].

27 You must not abandon the Levite who is within your cities (gates), for he has no part or inheritance with you.28 "At the end of every third year you should bring out the tithe of your produce of that third year and place it within your cities (gates). 29 The Levite, because he has no portion or inheritance with you, the foreigner, the fatherless and the widow who are within your cities, (gates), may come, eat and be satisfied. This is so that The LORD your God may bless you in all the works of your hand which you do. [ref Numbers 18:21-24].

Malachi 3:10-12 (ETB): 10 Bring all the tithes into the storehouse, So that there will be food in My Temple, Says The LORD of hosts. Use this to test Me, to see, "If I will not open for you The Windows of Heaven And pour out so much blessing for you, Such that there will not be enough room to receive it, [ref Genesis 8:22, Malachi 3:10, 2 Chronicles 31:3-10].

11 "Also, I will rebuke (stop, keep away) the devourer for your sakes, So that he will not destroy the fruit of your ground. Neither will the grape vines in the field fail to produce fruits for you" Says The LORD of hosts. 12 "And all the nations will call you blessed, For you will be a land of good pleasure," Says The LORD of hosts.

Luke 6:38 *(ETB): 38 Give, and it will be given back to you: in good measure, pressed down, shaken together to fill every empty space, and running over (overflowing) will people give into your lap. Because you will receive back again in the same measure (proportion) that you use in giving out", [ref Genesis 8:22, Deuteronomy 16:17, Proverbs 11:24-25, Malachi 3:10, Luke 6:38, 2 Corinthians 9:7, Mark 12:41-44, Luke 21:1-4].*

Explanation:

Offering or Giving to God is an act of worship and has been from the beginning, (Genesis 4:1-12). Both Abel and Cain brought their gifts before God. Then Abraham gave a certain proportion, one-tenth or ten percent, of all his spoils from the war to Melchizedek, (Genesis 14:18-19). Melchizedek was the king of Salem and priest of God Most High, who had come with bread and wine, to fellowship with Abraham, and to also bless Abraham.

On earth, we sow to reap (Genesis 8:22). This is a sure way God has established for us on earth to increase. Tithing, offering or giving are spiritual means through which we plant or sow and then get the harvest. It is a universal principle for everyone on earth and is not limited to just believers in

God. A non-believer who is generous gets blessed back.

No one goes to heaven or hell on account of tithing, offering or giving. It is faith in Yeshua The Messiah (Jesus Christ) that takes someone to heaven. However, God is a giver. Therefore, there is no one who would not be moved within them to give, if the person claims to be a child of God, has faith in Yeshua and the Holy Spirit is living in the person.

Tithes Under The Old Testament Law (Torah)

Tithe means one-tenth or ten percent. Under the Old Testament it was a legal number established for the Israelites, the physical descendants of Abraham. Of the tribes of Israel, the Levites worked full time for God. The remaining eleven tribes engaged in farming or business (Numbers 18:21-24). By the eleven tribes each bringing one-tenth, it ensured the Levites had the same amount as the rest, and no tribe was left poor. This was before they arrived and settled in Canaan.

In Canaan, the tithe was still to be paid by the Israelites. But now the tithe was not just for the benefit of the Levites only. Rather, it was also for the benefit of the widows, orphans and poor, as well as for the strangers, and even for the families bringing the tithe, (Deuteronomy 12:6-12, Deuteronomy 14:22-29). Together, they celebrated and enjoyed it before God. When the Israelites did this, they were then able to go and declare before God, that they had fully obeyed His command in giving their tithes to the Levite, the foreigners, the fatherless (orphans), and the widows, (Deuteronomy 26:12-15).

Generous Giving In The New Covenant

In the New Testament, Yeshua The Messiah (Jesus Christ) did not teach tithing. But He also did not say people should stop paying tithes or giving. What He said is to give as much as you can, whether as tithe, or offering or just giving with no name attached, (Luke 6:38). There is no percentage attached in the New Testament. You do it in proportion to your ability.

If someone has $10 and gives $2. And if another person has $10million, and gives $1million. Then before God, the one who gave $2 from $10, has given more than the one who gave $1million. But humans, including Pastors, will make more noise about the one who (in the eyes of God) gave less than you.

Also God does not regard what we give (offering, tithing or giving) and then complaining about. We should not give grudgingly, but happily or cheerfully (2 Corinthians 9:6-10). God prefers an offering, tithing or gift that is given willingly, (Exodus 25:2). That means we should not give beyond the point where we will start complaining or feeling unhappy in your heart. Giving should be voluntary. It should not be by coercion, or trickery, or creating guilt in the minds of people, or 'bullying' with harsh words or curses. The same is true of our worship or obedience to God.

Since giving is a means to sow and reap, a believer should not rob God and so rob himself by not giving, offering or tithing. They should bring these to the storehouse so that there would be food, (Malachi 3:8-12). But the Scripture did not say this food is only for the Pastor and Church workers. Rather it is also for the poor, the widows, the orphans, the strangers and those who have need for the 'food or fund'. Pastors who eat it alone or keep the best portion for themselves bring a curse on themselves, (Malachi 1:6-10).

Now, what the Church receives in offering, tithing or giving is not just meant for the Pastor. It is for five purposes or groups:

1): All workers in Church including Pastor, Choir, Musicians, Ushers, Gateman, parking attendants, etc. It includes all who work for the Church. It also include those sent out by the Church on mission work and are not receiving support where they are on mission, (3 John 1:7-8). And no one, including the Pastor should be paid more than the average income of members of the Church. Yeshua or the Apostles were not different from those around them. The exemption though was Judas Iscariot who was greedy for money. He was unconcerned about the poor and was stealing money for himself, (John 12:6). He represents leaders who are selfish and greedy for Church money.

2): The Widows, Orphans and poor people in the Church or community, should be provided for from the Church offering, tithing or giving

3): The Strangers. There two groups of strangers. The first categories are those in the community that are of a different faith and do not know the LORD. Examples are Moslems, Hindus, non-believers, etc. This is powerful evangelism to them because by this act, taste God's love and goodness and become open to accept Him. The other strangers are those who are new in a community and have not settled down and need help. It may also include traveling evangelists, Gospel or Mission workers.

4): Church Building Repair, Utility and Other Bills. An adequate or required amount should be set aside for this and other regular on-going Church costs, such as water, electricity, love feasts and uniforms for workers.

5): Yourself and your family members, including houseboys/girls. This could be through special love feasts organized on a regular basis by the Church. If a Church does not operate the biblical principles, then you have the right to distribute your money or goods directly for these purposes as may be required.

Finally, anything done with the money received by the Church from offering, tithing or giving belongs to all. It belongs freely to everybody including members and non-members or strangers in the community. This includes schools, hospitals, cars, planes, etc acquired with Church money. No one should be prevented or charged to use them!

CHAPTER 13

About "Baal, Bel, Molech And National gods, idols, deities"

Scriptural Verses:

Jeremiah 19:5 *(ETB):5 They have also built the pagan shrines in high places for Baal (the Canaanite male fertility god, idol). There, they sacrifice to Baal their sons (and daughters) as burnt offerings with fire. I did not command or speak about it to them. Neither did it ever come into My heart (to command them to do so), [ref Leviticus 18:21, 1 Kings 11:4-8, 2 Kings 23:10, Deuteronomy 12:29-31, Deuteronomy 18:9-11, Jeremiah 7:31, Jeremiah 19:5, Jeremiah 32:35].*

Jeremiah 32:34-35 *(ETB):34 Instead, they placed their abominations (idols) in the Temple which is called by My Name, to defile it. 35 They have also built the pagan shrine high places of Baal which are in the Valley of the Son of Hinnom. There, they make their sons and their daughters to pass through the fire and burned them in sacrifice to Molech. I did not command or speak about it to them. Neither did it ever come into My heart that they should commit such abominations to cause Judah to sin.' [ref Leviticus 18:21, 1 Kings 11:4-8, 2 Kings 23:10, Jeremiah 7:31, Jeremiah 19:5, Jeremiah 32:35].*

Explanation:

Pagan societies, both in ancient times and present time, have national gods, deities and idols they worship. Being part of their culture and practices, carved images of the idols or deities are proudly displayed in shrines, homes, restaurants, monuments. They do not know or worship the Most High God, who is the Almighty creator and possessor of the heavens and the earth, (Genesis 14:18-20).

Some of the images of the deities or idols are carved from stones, wood or molten metal and elaborately dressed in gold and silver, (Psalm 115:4-8, Isaiah 40:18-20, Isaiah 44:9-20, Isaiah 46:5-7, Jeremiah 10:2-7).

They make images of these idols or gods with their own hands, and begin to worship them. It was common in many nations of old, and still so in some nations even today. Many of them also engage in worship of the heavenly hosts of stars, moon, sun, planets, engaged in worship of idol images.

After the Israelites were freed by GOD Almighty, from their slavery in Egypt, they went on to possess the promised of Canaan, the land flowing with milk and honey, (Exodus 3:17). The LORD warned the Israelites, before and after they got to Canaan, against serving, bowing down, worshiping other gods or even swearing by their names in the land of Canaan, (Exodus 23:23-24, Leviticus 26:1, Deuteronomy 7:16-26, Deuteronomy 12:2-3, Deuteronomy 29:16-18).

In the land of Canaan were the Canaanites, Amorites, Hittites, Perizzites, Hivites and Jebusites. They worshipped Baal as the chief god (idol, deity). Baal was the male god of fertility, seen as having the power for reproduction of life (fertility) and also for harvest yield of crops.

The worship of Baal as chief god went beyond the land of Canaan. He was called different names in different nations. Among the

Canaanites, this deity was known as Baal. Among the Ammonites, Baal was also the chief god worshipped as Molech, Moloch, Milcom, or Malcam, (Leviticus 18:21, Leviticus 20:1-5, 1 Kings 11:4-8, 2 Kings 23:10, Jeremiah 7:31, Jeremiah 19:5, Jeremiah 32:35). In the Mesopotamian region, Baal was also known and worshipped as Tammuz (Ezekiel 8:14). Among the Babylonians and Chaldeans, Baal was known as Bel, their chief god worshipped in the Tower of Babel, (Isaiah 46:1, Jeremiah 50:2, Jeremiah 51:44). And there were other gods, deities among them such as Moredoch in the time of Nebuchadnezzar. And there was Nebo the god who presided over learning, and letters to the Babylonians, Hermes to the Greeks, Mercury to the Latins, and Thoth to the Egyptian.

The generations of Israelites that followed after the death of Moses, Joshua and those who came out of Egypt did not know God Almighty or worshipped Him wholeheartedly. The Israelites succumbed to the customs and practices of the Canaanites and surrounding nations, contrary to the warnings from God. On getting to Canaan, they abandoned God Almighty, the Creator of the heavens and the earth. Instead, they worshipped Baal and built many high places or pagan shrines for the worship of Baal.

Solomon built many temples for the worship of the gods of his many foreign wives, (1 Kings 11:4-8). The worship of Baal gained further prominence in the nation of Israel following the marriage of King Ahad to Jezebel, (1 Kings 16:30-34). Jezebel was the daughter of the king of the Sidonians, called Ethbaal (meaning with Baal). Prophet Elijab fought against Baal and his prophets who were under the care of Jezebel and Ahab. After their defeat in a contest, Elijah had 450 prophets of Baal slaughtered to bring purity back to Israel, (1 Kings 18:18-40).

Shrines for Baal and other gods were common places in the streets of Jerusalem and all over the cities of Judah before God sent them out on exile. The LORD had warned them not to let any of their offspring to pass through fire of ritual sacrifice for Molech, (Leviticus

18:21). Yet Israel, Judah and their kings went deeper into more despicable practices in their worship of Baal. In Judah, they built pagan shrines or high places at Topheth (the fire pit), which is in the Valley of the Son of Hinnom. There they committed all kinds of sexual immoralities, orgies, reveling in their worship of Baal and other gods. They also burnt their sons and daughters in fire, as sacrifice to Baal, also called Molech, Moloch (2 Kings 23:10, Jeremiah 7:31, Jeremiah 19:5, Jeremiah 32:35, Amos 5:27).

Like King Ahab and Jezebel of (the ten tribes of) Israel, King Manasseh of Judah was fully devoted to the worship of Baal, his consort Asherah (known also as the Queen of Heaven), and other pagan practices. (Refer to the commentary at the Chapter On "Asherah, Queen Of Heaven, Easter And Passover"). King Manasseh built wooden images (idols) for Asherah and brought it into the Temple of God, built by Solomon. He was also engaged in the worship of the heavenly hosts of stars, moon, sun, planets, engaged in worship of idol images, (2 Kings 21:3-7). He made his son pass through the fire, (burned as sacrifice) to Baal. He practiced soothsaying, witchcraft, and consulted spiritists and mediums.

Despite repeated warnings from God, Almighty, they refused to change. Therefore, God in His wrath, sent them out in exile from the land of Canaan. The ten northern trips of Israel, led by Ephraim were taken captive by Assyria, (2 Kings 17:4-24). The two southern tribes Judah (and Benjamin) were taken into exile to Babylon by Nebuchadnezzar, (2 Kings 24:13-20, 2 Kings 25:1-21).

There is idolatry now in many parts of the world, including in advanced western societies. Idolatry will continue to increase in the end time. Many of the ancient eastern pagan customs and practices will abound all over the world. Sorcery, spiritism, mediums, magic, witchcraft, soothsaying, etc will increase. Global alliances will be formed between many nations, enabling easy interchange and export of wicked and abominable practices between the east and the west, (Isaiah 2:5-9).

CHAPTER 14

About To Bless The LORD and The Blessed Person

Scriptural Verses:

Psalm 1:1-2 *(ETB): 1 Blessed (joyous, happy) is the person: Who does not listen to the advice (counsel, guidance, instructions) of the wicked; Or take his stand (makes a habit, persists, continues) in the way of the sinner; Or remain (stay, associate) in the company of the arrogant, (haughty, mocker, scornful).2 But his pleasure is in the law of The LORD (ADONAI). He meditates (ponders, reflects) in His law Day and night, [ref Joshua 1:8, 2 Corinthians 6:14-17, Deuteronomy 7:6, 1 Peter 2:9-10, Psalm 119:103].*

Explanation:

A Blessed Person:

A blessed person is joyous and happy! Is full of happiness, joy and contentment! Good things come from The LORD and His blessing makes a person full of happiness, joy and contentment. It does not come with sorrow, curse, mourning, or ruin. A person who fears The LORD is blessed. A person who meditates on the word of The LORD is blessed. For The LORD in turn draws near and delights in the revelation of Him, His Mightiness and goodness to such a person.

The LORD blesses us with His manifold blessings that make us joyous and happy. The blessings that come from The LORD include mercy, love, peace, joy, salvation, health, protection, provisions, comfort, satisfaction, contentment, answered prayer, father-child relationship with Him, being part of His Kingdom, etc.

To Bless The LORD:

The earth belongs to The LORD and the fullness in it. There is no material or wealth we can give Him which He does not already have or cannot create. And those come from Him to us. But we can bless Him with our obedience, praise and worship. To bless the LORD is to praise and worship Him in words or songs from the heart. It is not about material offering or money to Him. It is of the soul and being of a person praising his/her Creator.

To bless the LORD is to render words of praise, gratitude and appreciation of Him to Him from the heart. It could be spoken out aloud or in silence. Blessing the LORD in words or songs could be accompanied with dancing or kneeling or prostrating before Him, such as in the manner demonstrated in 1 Chronicles 29:20. It should be done in spirit and in truth, (John 4:24). It should be done with sincerity, wholeheartedly and voluntarily.

To bless the LORD is to offer praise and worship to Him from a heart of obedience. For obedience is better than sacrifice, (1 Samuel 15:22-23). A heart of disobedience is considered a wicked heart. Praise or worship from such a disobedient heart is as of hypocrisy and lip service, (Isaiah 29:13; Matthew 15:7-9, Mark 6:6-7). It is an abomination before The LORD. For God looks at the heart and delights in praise, worship or offering from an obedient heart.

CHAPTER 15

About The Revenge Of The Gibeonites

Scriptural Verses:

2 Samuel 21:1-2 (ETB): 1 There was a period during David's reign as king, when there was a famine that lasted for three years. So David at that time inquired of The LORD, (ADONAI). The LORD answered, "It is because of Saul and his bloodthirsty family, because he killed the Gibeonites", (2 Samuel 5:5, Numbers 35:33-34).

2 So the king called the Gibeonites and spoke to them. The Gibeonites were not part of the Israelites. They were from remnants of the Amorites. The Israelites had sworn to protect them. However, Saul had tried to kill them (wipe them out) in his zeal for the children of Israel and Judah, (Joshua 9:1-27).

Explanation

The Israelites were deceived by the Gibeonites to avoid being destroyed in Canaan, (Joshua 9:1-17). They failed to check with God, when the Gibeonites came. So they went ahead and made a covenant with the Gibeonites not to destroy them. The Gibeonites were to become servants of the Israelites as woodcutters and water carrier for the Temple of the LORD, (Joshua 9:18-27). And they were for a long time, from the time of Joshua to Samuel.

During Saul's reign as King over Israel, King Saul violated this covenant. He tried to wipe out the Gibeonites. This violation was a serious one before God. It brought about famine during the reign of King David, until their death was avenged on Saul's family, (2 Samuel 21:1-9).

God is a covenant keeping God. As His children, God expect us to honor all the vows we make before Him and to others. For this reason, we must be very mindful of the vows we make. The experience of Joshua and Israelites with the Gibeonites tells us, we should always check with God before we make agreement with others. And we must fulfill the vows we make to God. It is better not to make a vow, than to make it and not fulfill it, (Deuteronomy 23:21, Ecclesiastes 5:4).

Chapter 16

About Wisdom, Proverbs and Parables

Scriptural Verses:

Proverbs 1:1-7 *(ETB):1 These are the proverbs (parables) of Solomon, the son of David and king of Israel. They are:*

2 For learning about wisdom and discipline. For knowledge of the words (sayings) of understanding.

3 For receiving guidance on wisdom, Justice, judgment (decision making), and uprightness (fairness).

4 For the simple (ignorantly naive) person to learn how to take caution. For the young person to get knowledge and wisdom.

5 For anyone who is already wise to hear and still increase more in knowledge. For anyone who has understanding to reach a higher level of wise guidance.

6 For understanding proverbs and their interpretations. For understanding the saying and parables (dark sayings, riddles) of the wise.

7 Getting knowledge starts with fearing The LORD (ADONAI). But fools despise wisdom and correction,

[ref Proverbs 8:13, Job 28:28, Psalm 111:10, Proverbs 1:7, Proverbs 9:10].

Explanation:

Proverbs are also known as parables. They are short expressions of some wise, everyday godly truths and thoughts. Some are direct in their meanings, and some require wisdom to understand what the speaker means.

King Solomon was the son of King David. Most of the content of the Book of Proverbs are his sayings, though some were spoken by others such as by Agur the son of Jakeh (Proverbs 30), and King Lemuel's mother, (Proverbs 31).

God gave Solomon wisdom, exceptionally great understanding, and a great mind, (1 Kings 3:10-13, 2 Chronicles 1:11-12). People from all nations, including kings from all over the earth, who had heard of his wisdom, went to hear him. Solomon composed 3,000 (three thousand) proverbs, and 1,005 (one thousand and five) songs, (1 Kings 4:29-34). He also spoke of the rewards of wisdom, and foolishness, discipline, compassion, integrity, grace, as well as the evil of alcohol, pride, arrogance, self-praise, borrowing and collaterals, bad associations, pursuit of wealth, hot-temper, contention, wickedness, deception and falsehood, oppression, laziness, gluttony, gossips, slanders, immoral relationships (harlots and adultery by married women), etc.

Wisdom and Knowledge come from the fear of The LORD, (Proverbs 1:7, Proverbs 9:10, Proverbs 8:13, Job 28:28, Psalm 111:10). To fear The LORD is to hate what is evil! (Proverbs 8:13). Anything that makes God unhappy, or contradicts his command is evil. This includes pride, arrogance, deception, immorality, evil actions. Wisdom and Knowledge are for God's glory, and abide as long as we continue to fear him. The choice to fear God remains with us to decide. The enemy can take advantage, when people choose to disobey God. At some point, King Solomon who started well with the fear of God digressed into evil. He violated God's commands concerning foreign idolatrous women, and progressed from there to build temples for their gods and burned incense to them, (1 Kings 11:1-13, Deuteronomy 7:2-6, Deuteronomy 17:14-20, 1 Peter 2:9, 2 Corinthians 6:14). But the gift of God is without repentance of Him, (Romans 11:29). God is also no respecter of persons. God punished him for this, but his soul was saved (after repentance)! For Solomon through his actions had explored wisdom in the positive and foolishness in the negative sense, and himself came to a final conclusion, that the duty of all mankind is to fear God and keep His commandments, (Ecclesiastes 1:12-18, Ecclesiastes 12:13-14).

The Spirit of God rested on The LORD, the Messiah, the sinless perfect Lamb of God. Even the Spirit of wisdom and understanding, the Spirit of counsel and might, the Spirit of knowledge and of the fear of The LORD God, (Isaiah 11:2).

In the New Testament, The LORD, also used the method of parables for communicating when He was on earth. It was for the hearers to go and think about it. However, He would later explain to His disciples when they ask Him, (Matthew 13:10-13). The parables were earthly stories with meanings for the kingdom of God. Many of the hearers were not interested in hearing about the kingdom of God. Therefore, they did not understand. But those who were interested, received understanding.

In the same manner, the Spirit of wisdom, understanding, counsel, might, knowledge and of the fear of The LORD God rests in every believer through the Holy Spirit. It is the Holy Spirit that makes the fear of the LORD GOD possible. This is why the choice to be obedient every day to the Holy Spirit is critical to success. Solomon is a great example for us that our fear of God must be continuous, if we are to please God. The fear of God and obedience to Him are critical to finishing well!.

CHAPTER 17

About King Solomon And Shulamite

Scriptural Verses:

Song of Solomon1:5(ETB):5 I am black (dark-brown, sun-blackened) and beautiful, you daughters of Jerusalem!I am as the lovely tents of Kedar. As the beautiful curtains of (the tents) of Solomon.

Song of Solomon6:4-6(ETB):(He said):4 My love, you are as beautiful as Tirzah, lovely as Jerusalem, awesome (terrific) as an army with banners!5 Turn your eyes away from me. For they have overpowered me. Your hair is like a flock of goats coming down from Gilead. 6 Your teeth are sparkling like a flock of sheep that are coming out from their washing. Everyone of them is coupled (in pairs), and none is without an offspring.

Song of Solomon6:13(ETB): 13 Come back, Come back, Shulamite, (meaning "the perfect or the peaceful one"). Come back, Come back, to where we can look at you!

Explanation:

The Song of Solomon is the story of the romantic love life between King Solomon and a young lady. King Solomon was very much in love with her, just as she was. He gave her the nickname (pet-name)

Shulamite, which means "the perfect" or "the peaceful" one, (Song of Solomon 6:13).

King Solomon in his life time had 700 (seven hundred) wives who were princesses, and 300 (three hundred) concubines, (1 Kings 11:3). However, Shulamite was very special. King Solomon fell in love with Shulamite, after acquiring sixty queens, eighty concubines and countless virgins, (Song of Solomon 6:8).

Shulamite was especially flawless, perfect in all forms and very peaceful. She was well admired by other queens, concubines and women in King Solomon's life. While growing up, Shulamite's family protected her from being wayward until her marriage, (Song of Solomon 8:8-9).

Shulamite was black and very beautiful. She started life as a vineyard caretaker for her family and herself. She did this under the hot sun, which made her even much darker (tanned) and glowing than the other young women of Jerusalem, who were not exposed to the sun, (Song of Solomon 1:5-6). King David was another person who spent his early years under the sun as a shepherd for his family, (1 Samuel 16:11-12). David was described as radiant, glowing and ruddy. King Solomon shared a passion for the outdoor with Shulamite. Solomon, like his father king David, was also described as radiant (dazzling) and ruddy. King Solomon also had black hairlocks, which was thick, bushy, and wavy, (Song of Solomon 5:10-11).

Shulamite's love for Solomon was very passionate. It was described as a fierce fire that could not be extinguished by any amount of water or flood, (Song of Solomon 8:6-7). On his part, King Solomon loved her above all other women. His love for Shulamite was so deep that he spent much time with her and wrote about their romantic life. This was despite more than 1000 other queens, concubines and young women in his life, as well as his responsibilities as a reigning king over Israel and provinces.

CHAPTER 18

About Appearances Of God

Scriptural Verses:

Isaiah 6:1 *(ETB): 1 In the year that King Uzziah (Azariah) of Judah died, I saw The LORD (ADONAI) sitting on a throne. He was highly exalted and magnified. The Temple was filled with the train (bottom edge, hem) of His robe.*

Daniel 7:9-10 *(ETB): 9 "I watched as thrones were put in place, and the Ancient of Days sat down. His garment was white like snow, and the hair on His head was like pure wool. His throne was a flame of fire. Its wheels were like a blazing fire. 10 A stream of fire was flowing in His presence, pouring out in front of Him. A thousand thousands (millions) of angels ministered to Him. Ten thousand times ten thousand (many millions) stood in front of Him. The judgment court was seated, and the books were opened, [ref Daniel 7:10, Revelations 5:11].*

Revelation 4:2-3 *(ETB): 2 Immediately I was in the Spirit (entered into a vision). And Look! A Throne was set in heaven, and One was sitting on The Throne, [ref Isaiah 6:1, Ezekiel 1:26, Daniel 7:9].*

3 And The One who was sitting on The Throne was in appearance brilliant like a jasper (precious stone of various colors) and a sardius stone. And there was a rainbow around The Throne which looked like an emerald in appearance, [ref Exodus 28:17, Genesis 9:16, Ezekiel 1:28].

Explanation:

God Almighty, The LORD God of host in His natural state, is Spirit. No one can describe Him in His glory and appearance. He is too awesome, too magnificent, and too powerful beyond description in form and actions.

Also, no human being, can see God in His true or full glory and live. Moses who was highly favored and a friend of God, came close, but did not! God told Moses, "You will not be able to see My face, because no human being can look at Me, and remain alive", (Exodus 33:19-23, Numbers 12:6-8). So God allowed His glory to pass by, as He pronounced His Names, while covering the face of Moses. Even the Seraphim angels that Prophet Isaiah saw around His throne have six wings of which two are used to cover their faces, (Isaiah 6:1-2).

While no human can see God in His glorious form and live, God has however appeared to many of His servants as recorded in the Scripture. This is because when God appears to any human being, He does not do so in His full glory. God appears in a form that is more appropriate, convenient for us and for a purpose. He does so to convey a particular message. God created mankind from dust, in the likeness of His image and with His attributes, (Genesis 1:26-28). God appears in a physical form to us in human form, and as a man. For the scripture refers to God as a He.

God appeared to Abraham, who was His friend, in a simple human form and did not show off His power. He even ate with Abraham and they had conversations together as friends, (Genesis 18). God appeared to Moses many times, and in one occasion along with the seventy leaders of Israelites, who ate in His presence and did not die, (Exodus 24:9-11). This was at the period He was establishing His covenant and commandments with Israel.

In the case of Prophet Isaiah, He appeared as a King, (for He is the King of kings), who is Holy, righteous and enthroned on High. The revelation of the holiness of God shows our sinful nature in its raw form, deserving of death! This was why Prophet Isaiah exclaimed: "Woe is me, for I am undone (will perish, be destroyed). I am a man with defiled lips!, (Isaiah 6:5). But God is merciful. Isaiah's guilt and sin were taken away. God later sent His begotten Son, for the whole of mankind on earth, not to condemn us, but to redeem us from our sins, to give eternal life to all who will receive Him, (John 3:16-17).

Apart from Abraham, Moses, and Isaiah, God had also appeared to Daniel, Ezekiel and John in various forms, (Daniel 7:9-11, Ezekiel 1:26-28, Revelation 4:2-11).

The Most High God, The Father had also appeared, at least twice to His servant, (the one who wrote this and the End Time Bible, ETB). So have the Son and the Holy Spirit also appeared to him. In one instance, all three of them had appeared together. And in other times, the Son with the company of angels or alone.

God is purposeful. These appearances were to convey specific messages, concerning the coming arrival of the end time. For God does not do a thing (that affects mankind on earth) until He first informs His servants, (Amos 3:7). And the End Time Bible has not been written out of human will or desire. Rather, the End Time Bible has been written after The LORD Yeshua *(Jesus, Iēsous)*, who is also the Word of God, had by Himself appeared to assign and give the instruction for it to be written. He also confirmed it by The Holy Spirit.

In appearances, God the Father featured more to the prophets in the Old Testament times. The Son and the Holy Spirit were relatively silent at that time, unknown to them. They had not yet been revealed, and their ministry on earth had not yet been fulfilled. God has timing for everything He does. But all three are now part of us as His redeemed. We are truly blessed!

We must however be very careful about visions and messages. We must make certain to confirm the source. For not all visions or messages are from God. Falsehood and deception will multiply in the end time. Whatever visions or messages someone receives, whether directly from God Himself, or delivered through His angels, messengers, or prophets must always be confirmed. It must be confirmed with His Word. The Scriptural confirmation is the proof we must always look for. The Holy Spirit will always confirm with the Scriptures if we ask Him for help. It is one of His roles in the end time to reveal the truth to us. He will reveal or confirm that which is from the Father or from the begotten Son.

Obedience to His word is very important, much more than any sacrifice we can offer, (1 Samuel 15:22-23, John 14:15). In the end time, all faithful, obedient Saints will be taken away in rapture to heaven. There, all will stand before the throne of GOD to behold Him, and to sing praises along with angels to Him, (Revelation 7:9-11).

CHAPTER 19

About The Three Groups in Zion in End Time

Scriptural Verses:

Isaiah 35:10 (ETB): *The ransomed of The LORD will return. They will come to Zion with singing,*

Crowned on their heads with everlasting joy. They will be filled with joy and gladness. Sorrow and mourning (moaning) will not be found among them.

Revelation 19:14 (ETB): *14 And the Heavenly Armies were following behind Him on white horses. They were wearing fine linen, white and clean.*

Zechariah 14:5 (ETB): *5 Then you will run to escape through My mountain valley. For the mountain valley will reach to Azal. Yes, you will run to escape as you fled from the earthquake in the days of Uzziah king of Judah. This is how The LORD my God will come, and all the saints with You (Him).*

Isaiah 4:5 (ETB): *5 Then The LORD will create over the whole site of Mount Zion, and over those who assemble there: A cloud with smoke by day and the brightness of a flaming fire by night. For the glory will be a canopy (cover) over all*

Explanation:

Three groups will be with the LORD in Zion in End Time when He returns, after rapture, to reign on earth:

The LORD will return from heaven to earth with His Saints who have been taken to heaven in rapture. This is apart from the angelic host that will also accompany Him, (Zechariah 14:5b, Revelation 19:14, 1 Thessalonians 4:14-17, 1 Corinthians 15:51-55).

Thirdly, there are also those (humans on earth) who are also His redeemed, who have received Him as LORD. This did not go to heaven. But they are caught in Jerusalem in the final battle, the battle of Armageddon, of the armies of the world lead by the antichrist. This group of people in Jerusalem are displaced as they run to escape from the ruthlessness of the armies of the antichrist, (Zechariah 14:2).

After the LORD has done away with the enemies, (the antichrist and his world armies), the people displaced from Jerusalem will also return back to Zion. All will rejoice for the deliverance, (Zechariah 14:1-11, Revelation 19:11-21, Revelation 7:14-17).

CHAPTER 20

About When Righteousness Is or Not Filthy Rags

Scriptural Verses:

Isaiah 64:6 (ETB):6 But we are all like something that is unclean (filthy, defiled). And all our acts of righteousness are like filthy rags. We all wither like a leaf. And our iniquities have taken us away,

like the wind,[ref Zechariah 3:3-4, Isaiah 54:17, Romans 5:6-8, Ephesians 2:8-9, 1 Corinthians 1:30, 2 Corinthians 5:21, 2 Corinthians 5:17].

Explanation:

Righteousness or acts of righteousness can be like filthy or not filthy rags. Right from the moment of conception in the womb or birth, every child comes out wearing the garment of the nature of sin, (Psalm 51:5).

This garment of sin came from Satan through Adam and Eve when they fell in disobedience to God, when the Serpent tempted in the garden of Eden, (Genesis 3:1-13). Before then, there was no sin or unrighteousness in Adam or Eve. But from then on, every human being born, of man and woman, and not of the Spirit of God, goes through life wearing the filthy garment or nature of sin and unrighteousness. Cain, their first child, who was born after the fall, grew up to be a murderer, being consumed with jealousy of Abel, (Genesis 4:1-10).

Righteousness, is the standard of acceptance before God. Righteousness comes from God Himself. No amount of money can buy it. It has never been for sale from the beginning and will never be. Even if it was, no one can have enough wealth to buy it.

Righteousness is bestowed freely by God. But not everyone receives it. It is given only to those who meet His criteria.

Righteousness starts with the covering or removal of sins through forgiveness. In the old testament covenant, under which the Israelites of old operated, sin was covered or forgiven after the sacrifice of an appropriate animal blood. Even then, it was not everyone who received forgiveness, but only for a specific group. Anyone who was seen by The LORD to be humble (not arrogant, proud or haughty), and repentant (contrite, remorseful) of their sins, and fearful (obedient) when they hear the word of God, (ref Isaiah 66:2-3, Psalm 1:1-2). Everyone else outside of this group, who did not meet all the three criteria, did not receive mercy. Though, they may sacrifice the fattest bull or lamb with the most blood poured, their sins did not receive forgiveness or mercy of God. In fact, their very sacrifices of bulls or lambs were considered are likened to murdering a man or breaking the neck of a dog, (ref Isaiah 66:2-3).

But the underlying filthy garment of sinful nature was never removed for either group. Hence even Joshua, the high priest, who was perfect according to the standard of man, was still considered filthy. This was why Joshua was still accused by Satan before God, (Zechariah 3:1-5). This was because Joshua still had the garment of unrighteousness or sin on him. It came from Satan, in the garden of Eden, through Adam and Eve, who passed it to every of their offspring. But God in His mercy, removed the filthy garment of unrighteousness from Joshua. It was symbolic of what was to come later through His Son, the Branch.

Therefore, whatever is done wearing the old nature, without being covered by God's righteousness is like filthy rags. This was the situation in the Old Testament, even in the days of Isaiah and until God sent his son.

Under the new testament or covenant, God offered His own perfect sacrificial Lamb, who came as His begotten Son, for the forgiveness of sin, (John 1:29, John 1:36). Not only is sin forgiven through the sacrificial Lamb of God, but the very filthy garment, nature of sin or unrighteousness is also removed at the same time. This is why anyone in the Son (the Messiah or Christ) is a new creature, because old things (garments, nature of sin) is gone, and the person becomes new, (2 Corinthians 5:17).

While righteousness is both free and made available for everyone, under the new testament or covenant, but not everyone has it. Only those in the Son (the Messiah or Christ) receive the righteousness of God through Him. For He is the wisdom from God, the righteousness, sanctification and redemption for every believer, (1 Corinthians 1:30).

Only those who accept the Lamb, the Son of God in their hearts and confess their sins with their mouths, (John 3:16-17, Romans 10:8-10) are righteous before Him. They become born again through the Spirit of God. For these, the sinful nature and barrier to relationship with God are removed.

Under this condition, then rebellion, pride, arrogance, haughtiness, and disobedience to the word of God are done away with. In fact, such a believer operates with humility and total obedience to the word of God. Self interests or desires are gone. The only desire is to delight God with acts of righteousness. The true believer in essence has become like poured as sacrifice unto God. The believer no longer lives a life of their own, but a life in the Son, through the Son with the power of the Holy Spirit.

So, as long as we are wearing the righteousness of God through the Son (the Messiah or Christ), our righteousness or acts of righteousness are Not like filthy rags. But very pleasing, desirable and acceptable like a sweet aroma to God.

The only thing that can make the garment to become defiled or filthy again is a lifestyle of sin and disobedience. It comes when the person chooses to re-wear or put on again, the old nature, the garment of disobedience, sin or unrighteousness from Satan. Then, whatever is done is filthy, no matter how lavish or generous it may be, whether of material, wealth, time, etc.

We also must not be fooled by the increase of blessings (wealth) people enjoy through generous acts of giving. For the promised blessings that come from sowing or giving is universal for all of mankind under the sun on earth, (Genesis 8:22). It is for both believers and non-believers alike, regardless of their faith or religion. But regardless of the rewards from the sowing of seeds, the soul of the unbeliever (or disobedient believer), is doomed for destruction due to the unrighteous garment they are still wearing. It can only be saved through the sacrificial blood of the perfect Lamb of God and remain so through continued obedience to His word.

Chapter 21

About Asherah, Queen Of Heaven, Easter And Passover

Scriptural Verses:

Jeremiah 7:17 (ETB): *Do you not see what they do in the cities of Judah and in the streets of Jerusalem? 18 The children gather wood, the fathers kindle the fire, and the women knead dough, to make cakes for the Queen of Heaven. They pour out drink offerings to other gods, so that they may provoke Me to anger, [ref Jeremiah 7:18, Jeremiah 44:17-19, 1 Kings 16:31-33, 1 Kings 18:18-19, 2 Kings 21:1-9, 2 Kings 23:4-15].*

Jeremiah 17:19 (ETB): *19 Then the women added, "When we burned incense to the Queen of Heaven and poured out drink offerings to her, did we do so only by ourselves? Did we not make cakes for her, marked with her image, to worship her, and pour out drink offerings (libation) to her with the permission of our husbands?"*

Jeremiah 17:25-27 (ETB): *25 This is what The LORD of hosts, the God of Israel, is saying:*

'You and your wives have spoken with your mouths saying, "We will surely keep our vows that we have made, to burn incense to the Queen of Heaven and pour out drink offerings to her." You have also fulfilled

with it your hands to show you mean it. There remains no doubt you will keep your vows and fulfill your vows!' 26 Therefore listen the word of The LORD, all Judah who live in the land of Egypt: 'Look (know this), I have sworn by My great Name,' says The LORD, 'that My Name will no more be mentioned in the mouth of any man of Judah in all the land of Egypt, saying, "The LORD God lives." 27 Look (know this), I will watch over them to bring disaster and not for good. All the men of Judah who are in the land of Egypt will be destroyed by the sword and famine, until they are completely wiped out.

Explanation:

Asherah The Consort of Baal:

Baal the chief male god, deity or idol was popularly worshipped in various nations along with his consort, the mother-goddess of fertility, called Asherah, (1 Kings 16:31-33).

Asherah had her own shrines and priests dedicated to worship her. The idol image of Asherah was build and worshipped in shrines. Asherah was worshipped as the mother goddess of fertility. For example, in the days of Prophet Elijah in Israel, while there were 450 prophets dedicated to Baal, there were 400 prophets dedicated to Asherah, all under the care of Jezebel and Ahab, (1 Kings 18:19).

Both Baal and Asherah had many names by which they were known among the Canaanites, Ammorites, Babylonians, and other nations. For example Baal was known to the Canaanites, as Baal or Molech. To the Ammorites, he was known as Milcom (Molech or Malcam). To the Babylonians and Chaldeans, he was known as Bel the chief god they worshipped in the Tower of Babel.

Similarly, Baal's consort, the mother goddess of fertility, was also known by various names in different nations. She was known as Asherah, Ashtoreth, Astarte, Inanna, Ishtar, etc. The Babylonians, Assyrians and Akkadians worshipped her under the name Ishtar (pronounced Easter). While Baal was generally worshipped by both males and females, Asherah had a stronghold following among the women, who were encouraged by their men.

Asherah The Queen Of Heaven:

Asherah was worshipped as the Queen of Heaven. The Canaanites and the Israelites had special shrines for her. Apart from her idol images built in shrines, worn or sown to clothes by people, the women made cakes with her image to honor and worship her. They also poured drinks (libation) to appease her, (Jeremiah 7:18, Jeremiah 44:17-19, Jeremiah 44:25-27, 1 Kings 16:31-33, 1 Kings 18:18-19, 2 Kings 21:1-9, 2 Kings 23:4-15).

Solomon followed Asherah and Baal when he went astray from God through his many foreign wives, (1 Kings 11:4-8). The Israelites through their idolatry practices integrated her images and worship even into the Temple of God, such as in the reign of King Manasseh of Judah, (2 Kings 21:1-7). This was in direct disobedience to the warnings from God.

The pagan idolatrous worship and celebration of this mother goddess of fertility, known also as the Queen of Heaven, has been mixed into Christianity, through various disguises.

Ishstar / Easter vs Passover Celebration:

As the goddess of fertility, Asherah or Ishtar, is directly or indirectly celebrated among Christians through Ishtar celebrations. Ishtar is pronounced in English as Easter!. The celebration of Easter has overshadowed and replaced the celebration of Passover, which is the sacrificial death and resurrection of the Passover Lamb of God. In place of Passover, Easter is celebrated. And not surprising, it is filled with bunnies, hares, rabbits, easter eggs, etc which are all the symbols of the modern female goddess of fertility, Ishtar (Easter).

The Israelites were commanded to celebrate Passover, as instituted by God, (Exodus 12:1-28, Leviticus 23:5-8, Numbers 9:1-14, Numbers 28:16-25, Deuteronomy 16:1-8). The Passover or Feast of Unleaven bread was celebrated by The LORD and the Apostles,(Luke 22:15, John 13:1-3, John 2:13-23, Matthew 26:17-28, Mark 14:12-25).

The pagans non-Jews celebrated Ishtar or Easter. The celebration of Easter has been timed over the centuries by the Romans to coincide and confuse the celebration of Passover. The Passover had always been celebrated by the Israelites. However, there is no celebration known as Easter instituted by God. The Scripture says that King Herod had arrested Apostle Peter during the days of unleaven bread, the Passover time. This was after he had killed James, the brother of John which pleased the people, (Acts 12:1-3). Herod kept Peter locked up and intended to bring Peter out to be killed after the celebration of Easter! (Acts 12:4). Thus Passover and Easter were celebrated around the same time. But while Passover was known to the Jews, Easter was alien to them, being a pagan festival.

Over the centuries, Easter has been celebrated all over the world among Christians instead of Passover. The Romans brought this into Christianity. As a result, Easter instead of Passover is popularly marked as the death and resurrection of the LORD. But God instituted Passover not Easter! Easter is a pagan corruption of Passover. Furthermore, from ancient times till today, Easter is celebrated with bunnies, hares, rabbits, Ishstar or easter eggs, etc It is a continuation of the celebration and global tributes to the ancient mother goddess of fertility, called by several names in different nations, as Asherah, Ashtherot, Ishtar, Easter.

What have bunnies, hares, rabbits, easter eggs, egg hunts, etc in Churches got to do with the celebration of the death and resurrection of the LORD? Nothing except to make Easter more fun and acceptable without question. It is a spiritual corruption (a continuation of spiritual adultery or idolatry) of merging the mother goddess of fertility, the Queen of Heaven, with the death and resurrection of the LORD. It has effectively obscured what should be the right celebration, that is the celebration of Passover!

Fabrication Of Queen Of Heaven Into The Church:

The ancient idolatrous celebration of the mother goddess of fertility through Ishtar or Easter continues till this day. She is also worshipped as the Queen of Heaven, which God Almighty is completely against as recorded in the Scriptures. Going even a step further in this idolatrous practice, some have replaced or elevated Mary, the Mother of the LORD, to the position of the Queen of Heaven. Mary, like the Apostles and other Saints who died and in paradise, will be resurrected when the trumpet blasts at the coming of the LORD, (John 11:25-26, Romans 6:5-8, 1 Corinthians 15:19-21, 1 Thessalonians 4:14-17, Revelations 20:4-6, Revelation 20:11-15).

There is no such title or position as Queen of Heaven with God. Beside God Almighty, there has never been and would never be a Mother of Heaven. God Almighty has no consort, God has no wife or consort (unlike the pagan deity or god, Baal). In heaven there is no marriage, (Matthew 22:30). Neither angels, nor God nor resurrected Saints marry or have need for a wife or husband. No such concept in heaven.

Furthermore, our salvation comes through The LORD, His death and resurrection only and our confession of Him, (John 3:16-17, Romans 10:9-10). Our prayers are answered in His name only, (John 14:13-14, John 15:16, Matthew 18:19, Matthew 21;22, Mark 11:24) . There is no other intermediary between us and God (1 Timothy 2:15, 1 Corinthians 1:30)! There is no Scriptural basis for the Queen of Heaven. Furthermore, God has always expressed His displeasure about such an idea. The practice in such churches today is no different from the integration of image of Asherah into the Temple of God by King Manasseh (2 Kings 21:1-7). Such practice is an extension of idolatrous worship of the ancient Queen of Heaven, which God was and still against, (Jeremiah 7:18, Jeremiah 44:17-19, Jeremiah 44:25-27).

Chapter 22

About 70years of Captivity And the Three Kings Of Babylon

Scriptural Verses:

Jeremiah 27:17 (ETB): *11 And this whole land will be a ruin, and an object of horror. These nations will serve the king of Babylon for seventy years!, [ref Jeremiah 25:11, Jeremiah 29:10].*

Jeremiah 29:10 (ETB): *10 For this is what The LORD says: After your seventy years of captivity are completed in Babylon, I will visit you and perform My good promise toward you, And allow you to return to this place, [ref Jeremiah 25:11, Jeremiah 29:10].*

Jeremiah 27:6-7 (ETB): *6 And now I have given all these lands into the hands of Nebuchadnezzar the king of Babylon, as My servant. I have also given him the animals of the field to serve him. 7 So all nations will serve him, his son and his son's son, until the time comes for his land to be taken. Then many nations and great kings will make him serve them, [ref Jeremiah 25:11-12, 2 Kings 25:27-28, Jeremiah 52:31-32, Daniel 5:30].*

Explanation:

The LORD had decreed through the prophesies of Jeremiah that the Jews (Judeans, Judaites, Judahites, Jehudites) will be in captivity for seventy (70) years, (Jeremiah 25:11, Jeremiah 29:10).

The LORD also stated through Jeremiah that three kings, Nebuchadnezzar, his son and his son's son will rule over Babylon before Babylon is defeated, (Jeremiah 27:7). After this, then other kings and nations will start to rule over Babylon.

In fulfillment of these, Nebuchardnezzar was succeeded by Eveel-Merodach as king of Babylon, (2 Kings 25:27-28, Jeremiah 52:31-32). Then Eveel-Merodach was succeeded by Belshazzar who saw the handwriting on the wall of the end of his reign and Babylon, (Daniel 5:1-30). That night, Medes overthrew Belshazzar and Babylon, and pronounced freedom for the Jews, (Daniel 5:30).

Then during the first year of the reign of Cyrus (Koresh) king of Persia, the LORD stirred up his spirit. So as the new Medo-Persian king with Babylon under him, Cyrus (Koresh) pronounced freedom for the Jews (2 Chronicles 36:22-23, Ezra 1:1-4).

CHAPTER 23

About The Thirtieth Year In Ezekiel 1:1

Scriptural Verses:

Ezekiel 1:1 (ETB): *1 I was by the River Chebar in Babylon, among the captives of Judah, when the heavens were opened and I saw visions of God. This happened on the fifth day, of the fourth month, of the thirtieth year (since the discovery of a copy of the Torah in the Temple, and renewal of the Covenant and Passover during the reign of King Josiah of Judah), [ref 2 Kings 22:1-3, 2 Kings 23:30-31, 2 Kings 23:34-36, 2 Kings 24:6-8, 2 Kings 24:17-18, Ezekiel 1:2].*

2 It was also the fifth day, of the fourth month, of the fifth year of the captivity of King Jehoiachin in Babylon, (and of the reign of King Zedekiah of Judah), [ref 2 Kings 24:13-17].

Explanation:

The thirtieth year referred to by Prophet Ezekiel, in Ezekiel 1:1, is counted from the time of King Josiah of Judah. Josiah became King when he was eight years old. He reigned for a total of thirty-one years.

A little over half-way through Josiah's reign, on the eighteenth year of his reign, a copy of the Torah (Law) was discovered in the Temple.

It was found by Hilkiah the high priest, who gave it to Shaphan the scribe, who in turn took it to Josiah the King of Judah, (2 Kings 22:1-20).

Josiah went ahead to have the Torah read to himself. It was also read to all the people. Together they renewed the LORD's Covenant and abandoned idolatry. The Passover festival was also re-instituted, (2 Kings 23:1-3, 2 Kings 23:21-23, 2 Chronicles 35:1). This was thirteen years to the end of the reign of Josiah.

So Josiah reigned for thirteen more years, from when The LORD's Covenant was renewed.

Josiah was succeeded by Jehoahaz who reigned for only three months, (2 Kings 23:30-31).

Then Jehoahaz was succeeded by Jehoiakim who reigned for eleven years, (2 Kings 23:34-36).

Jehoiakim was succeeded by Jehoiachin who reigned for three months (2 Kings 24:6-8).

Then Jehoiachin was taken into captivity by Nebuchadnezzar, and succeeded by Zedekiah (2 Kings 24:17-18).

The LORD appeared to Ezekiel on the fifth day, of the fourth month, of the fifth year of the captivity of King Jehoiachin in Babylon.

Adding all the time from the eighteenth year of Josiah's reign to the fourth month, of the fifth year of the captivity of King Jehoiachin in Babylon, gives the thirty years. This was the thirty years to which the Prophet Ezekiel was referring.

Chapter 24

About Three Righteous Men Noah, Daniel and Job In Their Time

Scriptural Verses:

Ezekiel 14:14 (ETB): 14 *Even if these three righteous men, Noah, Daniel, and Job, were in it, they would deliver only themselves because of their righteousness," says The LORD God, [ref Genesis 6:8-9, Daniel 1:8-9, Job 1:1, Job 1:8, Job 2:3].*

Ezekiel 14:16 (ETB): 16 *Even if these three righteous men, (Noah, Daniel, and Job), were living in the land: As I live," says The LORD God, "they would not even be able to deliver either their sons or daughters. They would deliver only themselves, and the land would be desolate.*

Explanation:

Noah:

Noah was just and blameless in his generations. He found grace, (unmerited favor), in the eyes of The LORD, (ADONAI). As a result, Noah and his household were not destroyed in the flood, (Genesis 6:8-9).

Job:

Job lived in the land of Uz in his time. He was blameless and upright. He was someone who feared God and kept clear of anything evil (sinful), (Job 1:1, Job 1:8, Job 2:3). Job underwent an excruciating time of test by the devil to make him sin. Despite losing everything, including all his children, wealth, and position in the society. Despite his severe sickness that followed. Despite pressures from his wife and friends, Job held faithfully unto God. In the end God delivered him. The LORD restored what Job lost. Indeed the LORD gave Job double of the possessions he had lost. Job lived 140 (one hundred and forty) years. He lived long enough to see four generations of his descendants: his children, grandchildren, great-grandchildren and great-great-grandchildren. Job died old, and full of days, (Job 42:10-16).

Daniel:

Daniel was one of the first group of hostages taken from Judah into exile in Babylon by Nebuchadnezzar. He was taken along with Jehoiakim king of Judah (2 Kings 24:8-12, Daniel 1:1-2). On arrival in Babylon and in the kings service, Daniel consistently refused to be defiled or to sin against God. This was despite opportunities and pressures to compromise. He was thrown into the lion's den for his faith, but God saved him, (Daniel 6:1-28). He was a great prophet, with the gift of God for the interpretation of dreams. He became the second in command of the Babylon empire and lasted through the end of several kings in the Babylonian empire and into the Medo-Persian empire, (Daniel 1:1-2, Daniel 1:8-14, Daniel 6:1-28).

CHAPTER 25

About Gog of Magog And The Anti Christ In Two End Times

Scriptural Verses:

Revelation 19:19-20 (ETB): *19 Then I saw the Beast (Anti-Messiah, Anti-Christ), the kings of the earth, and their armies from all over the earth. They were gathered together to fight a war against The One who was sitting on the white horse and against His army, [ref Zechariah 14:1-3, Revelation 16:13-16, Revelation 19:19-21].*

20 And the Beast (Anti-Messiah, Anti-Christ) was captured. The False prophet was also captured along with him. It was the false prophet who performed miraculous signs in the presence of the Beast. He used it to deceive all those who received the mark of the Beast and those who worshiped his image. These two were thrown alive into the lake of fire burning with brimstone (sulfur), [ref Revelation 13:11-17, Revelation 19:20, Revelation 20:10].

Revelation 20:1-3 (ETB): *1 Then I saw an angel coming down from heaven. He was holding the key to the bottomless pit. He also had great chain in his hand, [ref Revelation 9:1, Revelation 20:1].*

2 He took hold of the Dragon, that Serpent of old, who is the Devil and Satan. The angel bound Satan for a thousand years (1,000 years), [ref Revelation 16:13-16].

3 Then the angel threw the Dragon into the bottomless pit. He locked him up and placed a seal on him. This is so that the Devil would not deceive the nations any more, until the thousand years were finished. But after that, it would be necessary to release the Devil for a little while (a short period of time).

Ezekiel 38:1-6 (ETB): *1 Now the word of The LORD (ADONAI) came to me, saying, 2 "Descendant of mankind, (Son of man, human being), turn your attention against Gog, against the land of Magog, against the chief prince of Rosh, Meshech, and Tubal (Japhethites northward of Israel), and prophesy against him, [ref Genesis 10:2, Ezekiel 38:15].*

3 Say 'This is what The LORD God says: "Look (know this), I am against you, Gog, the chief prince of Rosh, Meshech, and Tubal (and Magog). 4 I will repel you (turn you around), put hooks into your jaws and lead you away with your entire army. I will do so to all your soldiers, horses, and horsemen who are well equipped with all kinds of armor. They are a huge multitude (horde) of warriors with bucklers, shields and swords (killing weapons), [ref Revelation 20:7-9].

5 Also with them and well armed with their shield and helmet (war armors), are Persia, Ethiopia (Cushites), and Libya (Ludites). 6 Gomer (son of Japheth who fathered Ashkenaz, Riphath, and Togarmah) and all its armies will also join them. So will the entire armies of Togarmah living in the far north join. A multitude of troops will be with you, [ref Genesis 10:3].

Revelation 20:7-9 (ETB): *7 Now after the thousand years have been completed, Satan will be released from his prison in the bottomless pit, [ref Revelation 20:3].*

8 And he will go out again to deceive the nations in the four corners (every part) of the earth. They will follow Gog and Magog, and gather together to fight war. They are mighty armies, and are so many in number (countless) like the sand of the sea, [ref Ezekiel 38:1-17, Revelation 20:7-9].

9 They went over the broad plain of the land and surrounded the camp of the Saints, (the holy people of God on earth after the millennium). They also encircled the beloved city (Jerusalem). But fire came down from God out of heaven and devoured the armies.

Explanation:

The Beast (Antichrist) vs Gog of Magog:

The Beast (Anti-Messiah, Anti-Christ) is different from Gog of Magog. But they both have the same spirit, used by Satan to lead rebellions. They would come at two different end time periods. They will each be world ruler in their own times, in two coming end times.

The Antichrist will be at the end of this current generation, before the start of the Millennium reign. He will arise and rule the world for the last seven years. His reign will end at the end of the first rebellion of Satan, when The LORD returns with His Saints.

But Gog, of Magog will be at the end of the second rebellion of Satan. This would be sometime after the Millennium reign. This will be after Satan is released from prison, and goes out on a second deception and rebellion against God.

Gog of Magog And Future World Rule:

Noah had three sons, Shem, Ham and Japheth, (Genesis 10:1). The Bible often refers to people through their ancestral lineage. For example, the children, descendants or offspring of Jacob, whose name was changed to Israel, are referred to as Israelites (Genesis 25:23-27, Genesis 32:24-28, Genesis 35:10). Their ancestral line can be traced back through Abraham and then to Shem. Also, the descendants of Canaan, the youngest of the four sons of Ham, were called Canaanites, (Genesis 10:6). They were the founders or original occupiers of the land of Canaan. In the same way, Magog was the second of the seven sons of Japheth, (Genesis 10:1-2). The land or area occupied mostly by his descendants is referred to as Magog.

Gog who will come in the future will be a descendant or offspring of Magog, and hence of Japheth. Before becoming the world leader, Gog will emerge as the powerful chief prince (supreme leader) of the nations of Rosh and of nations formed by the descendants of Japheth. This will include descendants of Magog, Meshech, Tubal who were sons of Japheth, (Genesis 10:2, Ezekiel 38:1-3). Also, the descendants of Gomer, another son of Japheth will join Gog. Gomer's sons were Ashkenaz, Riphath, and Togarmah, (Genesis 10:3, Ezekiel 38:6).

The Magog region or countries occupied by descendants of Japheth are located northward, far away from the land of Israel and her immediate neighbors. They are in the far north of the world, (Ezekiel 38:15)

Gog and his mighty army will also be joined by other armies from the regions of Persia, Ethiopia, and Libya (Ezekiel 38:5). The Persia region includes India, Egypt, Thrace, Europe, North Africa, western Asia, Black Sea, the Caucasus, the Caspian, Jaxartes, Arabian desert, Persian Gulf, Indian Ocean

Leading this powerful, well organized and equipped world army, Gog will launch a ferocious attack on Jerusalem, Israel, and the people of The LORD, (Ezekiel 38:4-9). The number of Gog's world army will be so numerous, like the sane of the sea. This will happen sometime after the end of the Millennium reign. By then, Satan would have been released at the end of his 1000 years in prison or bottomless pit, (Revelation 20:7-9). Satan will be released for a period. He will embark on a second rebellion. During that period he will go to test and deceive the people throughout the whole earth, (Revelation 20:1-3). He will use Gog and Magog to assemble a very powerful world army.

Gog will conceive an evil plot. The motivation for Gog's army would be hatred for the people of God, to shatter their peace and eliminate them, following the Millennium. He will also seek to acquire their wealthy possessions which God will bless them with, (Ezekiel 38:10-13).

They will however fail. For LORD God Almighty will turn the world army of Gog to attack each other. In His fury, the LORD God will also send against them, flooding rain, great hailstones, fire, and brimstone, down from heaven (Ezekiel 38:21-22, Revelation 20:9).

Due to their great number, it will take seven months to bury them and cleanse Israel. Their destroyed weapons will provide fuel for the fire for seven years. (Ezekiel 39:9-16).

It is after this second rebellion that Satan will be finally thrown into the lake of fire, (Revelation 20:10).

The Antichrist And Future World Rule.

The Antichrist will be different from Gog and in a much earlier era. He will be possessed and empowered by the Satan. He will reign over the entire world, be blasphemous against God Almighty and be worshipped before the second coming of the LORD, (Revelation 13:1-8). He will reign for seven years. He will make himself known with the abomination that causes desolation after three and half years. Then he will reign for another three and half years during which he will severely persecute (in great tribulations) the Israelites and Saints of The LORD in Jerusalem, Israel and all over the world, (Daniel 7:25, Daniel 9:27, Revelation 11:1-2, Revelation 12:6, Revelation 12:14, Revelation 13:5). He will intensely hate the things of God and overpower the Israelites and Saints of God on earth until God intervenes, (Daniel 7:21-22).

This will be before The LORD returns to rule on earth for the 1,000 years of the millennium rule. The Antichrist will assemble a very powerful world army to attack Jerusalem, Israel and the Saints of God. At the end of his seven years reign, the Antichrist will be captured with his false prophet and thrown into the lake of fire, (Revelation 19:17-21). Following this, his master, Satan also known as the dragon, the old serpent, the Devil will be arrested, chained and thrown into hell or the bottomless pit (but not lake of fire) for one thousand years, (Revelation 20:1-3). During that time, The LORD will reign on earth in what is referred to as the 1,000 years or millennium reign of The LORD. The Devil being in prison will not be able to deceive the people on earth.

After the 1,000 years are over, Satan will be released for a little while to test and deceive the people throughout the whole earth, (Revelation 20:3, Revelation 20:7-9). It is during this time Gog of Magog and his world army will launch another attack on Jerusalem, Israel, and the people of The LORD, (Ezekiel 38:1-9, Revelation 20:7-9).

The LORD God Almighty will turn the world army of Gog to attack each other. In His fury, the LORD God will also send down from heaven against them flooding rain, great hailstones, fire, and brimstone, (Ezekiel 38:21-22, Revelation 20:9).

This second rebellion is another proof that Satan cannot change. This is despite his 1000 years in the prison of cell.

Finally, Satan will be judged and thrown into the lake of fire to join the antichrist and his false prophet, (Revelation 20:10). They will burn there forever and ever. Other followers of Satan will also be judged and thrown into the lake of fire, followers, (Revelation 20:11-15).

CHAPTER 26

About King Jehoiakim And Daniel

Scriptural Verses:

Daniel 1:1-3 (ETB): *1 Nebuchadnezzar the king of Babylon came to attack Jerusalem and besieged it. This was in the third year of the reign of Jehoiakim the king of Judah, [ref 2 Chronicles 36:5-7, 2 Kings 23:34-36, 2 Kings 24:1-6, Jeremiah 36:6-9].*

2 The LORD (ADONAI) gave him victory over Jehoiakim the king of Judah. He also permitted him to take some of the articles from the Temple of God. Nebuchadnezzar carried them off to the temple of his god in the land of Shinar, (ancient name of Babylon or Chaldea). He took the articles to keep in the treasure house of his god, [ref Jeremiah 27:20-22, Ezra 1:7-11].

3 Then Nebuchadnezzar the king of Babylon gave instruction to Ashpenaz, his chief officer in charge of his eunuchs. Ashpenaz was to bring (to the palace) some of the Israelites. He was to also bring some of the offspring of the king of Judah, and some of the princes (noblemen with royal descent) he had taken to Babylon.

Daniel 1:6 (ETB): *6 Among them were four young men from the tribe of Judah whose names were Daniel, Hananiah, Mishael, and Azariah.*

Explanation:

King Jehoiakim succeeded his brother Jehoahaz who reigned over Judah for just three months. They were both sons of King Josiah, whose death was followed by rapid decline of spiritual state, welfare and power of Judah, due to sin. Pharaoh had Judah under his domain after the death of Josiah. He removed Jehoahaz and took him to Egypt, where he was placed in prison till he died, (2 Kings 23:31-34, 2 Chronicles 36:1-4). He then put Jehoiakim as king over Judah. He also changed his name from Eliakim to Jehoiakim.

The defeat of Egypt and then Judah by Nebuchadnezzar the king of Babylon brought King Jehoiakim under him and served him. Three years later, King Jehoiakim rebelled and refused to serve or pay the tribute to Nebuchadnezzar any longer. King Nebuchadnezzar responded by going to attack Judah and Jerusalem in the third year of the reign of King Jehoiakim, (2 Kings 24:1). Following the defeat of King Jehoiakim. he was chained to be carried to Babylon, (2 Chronicles 36:5-7). However, King Jehoiakim continued as the vassal of Nebuchadnezzar and his reign over Judah for eleven years, (2 Kings 24:1-6).

King Jehoiakim himself did not live in captivity in Babylon. However, Nebuchadnezzar collected tribute from the treasury in Jerusalem and took some of the articles from the Temple of God. He also took some members of the royal family of Jehoiakim, some other nobles of royal descent, along with some of the people from the tribe of Judah as plunders, prisoners and captives to Babylon, (2 Kings 24:1-12, Daniel 1:1-3).

Daniel and his three friends Hananiah, Mishael, and Azariah were among those taken to Babylon, according to the plans of God. God used Daniel who remained faithful to Him throughout the successive reigns of the three kings of Babylon. Namely Nebuchadnezzar, his son Eveel-Merodach, and grandson Belshazzar , (Jeremiah 27:5-7).

King Jehoiakim And Daniel

They ruled Babylon until conquered by King Cyrus of Medo-Persia, during the reign of Belshazzar, (Daniel 5:1-30).

During the reign of Jehoiakim as king over Judah, he did evil in the sight of The LORD. He also burnt the first scroll of prophesies written by Jeremiah, (Jeremiah 36:1-32). After his eleven years of reign, Jehoiakim was succeeded by his eighteen year old son Jehoiachin who ruled over Judah for only three months. He was taken into captivity to Babylon. There he was put in prison, where he remained for thirty-seven years until freed by Eveel-Merodach king of Babylon, who succeeded Nebuchadnezzar his father, (2 Kings 24:8-12, 2 Kings 25:27).

CHAPTER 27

About The Little Horn And Hanukkah At End Of The Greek Kingdom

Scriptural Verses:

Daniel 8:23 (ETB): *23 "At some point in the future, during the latter time of the reign of their kingdom, when the rebellion from the rebels has reached the peak, a king will arise, Having fierce (arrogant, aggressive) demeanor, And skilled in double dealing (manipulation, intrigues, sinister schemes).*

Explanation:

The little horn, the AntiChrist ruler, will come at the end time and reign for one week of seven years (Daniel 9:27). However, Daniel, received a vision in the third year of the reign of King Belshazzar (grandson of Nebuchadnezzar) of Babylon Kingdom. Gabriel had informed Daniel a little horn, a king, would come at the latter end of the Greek Empire (Daniel 8:23). The king will have a fierce (arrogant, aggressive) demeanor, very skillful in deception, double dealing, manipulation, and sinister schemes.

He will wield a lot of power and destroy many people, including the holy people. He will be successful and accomplish whatever he wants. Falsehood, lies and deception will become the acceptable norm during his time. He will be full of pride and boastful. He will even pitch himself against The LORD as he takes over the Temple and stops the daily Sacrifices, (Daniel 8:23-26).

This prophecy was fulfilled, almost 400years after Daniel had prophesied. The little horn or king was Antiochus IV Epiphanes who ruled as the king of the North from 175-164 BC. Antiochus IV Epiphanes was the eighth in a succession of twenty-six kings from the fourth horn, the Seleucid part, of the Greek Empire. Antiochus IV Epiphanes rose to power as he usurped Heliodorus and Demetrius and became the new King. Antiochus gained influence, power and obtained the kingdom through flatteries.

When Antiochus IV Epiphanes had became king in 175 BCE, he overthrew Israel's legitimate High Priest Onias III who was of the priestly lineage, as recognized by God and Israel. He was therefore, like a star of heaven, who represented God in leading the Jews on the path of righteousness. Antiochus IV Epiphanes first replaced Onias III with his brother Jason who was himself replaced by Menelaus. But Menelaus was a Benjamite, and a non-member of the priestly Levite family. Thus, Antiochus IV Epiphanes removed the true High Priests of God, replaced him with his own and so brought to end God's divine order of things in His temple. This was equivalent to growing up to the host of heaven, casting down some of the host and the stars of heaven to the ground, and trampling them as prophesied by Daniel.

History has it that Antiochus IV Epiphanes plundered and desecrated the holy land and Temple. He was violently bitter against the Jews, and was determined to exterminate them, their religion and worship of God. He devastated Jerusalem, defiled, and prohibited Temple worship. After taking over Jerusalem and the Temple with the help of his military forces, He caused the Temple sacrifices to cease as he took away the regular burnt offering. He issued decrees that forbade Jewish religious practice and completely halted the sacrifices. He outlawed the observances of Sabbath, designated Holy Days and circumcision.

He compared himself with one of the Greek gods, Zeus and gave himself the surname "Epiphanes" which means "The Illustrious One, The Magnificent One, The visible god". He demanded to be worshiped as a god four times a year. He was a contemptible person, who acted as though he really were Zeus or Jupiter and the people called him "Epimanes" meaning "the madman".

He setup a statue of Zeus/Antiochus in the Temple above the altar. The most detestable animals (the pig) were brought and sacrificed upon the altar. Then taking the broth of the pig and sprinkled it around the sanctuary, thus defiling it.

The righteous ones among the Jews who resisted him suffered intense persecution. Many were killed. He also sold many, thousands of Jewish families into slavery. He destroyed all copies of Scripture that he could find and slaughtered everyone discovered in possession of such copies. He preferred and protected those who "violate the covenant"

Daniel heard a voice asking "How long will be the duration, when the vision is being fulfilled, regarding the cancellation of the daily sacrifices and the rebellion of desolation (devastation, horror), when both the Sanctuary (Temple) and the host (leading Saints) are to be trampled underfoot?" The answer was given as 2300 morning and evening sacrifices.

By 165 BC the Jewish revolt led by Judas Maccabeus against the Antiochus IV Epiphanes and the Seleucid monarchy was successful. The Jerusalem Temple was liberated, purified, rededicated with a new altar along with new holy vessels on 25th of Kislev (December 14, 164 BCE). The celebration of Hanukkah every year for eight days was instituted by Judas Maccabeus in 165BC to commemorate this victory over Antiochus IV Epiphanes. The Jews still celebrate Hanukkah to this day.

A complete fulfillment of this prophecy of a powerful little horn will occur in the future with the coming of the AntiChrist in the end time. Antiochus IV Epiphanes exhibited many traits of the End Time Antichrist. But he is different, and so just a shadow forerunner of the end time Antichrist. The total period when he desecrated the Temple to when it was cleansed was 2,300 days (almost 77months, or more than 6years). The end time Antichrist will commit the abomination of desolation for three and half years. And there is no mention of the cleansing of Temple at the end time Antichrist.

CHAPTER 28

About The Kings Of The North And South From Greece Kingdom

Scriptural Verses:

Daniel 11:3-4 (ETB): *3 Then at that time a very powerful king will arise (to reign over the kingdom of Greece). He will rule with great authority (dominion) and do whatever pleases him.*

4 After he is firmly established, his kingdom will be broken up and divided toward the four winds (corners, directions) of heaven. However, it will not be among his descendants or have the same authority (dominion) with which he ruled. For his kingdom will be uprooted, and taken over by successors besides them, [ref Daniel 8:21-22].

Explanation:

Following the rise and death of Alexander the big horn and king of the Kingdom of Greece, the kingdom was divided into four parts, headed by his four Generals, (Daniel 11:3-4). For biblical reference, regions are described as North or South relative to Jerusalem. With this in mind, the four Greece regions were: 1). Seleucus (to the North), consisting of Babylon, Persia and Syria 2). Ptolemy (to the South), consisting of Egypt and Palestine, 3) Cassander (to the

THE KINGS OF THE NORTH AND SOUTH FROM GREECE KINGDOM

West) consisting of Macedonia, Greece. 4). Lysimachus (to the East), consisting of Thrace, Asia Minor. Seleucus also added Asia Minor from Lysimachus to his own. So the Seleucus to the North and Ptolemy to the South of Jerusalem were the two most prominent.

In Daniel 11:5, the king of the South referred to was the Ptolemy dynasty, reigning over the southern territory, relative to Jerusalem, with capital in Alexandria in Egypt.

In Daniel 11:6, the daughter referred to was Berenice, the daughter of Ptolemy II who was given in marriage to the king of the north, Antiochus II Theos. This was with the hope of bringing peace between the two powers. To marry Berenice, the King of the North put away his own wife, Laodice, He later restored Laodice after Bernice lost favour/favor with him. In revenge for what was one to her, Laodice had her husband poisoned. She also killed Berenice, her children, attendants and supporters.

In Daniel 11:10, the two sons of the king of the North (Antiochus II Callinicus) were stirred up to redeem the honor of their father, by regaining the lost territory of the "king of the North". The younger, Antiochus III Magnus, regained much of the lost territory and then assumed the Seluecid throne.

In Daniel 11:11-12, history has it that the ruler in the South at that time (Ptolemy IV Epiphanes), went to fight against the king of the North (Antiochus III). The North was defeated and lost ten thousand soldiers. Yet nothing was gained by the battle.

At this stage, the Romans, who took over from Greece, had begun to exercise some influence from the North. The Roman armies confronted the Seleucid king, Antiochus the Great (Magnus) and in 190 B.C. defeated him at Magnesia. Decades later they took over Corinth and Carthage from Greece, and later Egypt in 168 B.C.

In Daniel 11:17, the daughter of women referred to was Cleopatra, who Julius Caesar met in Egypt. She was made queen, but did not stay loyal to Julius Caesar. She joined with Anthony, his rival.

In Daniel 11:27-35, the Little horn of the end of the Greece Empire, a king of the North came up (Daniel 8:23). His defeat brought about the yearly Celebration of Hanukkah by the Jews since December 14, 164 BCE. Refer to the Chapter About The Little Horn And Hanukkah At End Of The Greek Kingdom.

The land of Israel came under Roman rule in 63 B.C. The Romans went on to kill The Messiah (Daniel 9:26). This was in in April 3, 33AD. They also went on to destroy the Temple, the city of Jerusalem, killed many of the people and sent most of the rest of the people of Judah into exile in 70AD, (Daniel 9:26). The real Judeans / Israelites left Jerusalem desolate for almost two thousand years, since 70AD till 1948AD. During this time, the Romans, their descendants, other Europeans, including the British and others occupied it. As prophesied, the Romans are the people of the little horn prince, the Antichrist, who is to come in the end time, (Daniel 9:26-27). Indeed, the end time little horn or Antichrist, came out not from the third beast (Greece) but from the fourth beast, the Roman Empire, (Daniel 7:7-8).

In Daniel 11:36-43 is a description of some of that would be the fulfilled by the Little Horn of the End Time, including his conquests, and end. His time will suddenly come to an end, and there will be no one to help him, (ref Daniel 7:11, Zechariah 14:2-5, Zechariah 14:12-15, Revelation 19:11-21).

CHAPTER 29

About The Day Of The LORD In End Time

Scriptural Verses:

Zechariah 14:6-7 (ETB): *It will come to pass on that Day that there will be no light. The lights will diminish. 7 It will be one day which is known to The LORD. There will be neither day nor night. But by evening time there will be light,* [ref Zechariah 14:6, Luke 21:25, Matthew 24:29, Matthew 24:36, Amos 5:18-20, Zephaniah 1:15-18, Malachi 4:1-3].

Amos 5:18-20 (ETB): *18 Woe (a pity) to you who want to see the day of The LORD! For what good is the day of The LORD to you? It will be darkness, and not light. 19 It will be as though a man escaped from a lion, and a bear met him! Or as though he went into the house, leaned his hand on the wall, and a serpent bit him! 20 Is the day of The LORD not darkness, instead of light? Is it not very dark, with no brightness in it?,* [ref Amos 5:16-20, Zephaniah 1:15-18, Zechariah 14:6, Malachi 4:1-3, Luke 21:25, Matthew 24:29, Matthew 24:36].

Malachi 4:1 (ETD): *1 "Look (know this), for the Day is coming. The day is burning like a furnace. It is the day when all the proud, yes, all the evildoers will be like dry straw. They will be burned up on the day that is coming. Their roots or branches will not survive", Says The LORD of hosts.*

Explanation:

The phrase "The Day of The LORD" has been used in the Scriptures in three distinct evens that will occur at different times in the end time:

#1) The Saints Taken Away from Earth or Rapture Day of The LORD;

#2) The Start of Millennium Day of The LORD;

#3) The Judgment Day Of The LORD.

Therefore, the Day of The LORD should be understood in these separate contexts where they appear in the Scripture. Let us look at them in the order in which they will occur:

#1 The Saints Taken Away from Earth or Rapture Day of The LORD.

This can also be referred to as The First Resurrection Day of The LORD. This is when The LORD will suddenly appear in the cloud. The purpose is for The LORD to take the Saints away to heaven, as He has promised, so they could be with Him, (John 14:3, Matthew 24:30-31, Acts 1:9-11). The day will be a surprise to the believers on earth, (Matthew 24:36-44, Mark 13:32, 1 Thessalonians 5:2, Revelation 3:3, Revelation 16:15).

He will not come to stay on the earth. This event will happen in the air (atmosphere). The LORD will suddenly appear in the cloud. There will be a very loud blowing of the trumpet (shofar) of God by an archangel, (Matthew 24:30-31, 1 Thessalonians 4:13-18). Those who have fallen into sleep (of dead people), who are in The Messiah, will rise up first. This is also referred to as the first resurrection, and it is only for the Saints, (Revelation 20:5-6). At the same time, in the twinkling of an eye, those who believe in Him, who are still alive and remain in The LORD, will be taken up together with them in the clouds. They will all go to heaven together with The LORD and be with Him forever, [ref Matthew 24:30-31, 1 Thessalonians 4:13-18, 2 Thessalonians 2:1-12, Matthew 22:23-33, Mark 12:18-27, Luke 20:27-40, 1 Corinthians 15:12-23, Daniel 12:1-2, Acts 1:9-11, John 14:3, Matthew 24:36-44, Mark 13:32, 1 Thessalonians 5:2, Revelation 3:3, Revelation 16:15,].

#2 The Start Of Millennium Day of The LORD.

This day will also come as a surprise for the world. It will be terrible for the enemies of The LORD like in the past. The Day the flood came was a Day of the LORD in Noah's time, (Genesis 7:10-12). That was all over the earth. The day Sodom and Gomorrah were destroyed was another day of the LORD (Genesis 19: 23-25).

However, this Day of the LORD coming in the end time is when The LORD will return back to earth with The Saints. He will come back in glory as The Messiah, The King of kings and the LORD of lords, to be the Prince (Ruler) and Priest of God on earth. He will remain physically on earth but in glorious form, along with His Saints. This would be for one thousand (1,000) years or Millennium reign. On that Day, The LORD Himself will arrive with His angels, and the Saints from heaven. The Saints (dead or alive) who have been taken in rapture to heaven, would have finished celebrating the marriage feast of the Lamb. It is the heavenly celebration of Passover, the Holy Union or Communion, the physical togetherness of the LORD as the head and His Saints as His body, (1 Thessalonians 4:15-17, 1 Corinthians 15:51-52, Revelation 19:6-9).

The day of His coming to reign will be a day of doom for the antichrist, his false prophet and millions of their soldiers on earth. The LORD will set foot on Mount Olives, (Zechariah 14:1-4, Matthew 24:3, Acts 2:9-12, Luke 21:25-28). There will be the battle of Armageddon to eliminate the armies of the antichrist and false prophet, (Revelation

19:11-21). They stand no chance and will be caught by surprise. The antichrist and false prophet will be captured and thrown into the lake of fire. His millions of army will be destroyed by the sword (word) coming out of the mouth of the LORD. It will include kings (leaders of nations) of the earth, the great men, the rich men, the military commanders, the mighty men, the slaves and the free men. They will be devastated with a major plague sent by the LORD on the wicked people and animals, (Zechariah 14:12-15, Revelation 19:11-21).

It will also be a day of doom for Satan and his angels who will be chained and thrown into hell (not lake of fire). Satan will be captured, bound and imprisoned in the bottomless pit of hell. He will stay there although the millennium reign, (Revelation 20:1-3).

After the elimination of the evil and evil doers from earth, and the arrest of Satan, the Devil, then the Kingdom of The LORD on earth will start, (Revelation 20:1-3).

At the end of the one thousand years Millennium reign, Satan will be released for a short while to deceive people. [ref Revelation 19:11-21, Revelation 20:1-3, Revelation 20:7-9). Then there will be another Day of the LORD, which will be followed with judgment. Refer to the commentary at the end of Ezekiel 38 Gog of Magog And TheAntiChrist In End Time.

#3 The Judgment Day Of The LORD:

This is the last event that will occur. The day will also come as a surprise. This Judgment Day of the LORD will be a day of darkness, gloom, trouble, distress, trepidation, devastation for the evildoers. It will a day burning with the fierce anger of the LORD like a furnace oven.

Satan will now also be thrown into the lake of fire,(Revelation 20:10). On this Day God will also pour His fierce anger on the children of disobedience on earth. The wicked will be like straw and will be completely destroyed from the earth, (Amos 5:16-20, Zephaniah 1:15-18, Malachi 4:1-2). That fierce anger of God has been building up but being held in check until the Judgment Day of the LORD. It will be global, and affect all nations on earth.

On this day, The Judgment Throne of The LORD will be set up. There will be the second resurrection, which is of the wicked, to arise for judgment. The sea, the earth, Death and Hades (Hell) will release the dead held in them. All the dead, small and great, will stand before God, and books will be opened. The dead will be judged according to their works, which are written in the books. There will be another book opened, called The Book Of Life. Then Death and Hades (Hell) will be cast into the lake of fire. This is the second death. And anyone whose name is not found written in the Book of Life will also be cast into the lake of fire, (ref Revelation 20:11-15). On The Judgment Day of The LORD, the heavens will pass away with a loud noise. Every element that makes up the heavenly bodies will be burned up with fire. Both the earth and all the things in it will be burned up, (2 Peter 3:10-12).

After all these things, then there will be the New heavens and the new earth, with the new Jerusalem (2 Peter 3:13, Revelation 21:1-4).

CHAPTER 30

About The Scribes, Pharisees, Sadducees, Essenes and Herodians In Israel

Scriptural Verses:

Matthew 3:7 (ETB): 7 But when he saw many of the Pharisees and Sadducees also coming to his baptism, he said to them: "You generation of vipers! Who warned you to run away from the (judgment of God coming with) fierce anger?

Luke 5:17 (ETB): 17 One day, Yeshua(Jesus, Iēsous) was teaching the people. Also some Pharisees and Scribes (Torah law teachers) were sitting there. They had come from various towns of Galilee, Judea, and from Jerusalem. The healing power of The LORD (ADONAI) was present.

Explanation:

The Scribes, Pharisees and Sadducees were prominent in Israel in the days of Yeshua The Messiah.

The Scribes

The Scribes were the teachers and interpreters of Torah (the five books of Moses, namely Genesis, Exodus, Leviticus, Numbers and Deuteronomy). They were well trained and learned as teachers, interpreters and lawyers in the Law of Moses (Mosaic Law) and sacred writings. They provided interpretation to the difficult and subtle questions of the Torah. For this reason, they were also part of the Sanhedrin, and work closely with the priests, the Pharisees and leaders of the people.

The Pharisees

The Pharisees were a sect in Israel, who started after the Jewish exile. They are the fathers of modern day Judaism. They believe in the Old Testament, along with Jewish oral traditions, beliefs and way of life. The Pharisees believe in the existence of good, evil, angels and demons, and in the coming of The Messiah. The Pharisees believe in the resurrection of the dead, existence of hell, fire and reward for each person according to his individual deeds. They seek for praise through outward observance of external rites and forms of religious devotions such as ceremonial washings, fasting, prayers, and alms giving. They mingled with the common people while taking advantage of them. They prided themselves on their good works, which they publicly advertise for all to see. They tell people to do what they themselves will not do. They enjoyed placing heavy burdens and demands on people. They did all their works of the commandments as a show off in public, to be seen and praised by all people. They loved to wear on their arms extra large prayer patches (phylacteries) with passages of Torah written in them. Also, they wore robes with extra long tassels. They took the extra effort to make them conspicuous so that they will look more pious than the other people about the law of God. They loved the high tables and places of honor at feasts and the best seats in the synagogues. They loved being greeted in the marketplaces, and addressed as 'Rabbi, Rabbi' by the people, (Matthew 23:3-8).

Yeshua The Messiah also further spoke of the multiple sins of the Scribes and Pharisees, their hypocrisy and double standards, pretenses, focus on the outside while the inside if filthy, focus on smaller things and ignoring what really matters, false teachings, wickedness, bloodsheds of the righteous and prophets, persecutions the Saints, etc (Matthew 23:13-36).

The Sadducees

The Sadducees(meaning "the righteous") were a religious party among the Jews. They were wealthy, hated the common people, and were opponents of the Pharisees. They did not believe in traditions. They believed in Torah as written, and only as it relates to faith and moral conduct. Unlike the Pharisees and Scribes, the Sadducees did not believe in resurrection of the body, immortality of the soul, the existence of spirits and angels and future judgment because they were not covered in the Torah. They also denied the oral laws, the prophets and psalms as revelations of God.

Yeshua The Messiah chastised the Sadducees for their lack of knowledge and understanding of the Scriptures or the power of God. He used the scripture to teach them about the resurrection of the dead, and also why there is no marriage, no one will marry or be given in marriage after resurrection, (Matthew 22:23-33).

The Essenes

The Essenes came as a third option to the Pharisees and Sadducees. They moved out of Jerusalem, fearing the corruption of the Pharisees and Sadducees. They lived a secluded life style in the desert. They taught righteousness, adopted strict dietary laws and a commitment to being eunuchs and celibacy, (Matthew 19:7-12). Not much is written about the Essenes in the Scriptures.

The Herodians

The Herodians were followers of Herod. They were mentioned in the Scripture and always in conjunction with the Pharisees (Mark 3:6, Mark 8:15, Mark 12:13, Matthew 22:16). The Herodians were a political party and a sect of Hellenistic Jews. Their objective was to restore a Herod to the throne in Judea as well as in other areas ruled by Herod the Great. Like the Pharisees, they severely opposed Yeshua The Messiah, and plotted together to have Him killed.

CHAPTER 31

About Family Division, Love And Hate

Scriptural Verses:

Matthew 10:34-39 (ETB): *34 "Do not imagine that my coming to earth is all peace. My coming will not be all peace but war, ([a division between those who do not love Him and those who love Him]). 35 For my coming will:*
'set a son against his father,
a daughter against her mother,
and a daughter-in-law against her mother-in-law'.
36 And 'the enemies of a person are the people of his own household', [ref Micah 7:6, Matthew 10:34-39].
37 Whoever loves his father or mother more than Me is not worthy of Me. Also, whoever loves his son or daughter more than Me is not worthy of Me. 38 And whoever does not take his cross (self denial, death of self, giving up self) and follow after Me is not worthy of Me. 39 Whoever finds (lives, clings to) his own life will lose it. But whoever gives up his life for My sake will find it,

[ref Matthew 10:34-39, Luke 12:49-53, Luke 14:25-27, Matthew 16:24-26, Mark 8:34-38, Luke 9:23-27]

Family Division, Love And Hate

Explanation:

God is love. He is the God whose love is so wide, long, high and deep and cannot be fathomed. He manifested His love for us through His only begotten Son by sending Him to come and die for us, so that we might live through Him. The gospel of good news brought by Yeshua from God is rooted in love. He wants us to also show that love to others. Every believer in Yeshua must love. Whoever does not love is not born of God and does not know God, (John 3:16, 1 John 4:7-12, Ephesians 3:18).

It is Yeshua's desire for us to have abundance of peace. Yeshua is the prince of peace. He gives peace, the like of which, no one else can give, (Isaiah 9:6, John 14:27).

Despite these, Yeshua has warned that His coming is not all for peace on earth. Rather, it will kindle fire on earth. The fire of conflict, division and hate even within the family. He said the father will be divided against son and son against father; the mother against daughter and daughter against mother; the mother-in-law against her daughter-in-law and daughter-in-law against her mother-in-law, (Matthew 10:34-39, Luke 12:49-53).

The reason for this is because not everyone will accept Him or accept God as their LORD! If everyone in a family were to accept the lordship of The Messiah or God in their lives, there will be no conflict or division amongst family. But opposition to the things of God comes when people do not accept Him. Those who do not accept Him will oppose those who do. This will inevitably bring about conflict, hate and division within the family, between parents and children, between siblings, and between neighbors and friends. In some cases, it can bring about persecution, rejection or even death of the believer. This is the fire and division Yeshua says His coming brings to earth.

God has given each person the freedom of choice. Following The Messiah and obeying God is a choice each person must make. There will be some who choose to follow and obey God. There will be some who will choose not to follow or obey Him. For this reason, conflict, tension, division will arise between the peoples on the opposite side of the choice. When people are on the opposite sides of this choice, conflict may arise between pleasing God or pleasing people. Conflict may arise between following human traditions and obeying what God says in His word.

Hate, rejection and persecution may arise against a believer because he has decided to follow The Messiah and obey God. Those who reject The Messiah are inevitably against Him and His followers. They are on the side of the Devil. With the Devil comes hate and even death. Just as the Devil comes to steal, kill and destroy, his followers are prepared, if possible, to destroy the follower of The Messiah and God, (John 10:10). They are known by their fruit, whether they are of God or of the Devil, (Matthew 7:16, Matthew 7:20).

Yeshau also said if anyone follows Him as The Messiah, and does not hate his father and mother, wife and children, brothers and sisters, and even his own life also, he cannot be His disciple! He said such a person must completely deny himself, take up his cross and follow Him, (Luke 14:25-27, Matthew 10:38-39, Matthew 16:24-26, Mark 8:34-38, Luke 9:23-27). He said whoever loves his father or mother more than Him is not worthy of Him. Whoever loves his son or daughter more than Him is not worthy of Him. In other words, the love for God must take first place over and above all else. It must be more than the love for the family. There must be self denial, death of self and giving up of self, family and what the person loves or treasures.

To "hate one's family" is not and never to be violent against anyone. It is also not and never to hold resentment, hate, grudge or unforgiveness against anyone. For those who harbor resentment or violence in their hearts are not of God! And those who refuse to forgive will not receive forgiveness from God, (Matthew 6:14-15). God is love, and a believer in The Messiah who follows God must show love all the time. To love God is to completely listen, obey Him, and live according to His word, (John 14:15). It is to put Him and His word above all else and be prepared to reject all others if and when a conflict arises.

To "hate one's family" is to love God more than them. It is to be prepared to reject, disobey, refuse, ignore, disagree, or completely walk away from them if their ideas, requests, desires, practices, customs, traditions are in conflict or contradiction against the word of God.

To "hate one's family" is to hate and reject the bad habits of a person and not the person! The believer is still to love them and show them God's love. The believer in The Messiah has to make a hard choose between obeying God or pleasing the family when there is a contradiction! To "hate one's family" is for the believer in The Messiah, to make a decision against pleasing the family outside of God's command!

Every true believer in The Messiah must continue to show God's love and pray for others, for their salvation. God does not want anyone to perish but to come to the knowledge of His love and salvation through His Son. Every believer must have this mind set! But there is one limit to showing God's love to others. The love must not go beyond the point where the believer will have to compromise in his obedience to God, and so loss his own salvation and soul. God does not desire for any soul to perish or go to hell. The believer must therefore, first save his own soul by living in the righteousness of God and total obedience to Him. Then the believer must extend God's love to others and labor in that love to save other souls from perishing. This is by continuing to share the good news of God's kingdom and leading them to also know and live in God's righteousness and obedience to God. Where this is not physically possible or it puts the salvation of the believer in potential jeopardy, then the believer should just pray for them, wherever he is, away from them. God will raise somebody else as a messenger to them because of His love and the believer's prayers to God for them. And always remember, a human being can preach to another, but no human being has the power to convert another one to follow The Messiah. It is the Holy Spirit that does every true conversion and seals the believer.

CHAPTER 32

About Matthew, Mark And Luke Minor Differential Emphasis of Details

Explanation:

There is little or no difference, except in areas of emphasis, between the accounts of Matthew, Mark and Luke. Apostle Matthew was the writer of the Gospel of Matthew. He was originally a tax collector before accepting Yeshua into his life, (Matthew 9:10-13, Mark 2:13-17). Then he became one of the disciples and an Apostle, (Matthew 10:1-4, Mark 3:13-19). Apostle Matthew was thus a first eye witness of what happened.

John Mark, was the writer of the Gospel of Mark. He was the son of a widow named Mary (Acts 12:121-17). Mary's home was a meeting place for the disciples to fellowship and pray. While Mark was not one of the twelve disciples, his closeness to them enabled him to gather much information from the disciples. John Mark later accompanied Paul and Barnabas on their missionary journeys, (Acts 12:25).

The accounts of the scenes, purposes, actions and outcomes of the events given by Matthew and Mark were exactly the same. They collaborated each other. Occasionally, and only in a few cases, did they have differences in areas of emphasis of the same event. There are six such places that can be observed in the books of Matthew and Mark where such occurred. They are explained below for greater understanding.

#1 Lawful To Do Good or Not on Sabbath (Matthew 12:10, Mark 3:4, Luke 6:7-9):

Matthew stated the people asked Yeshua (Jesus, Iēsous), "Is it permissible by the Law (Torah) to heal on the Sabbath?". Their purpose was to lay a trap with which they could accuse Yeshua. The account of Mark stated Yeshua said to the people: "Is it permissible by the Law (Torah) to do good or to do evil, to save life or to kill on the Sabbath?" The questions were both the same in both accounts.

Luke reported that the Scribes and Pharisees were closely watching Yeshua to see if He would heal on a Sabbath. They were looking for an opportunity to accuse to Him. So Yeshua knowing their thoughts, turned round to ask them the question, (Luke 6:7-9). He knew the question in the minds of the people, some silently voicing it. So He was in essence rhetorically echoing or asking back the question before He went on to answer it.

However, and more importantly, the scene, purpose, action, teaching and outcome were both the same in both the accounts of Matthew and Mark.

#2 Casting Out Of Legions Of Demons (Matthew 8:28-34, Mark 5:1-17, Luke 8:26-39):

Matthew had direct personal experience working with The LORD as a disciple and an Apostle. There has been a lot of confusion on this as to whether there were two men or just one man possessed by demons and delivered by Yeshua.

Both Mark and Luke mentioned of a man that came out to meet Yeshua. Their report contained the word 'a man or the man'. They continued their report on this man and the legions of demons that were cast out from him.

At the beginning of Matthew's account, he used the word 'two'. Then in the same verse, Matthew went on to add "possessed with demons, coming out of the tombs, exceeding fierce, so that no one could pass through that way", (Matthew 8:28). Matthew may have been referring to two men, and many readers have assumed and interpreted it as such. However, unlike his reports about people in other areas, here he did not use or add the word 'men', 'two men or people'.

The word 'two' may also be referring to the dual or double situation here. For in all the deliverances of demon-possessed people by Yeshua as reported in the Scriptures, this was the only case reported of not just being demon-possessed but also extremely fierce and dangerous to the people around. This may be what Matthew was referring to. That is, a combined dual, two, twain situation of one being 'both' demon-possessed and extremely fierce. The word interpreted as 'two' here, without the word 'men or two men', could also have meant 'both". That is the presence of 'duo', 'dual', 'two' or 'twain' situations. Such as one being 'both' demon-possessed and extremely fierce.

Also, in the rest of the Matthew's account of this deliverance from Matthew 8:29-34, the word 'two men' or 'men' or 'man' were never used! Instead, Matthew immediately began and continued to use the word 'us', or 'they' to represent the unusual presence of multiple demons. For example in Matthew 8:29, it says 'they cried out, saying: have you come to torment us before the time'?. This was clearly of the multiple demons speaking, and pleading their case with Yeshua. Both Mark and Luke also confirmed there were multiple demons, which spoke and pleaded together that they should be sent to the herd of swine. Mark and Luke also used the word 'a man', 'the man' to indicate there was only one man, whose body had been the home to the legions of demons.

So Matthew in his opening sentence on this account, informed us of the dual presence or situation of being both demon-possessed and extremely fierce. And the accounts of Mark and Luke helped in further clarifying for us to understand there was just one man, who was both demon-possessed and extremely fierce with legions of demon. In that case, both Matthew, Mark and Luke were all in perfect agreement, filling in the missing gaps, as they did in many other reports.

Again, and more importantly, in the accounts each by Matthew, Mark and Luke of the casting out of legions of demons in Gaderenes, the scene, purpose, action, and outcome were all the same. This is what is more important to believers. And Yeshua had the power to and could have done this to one, two, three or a crowd of people all demon-possessed at the same time.

#3 Walking stick or Rod for Journey (Matthew 10:10, Mark 6:8):

When Yeshua (Jesus, Iēsous) was sending out the twelve disciples on evangelism in the surrounding towns, He instructed them on how they should go, what to take or not take. In the account of Matthew, they were not to take "extra change (but just one) of clothes, shoes, or walking sticks (staff, rod like shepherd's)". The account of Mark stated "except a walking stick", meaning not more than one walking stick or staff. Both accounts agree with each other. In both accounts, not more than one shepherd-like staff or rod was allowed of them. Again the scene, purpose, action, and outcome were both the same in both the accounts of Matthew and Mark.

#4 The Special Request for James and John (Matthew 20:20-24, Mark 10:35-41):

Matthew gave more details on the participation by the mother of the sons of Zebedee, on this request for the benefit of her two sons. The request related to both her sons James and John, who were also disciples. Mark focused on just James and John, the two disciples involved and with whom the other disciples were displeased. Mark ignored the part of the mother, who initiated it. In the accounts of both Matthew and Mark, the two disciples James and John participated in the making of this request to Yeshua (Jesus, Iēsous). They both confirmed their willingness to do whatever it takes, (Matthew 20:22, Mark 10:38-39). The scene, purpose, action and outcome remained the same as reported by both. The mother of James and John, whose name was Salome, was a very faithful follower of Yeshua, along with other women, who ministered to their needs till the very end. She was with the other women during the death on the cross and resurrection of Yeshua, (Mark 15:40, Mark 16:1).

#5 The healing of Blind men in Jericho (Matthew 20:29-34, Mark 10:46-52, Luke 18:35-43):

The accounts of Mark and Luke were both focused on the blind man who was healed as Yeshua was entering into Jericho, (Mark 10:46, Luke 18:35). The blind man's name was given as Bartimaeus in the report of Mark.

On the other hand, the account of Matthew was focused on two blind men who were healed after Yeshua had entered and was leaving Jericho for Jerusalem, (Matthew 20:29). The blindman, named Bartimaeus, was sitting and begging at one end of the city, the entry way taken in by Yeshua and His disciples. They were coming from the Jordan end. The other two blind men were on the other end of the city, the side leading to Jerusalem where Yeshua was headed.

Again, the focus is not the number of blind men. The key thing, which is most important, was that the blind was healed as confirmed by both Matthew, Mark and Luke that the healing of the blind took place. In both cases, the blinds who desperately needed the healing, shouted on top of their voices and refused to be silenced or intimidated by the crowd. Again the scene, purpose, action, and outcome were both the same in both the accounts of Matthew and Mark.

#6 The Donkey and the Colt In Triumphant Entry(Matthew 21:2-11, Mark 11:2-10):

While Matthew mentioned both the donkey and her colt (young donkey) together, Mark focused on just the colt. Mark's account does not negate or disprove the existence of two donkeys, the mother donkey and the young colt. Yeshua rode on the colt which had not been ridden on before. Again the scene, purpose, action, and outcome were both the same in both the accounts of Matthew and Mark. The important thing was The Messiah triumphantly rode on a donkey into Jerusalem and fulfilled the prophecy by Zechariah, (Zechariah 9:9).

CHAPTER 33

About A Hundred Fold Return For Losses For The Kingdom Of God

Scriptural Verses:

Matthew 19:27-30 (ETB): *27 Then Peter replied and said to Him, "See, we have left everything and followed You. Therefore what will we have?" 28 So Yeshua said to them:*

"Of a truth I tell you, that in the regenerated world to come, when the Son of Man sits on the Throne of His glory, you who have followed Me will also sit on twelve thrones with power to judge (rule) over the Twelve Tribes of Israel, [ref Matthew 19:28, Luke 22:30, Revelations 2:26-27, Revelations 21:10-14].

29 Also everyone who has left houses or brothers or sisters or father or mother or wife or children or lands, for the sake of My Name, will receive a hundred times over, and will obtain eternal life.

30 But many who are first (greatest in ranking in this world) will be last (least important in the regenerated world to come), and many who are last (least important in this world) will be first (greatest in ranking), [ref Matthew 19:27-30, Mark 10:29-31, Luke 18:28-30, Matthew 12:48-50, Mark 3:33-35, Luke 6:38, Acts 2:44-46].

Mark 10:28-31 (ETB): *Then Peter began to say to Him, "See, we have left everything and followed You." 29 So Yeshua replied and said:*

"Of a truth I tell you, no one who has left house or brothers or sisters or father or mother or wife or children or lands, for My sake and of the gospel of good news, 30 that will not receive a hundred times over, in this present age, houses and brothers and sisters and mothers and children and lands, along with persecutions. And will also receive eternal life, in the age to come.

31 But many who are first (greatest in ranking in this world) will be last (least important in the world to come). And many who are last (least important in this world) will be first (greatest in ranking), [ref Matthew 19:27-30, Mark 10:29-31, Luke 18:28-30, Matthew 12:48-50, Mark 3:33-35, Luke 6:38, Acts 2:44-46].

Luke 18:28-30 (ETB): *28 Then Peter said to Him, "See, we have left everything and followed You"*

29 So Yeshua said to them:

"Of a truth I tell you, there is no one who has left house or parents or brothers or wife or children for the sake of the Kingdom of God, 30 who will not receive many times over, in this present age, and also receive eternal life, in the age to come, [ref Matthew 19:27-30, Mark 10:29-31, Luke 18:28-30, Matthew 12:48-50, Mark 3:33-35, Luke 6:38, Acts 2:44-46].

Explanation

The LORD will reward all the sacrifices and losses for the sake of the gospel of good news of the King of God, (Matthew 19:27-30, Mark 10:28-31).

He said everyone who has left house or brothers or sisters or father or mother or wife or children or lands, for My sake and of the gospel of good news, will receive a hundred times over, in this present age, houses and brothers and sisters and mothers and children and lands, along with persecutions. Then in the age to come, they will receive eternal life and some would be rulers, (Matthew 19:27-30, Mark 10:29-31, Revelations 2:26-27).

Simply put, every effort or sacrifice made for the Kingdom of God will be recognized and rewarded. And God is more than able to meet and exceed the needs of each person.

House lost could be actual house or home. Brothers, sisters, father, mother, wife or children are family members or relatives. Land could be a parcel of land, field or a country or nation where the person was born.

About Hundredfold Father, Mother, Sisters And Brothers:

First, let us understand, who is a family. In the strict sense, a family member is one related by blood. In other cases, they may be family through marriage or adoption. Every believer in The LORD has been reborn (redeemed) by the Blood of the LORD Yeshua Himself. All believers have thus become related and members of one big family in the Kingdom of God.

God is the father, who is a hundred times more than any other earthly father. He is the father for all believers in Yeshua The Messiah.

Secondly, Yeshua also clearly explained who is His brother, sister or mother. One time, His earthly blood mother and blood brothers came looking for Him while He was preaching the gospel. He stopped, looked around the people and explained to them He already had his mother and brothers around there with Him. "For whoever does the will of God is My brother, My sister and mother", (Matthew 12:46-50, Mark 3:31-35).

Thirdly, while He was on the cross, He told Mary His mother: "Woman, look! Your son!". At the same time, He also said to the disciple (John) "Look! Your mother!" And from that time on, the disciple took her to his own home, (John 19:26-27). They had become one family through The LORD.

So, every believer in the LORD already has more than a hundred fold gain of brothers, sisters, father, mother, wife or children This is whether they still have their earthly families with them or not. The desirable thing is for the blood family members to join this bigger family by coming under Yeshua The Messiah as LORD and savior. Even where there has been no physical loss, there is still a gaining of a more than a hundred fold of new family members.

Now, there are actually those who have lost their earthly families of brothers, sisters, father, mother, wife or children. The LORD in the Scripture already explained this could and would happen. A person may through devotion to the gospel suffer loss of contact with families; Or has no family home to go to back to because of constant moving around (Matthew 8:20); Or his or her family may be killed through persecution; Or may through rejection by relatives, be cut off or become an outcast by parents or other family members or relatives. Clearly, the person cannot get back to those members of his family or household he is related to by blood. Yeshua warned that His coming will bring about a conflict, rejection, separation between families members as some will accept or oppose, (Matthew 10:35-38, Luke 12:51-53).The desirable thing is for the blood family members to also accept Yeshua The Messiah as Lord and savior. Then they can continue as one in Him. God does not want anyone to perish (John 3:16, 2 Peter 3:8-10).

Those who have lost physical or earthly family gained more than one hundredfold reward by remaining with the body of believers in The LORD, and in fellowship. They gain new family brothers, sisters, father, mother, wife or children in The LORD.

In the example of the early disciples and believers, they came together as one family, new brothers and sisters, sharing everything together as one, (Acts 2:44-46, Acts 4:32-35). They had fellowship together, and freely moved among each others. Every believer gains this new family of brothers, sisters, of believers as one in the LORD, with God as the father. This is much bigger, than those who are family members by human blood. This is how it should be seen in the body of The LORD. Not just in a small Church with few members, but looking at the bigger body of The LORD.

About Possessions, lands and properties:

The silver, the gold, all of heavens and earth belong to God (Haggai 2:8, Psalm 24:1, Psalm 115:16, Isaiah 66:1). He is more than able to reward each person more than a hundred fold of their losses for the Kingdom of God. But He also said, what will it profit a person if he gains the whole world and loss his soul, (Matthew 16:26, Mark 8:36-38). He said sell what you have and give to the poor. He further said, everyone should lay up their treasures in heaven where there is no moth, rot or thieves, and where your treasure is where your earth is (Matthew 6:19-21, Luke 12:33-34). He told the rich man, if you want to be perfect, go and sell all your possessions, give them to the poor, come, take up your cross and follow Me (Matthew 19:21, Mark 10:21). He said, it will be difficult for the rich to enter the Kingdom of God, and even more so for them than for a camel to pass through the hole of a needle, (Mark 10:23-25.

While He wants us to be rich and fully provided for, He emphasizes contentment and His ability to meet our daily needs, and our sharing with the poor. His teaching about the Kingdom of God is not of poverty. But it is of being well provided for. Neither is it about accumulation of materials, wealth and possessions. But it is of sharing. It is of being a conduit, a channel for God's blessings to flow and be shared with those who have need. As an example, He did not accumulate wealth while on earth. Also none of His disciples, apostles or early believers accumulated wealth, houses, properties, etc. Indeed, they could have taken advantage of their great miraculous, healing or even prophetic powers to accumulate wealth for themselves from the people. But they chose to be like the others, shared whatever they had with them, while laying up treasures in heaven. This is the model for every true believer. The present global accumulation of riches in the churches by leaders using God endowed miraculous or prophetic powers, or accumulating wealth through seeking for donations, tithes and offering is alien to the Scripture! They are no better than the girl possessed with spirit of divination who brought much wealth to her master until Paul put an end to it, (Acts 16:16-18). They are not better than prophet Balaam (Numbers 23-24) who used his power to gain wealth. They are not better than Gehazi the greedy servant of Elisha the miracle working prophet of God, (2 Kings 5:20-27). Neither are they better than the Pharisees or Scribes who twisted the gospel and used their positions as leaders to accumulate much wealth for themselves, (Matthew 23:3-8, Matthew 23:13-15).

In the early Church, there was great love. The believers had all things in common. In a single Church location they shared all together. When they moved to another place they still had access. The Apostles and believers travelling around did not have to acquire houses and properties. They simply went to the home of another believer and stayed with them. And there could be hundreds, if not thousands of such believers' homes and properties where the believers have such joint access. Believers open up their homes and possessions to other poorer believers.

Believers are promised eternal life and mansions in heaven. Indeed, there are many mansions in heaven, enough for all believers, (John 14:2). And everyone who makes it to heaven become like an Angel, (Matthew 22:30, Mark 12:25, Luke 20:35-36). Therefore, people who see themselves owning many mansions in heaven is an extension of their human values or expectation. It has no place in Heaven. What is the purpose or need for people need to accumulate mansions, houses or properties in heaven(like on earth)? It is ridiculous. Its is trying to transfer human, earthy value system into heaven! For Angels do no accumulate any of these. The Kingdom of Heaven is one big family of God, all united. Accumulation on earthy is an insurance against when supply runs out. But in heaven, they have no need to accumulate material, possessions, or food as humans do on earth. This is because in the Kingdom of God, He makes everything available to them if and at the instant they need anything. They never lack anything. The LORD gave us a little glimpse of that while He was on earth, He never accumulated. He simply asked The Father for whatever He needed, whenever He needed something. And in heaven, nothing is lacking, and even if there is, the Father is right there to provide instantly (before one asks)! If in heaven they never lack anything and if what God has is available to them at anytime they ever have need, then there is no need to accumulate. Since there is never lack of anything they need from the Father, they have no need to accumulate (as insurance for when it finishes). For in the angelic state, they can move around, at great speed, to anywhere, and stay anywhere (if necessary). If they eat or change clothes as we do, (which is doubtful), they can do any of these at will, at anytime, automatically, without the need for wardrobes or pantries or storage barns for accumulation.

CHAPTER 34

About Stars Falling From Heaven

Scriptural Verses:

Matthew 24:29 (ETB): *29 "Immediately after the tribulation at that time: the sun will be darkened. The moon will also not give its light to the earth. The stars will fall from heaven, and the heavenly powers will be shaken, [ref Isaiah 34:4, Matthew 24:29, Revelation 6:12-13, Revelation 12:7-9].*

Explanation

On the Day of The LORD, the sun that gives light to the earth will be darkened. The moon that also gives light to the earth will not give its light. There will be actual darkness for a day on the earth, (Isaiah 24:23, Zechariah 14:6-7, Matthew 24:29, Acts 2:20).

The Messiah in His revelation and prophecy also said that Stars will fall from heaven, and the heavenly powers will be shaken, (Matthew 24:29). This statement is part a metaphor and part literal.

A small asteroid or rock falling from the sky to the earth would cause a major destruction. As for stars, there are billions, countless number, of them in the sky. They are each much bigger than our sun, moon or earth. One or some of the stars falling to the earth will shatter the whole earth into small pieces. The Messiah is coming back to the earth. The people on earth will see Him, and He will rule over all the earth as King and Priest of God.

Therefore, stars falling from heaven are not literal stars. Rather the statement of 'stars falling from heaven' is a metaphor referring to divine heavenly beings, who will fall down from their lofty positions in heaven. Prophet Isaiah spoke about Satan's fall, saying: 'How you have fallen from heaven, you son of the Dawn, O Lucifer. How you are thrown down to the earth', (Isaiah 14:12). The literal meaning of Lucifer is 'Light bearer, shinning one, morning star'!

The stars falling from heaven in the end time will include Satan, and other bad angelic principalities, powers, and rulers in heavenly places, (Ephesians 6:12, Daniel 10:13). They would fight to remain in the heavenly realms but will be defeated and thrown down, fall down to the earth, (Revelations 12:7-9). As they fall from their domains or positions of power, the powers of heaven, rulers or 'gods' will be shaken and not be like before. (Also Refer to the Chapter about 'idols, gods, and God of gods' at the bottom of Deuteronomy 10).

The LORD, The Messiah, once told His disciples He beheld Satan falling like lightning from heaven, (Luke 10:18). In the end time, Satan will further be bound with chain and thrown down into the bottomless pit, (Revelation 20:1-3). The bottomless pit or hell will be his prison for one thousand years, before the Millennium reign of the LORD on earth. It is the initial place, before going to lake of fire, for all fallen stars or divine beings, who have violated their first estate.

Prophet Isaiah also said: 'The LORD will punish in heaven above the 'gods' (divine heavenly beings, angelic), And on the earth the kings of the earth. They will be rounded up together, as prisoners are rounded in the pit. They will be put in the prison. And finally, they will be punished, (Isaiah 24:21-22). Ultimately, they will later end up in the lake of fire, which had been prepared for them, (Revelation 20:10, Matthew 25:41, Jude 6, Revelation 20:11-15).

The antichrist is not one of the stars of heaven or divine heavenly being. He will start initially as a man of sin, who will become adopted by Satan for his use. He will go straight into lake of fire along with the false prophet, (Revelation 13:3-8, Revelation 19:20).

CHAPTER 35

About Resurrected Saints Seen In Jerusalem

Scriptural Verses:

Matthew 27:51-52 (ETB): 52 *Also the graves were opened. The bodies of many of the saints (holy people) who had fallen asleep were raised from the dead. 53 And after Yeshua's resurrection, they came out of the graves and went into the holy city, where many people saw them, [ref 1 Peter 3:18-21, Ephesians 4:8-10; Hebrews 2:14-15, John 11:25, Revelations 1:18].*

Explanation

One of the major events that happened during the death and resurrection of Yeshua The Messiah was the resurrection of the Saints, (Matthew 27:52-53). He is the resurrection and life and holds the keys of death and hell, (John 11:25, Revelations 1:18).

While He was on the cross, He cried with a loud voice the second time and released His spirit. Some events followed this. First, the Temple Veil was torn from top to bottom. There were two veils or screens. There was the outer veil or screen called the Temple Veil. It separated the Tabernacle from the main Temple area where the

Altar of burn offering was, (Exodus 26:36, Exodus 40:28-30). The second veil or screen was within the Tabernacle. The Tabernacle had two sections, the Holy Place and The Most Holy Place, which were separated by the second veil or Screen, (Exodus 26:31-35, Exodus 40:21). The Scriptures only mentioned the Temple Veil being torn.

While the Temple Veil being torn, there was also earthquake and the splitting of rocks in Jerusalem. In addition, the graves were opened.

Yeshua The Messiah was the first fruit to be raised from the dead with immortality, (1 Corinthians 15:20-23, Revelation 1:5, Luke 24:39). Then after His own resurrection, many bodies of the Saints that were dead were also raised from the dead. They were seen by the people in Jerusalem city, because they appeared to many, (Matthew 27:50-53).

The Scripture does not say if other cities also had the bodies of the dead Saints raised to life, as in Jerusalem. During His ministry on earth, The Messiah raised many people bodily, from the dead, and they lived with their families. If the Saints whose bodies were brought back to life were all of that generation, and had no immortality in the manner of Lazarus, then it is conceivable they went to be with their families, (John 11:1-45). Then they would live in their bodies until their death.

However, the Saints were some of the multitude of captives set free from Satan by The Messiah. The Scripture tells us that The Messiah led the captives captive when He ascended on high. Their souls await the time of the sound of the trumpet call of God. Then the dead in The Messiah will rise first, and their souls will be reunited with glorious bodies. Those who are alive in Him, will join them and be caught up together in the air with The Messiah, (1 Thessalonians 4:15-17, 1 Corinthians 15:51-52)

Until the death and resurrection of The Messiah, the souls of the Saints who died were held in a paradise below the earth. The souls of the unrighteous were also below in hell, in a separate compartment. They could see and communicate with each other, but could not help or change their status, (Luke 16:19-31)

Also from after the resurrection of The Messiah, when any Saint dies, the soul no longer goes to a paradise in the lower part of the earth. Rather the soul of the righteous goes to the paradise in the heavens above, to await the resurrection of the body, (Revelation 6:9-11, 2 Corinthians 5:8, Philippians 1:21-24, Hebrew 12:22).

As for the unrighteous, they will continue to go to hell, below the earth, where they are held until their own resurrection for judgment, (Revelation 20:11-15).

CHAPTER 36

About Elijah And John The Baptist Identical Ministry

Scriptural Verses:

Isaiah 40:3(ETB): *3 The voice of one crying in the wilderness: "Prepare the way of The LORD. Make a straight highway In the desert wasteland for our God,*

[ref Isaiah 40:3, Matthew 3:3, John 1:23].

Malachi 3:1 (ETB): *1 "Look (know this), I will send My messenger, and he will prepare the way ahead for Me. The LORD, whom you seek, will then come suddenly to His Temple, even the Messenger of the covenant, in whom you take pleasure. Look, He is coming," Says The LORD of hosts, [ref Isaiah 40:3, Matthew 3:3, John 1:23, Malachi 3:1, John 2:13-17, Matthew 21:12-13].*

John 1:22-23 (ETB): *Then they said to him, "Who then are you? What answer should we take back to those who sent us? What would you say about yourself?" 23 He said: "I am, as the prophet Isaiah said": "The voice of one crying in the wilderness: 'Prepare the way of The LORD (ADONAI). Make His path straight'". [ref Isaiah 40:3, Matthew 3:3, Mark 1:3, Luke 3:4, John 1:23].*

Elijah And John The Baptist Identical Ministry

Malachi 4:5 (ETB): *5 Look (know this), I will send you Elijah the prophet before the coming of the great and dreadful Day of The LORD, [ref Zechariah 4:11-14, Revelation 11:3-4, Malachi 4:6, Matthew 11:10-15, Matthew 17:10-11].*

Explanation

Elijah and John the Baptist were different prophets for different times. But they had similar kind of assignment and operated with the power of the same Spirit. They have special ministry to do with the coming of the Messiah. There are two comings to the earth of The Messiah. Each of these two comings have a messenger to herald and prepare the way. This is the assignment of John The Baptist and Elijah.

His first coming of The Messiah was as The Lamb of God. He was to come, suffer, be killed, and rise up from the dead on the third day, (John 1:29, John 1:36, John 3:16-17, Luke 24:44-47). He repeatedly told His disciples about this, (Matthew 16:21, Mark 8:31, Luke 9:22, Matthew 17:22, Mark 9:30-31, Luke 9:44-45, Matthew 20:18-19, Mark 10:33-34, Luke 18:31-34).

The purpose of this first coming was to bring about repentance, be the sacrificial Lamb, the ransom for the forgiveness of sin and salvation to the world, (John 3:16-17, Luke 24:47).

Ahead of this first coming of the Messiah, a messenger was to be sent as prophesied in the Scriptures. The role of the messenger was to prepare the way, to warn the people. He was the herald, the announcer. He was to come ahead and prepare the people. (Isaiah 40:3, Malachi 3:1, Matthew 3:3, Mark 1:2-3, John 1:23).

John The Baptist was the messenger ahead of the first coming of The Messiah as Sacrificial Lamb of God. He lived a secluded life in the wilderness. After many centuries of no prophets in Israel, He was born and then rose as the lonely voice in the wilderness. He rose to announce through his preaching of the arrival of the Messiah, who will save the world from sin. He baptized, (totally immersed, dipped inside, submerged), the Messiah and revealed Him to the Israelites.

There is an interval between the first and second coming of The Messiah. After the first coming of the Messiah, and having accomplished the purpose of salvation for the world, He would go back to heaven and stay for a while. Then at the appointed time, He will come back again, the second time. This time would not be as the sacrificial Lamb of God, but as The King of God to reign on earth. He will reign and rule on earth as The King of kings and LORD of lords, (Revelation 19:11-21). He will both King and Priest of God on earth (Zechariah 6:12-13).

The day He appears would be The Day of The LORD on earth. For He comes to put an end to sin, and would eliminate the rebellious, the disobedient, (Zechariah 14:1-4). It will be a day of doom for the antichrist, his false prophet and millions of their soldiers on earth, (Revelation 19:19-21). It will also be a day of doom for Satan and his angels who will chained into hell, (Revelation 20:1-3). Refer to the commentary at the Chapter About The Day Of The LORD in End Time.

Like the first coming, His second coming will be specially heralded by messengers. This time, there will be two messengers. One of them would be Prophet Elijah, (Malachi 4:6, Revelation 11:3-4, Zechariah 4:11-14, Matthew 11:10-15, Matthew 17:10-11).

Elijah was around during the time of Ahab and Jezebel, (1 Kings 17:1-24, 1 Kings 18:1-40). He had defeated the false prophets led by Jezebel and brought revival to Israel. Prophet Elijah did not die, but was parted from Elisha his servant and then taken away in a chariot, (2 Kings 2:11-12). He was taken away but will come back to play a major role as a messenger ahead of the second coming of the Messiah in the end time. Elijah and Moses appeared and discussed with The LORD Yeshua during the transfiguration, (ref Matthew 17:1-9, Mark 9:2-10, Luke 9:28-36).

Apart from Elijah, the other prophet who did not die as reported in the Scriptures was Enoch, (Genesis 5:24). He was of the first world or generation, which started with Adam and was destroyed in the flood in Noah's time. Whether it is Enoch or Moses or one of the Apostles of the LORD or someone else who joins Elijah would be as determined by the LORD, who knows what is best in His plans. Refer to commentary at the end of Revelation 11 about the two witnesses in the end time.

The purpose of Elijah and of the other messenger in the end time would be like that of John the Baptist. His purpose is to prepare the Israelites, who had rejected Him when He first came. His purpose is to help them avoid the fierce anger and judgment of God, through getting them to repent and accept The Messiah. His purpose is to be witness, who testifies of The LORD.

When The Messiah came the first time, the Pharisees, chief priests, Scribes and rulers of the Israelites of old rejected Him. They rejected and crucified Him the first time. The people of Israel also rejected Him and have largely remained desolate and in apostasy since them till now. Meanwhile the message of good news of the Kingdom of God went out through the Apostles and disciples of the Messiah to the world. The Gentile nations have accepted The Messiah. Today, as in other times, some few individual Jews have accepted Him, just like His few disciples of old. But in general, the apostasy of Israel as a nation will continue until just before His second coming.

Elijah will come as a messenger ahead of that second coming, (Malachi 4:6). Elijah and one other witness will arise to preach, (Revelation 11:3-4). The Antichrist will also severely persecute the Israelites. The combination of these will bring about the unparallel repentance and mourning by the Israelites as a nation, ahead of The Messiah's return, (Zechariah 12:10-14).

In the second time, He is not coming as a Lamb to take away sin. Rather, He is coming as a ruler and priest of God on earth. He will reign over the whole world from Jerusalem.

CHAPTER 37

About The Roman Empire, Syria And Jerusalem

Scriptural Verses:

Luke 2:1-3(ETB): 1 In those days, a decree went out from the Emperor Caesar Augustus that a census should be taken in the entire Roman world for taxation. 2 This was the first census conducted while Quirinius (Cyrenius) was governor of Syria region, 3 So everyone went to his own ancestral city to be registered.

Explanation

In the Old Testament, the Syria region was known as Aram. During the time of Yeshua and John the Baptist, the Syria region was part of the Roman Empire. Syria region with capital in Antioch was a large Asia province of the Roman Empire. The Syria region was bounded in the north by Taurus and Amanus ranges, in the south by Palestine, in the east by the Euphrates and Arabia, and in the west by the Mediterranean. Judea, Galilee, Idumea and Samaria were part of Palestine in the Syria region.

Also, at that time of the birth of Yeshua, the governor of Syria region was Quirinius (Cyrenius) who conducted the first census. Caesar Augustus (27 BC to 14AD) had been reigning as the first Roman emperor at the time of the birth of John and Yeshua. He was later succeeded by Tiberius Caesar as the second Roman Emperor (from 14AD to 37AD).

John The Baptist started his ministry of preparing the way for The LORD during the fifteenth year of the reign of Tiberius Caesar, (around 28AD or 29AD. At that time Pontius Pilate was the governor of Judea, Herod was tetrarch of Galilee, the high priests in the Temple in Jerusalem were Annas and Caiaphas, (Luke 3:1-2).

Yeshua had prophesied the complete destruction of Jerusalem and the Temple, (Matthew 24:1-2, Mark 13:1-2, Luke 19:41-44). This was fulfilled in 70AD during the reign of Vespasian (Titus Flavius Vespasianus) as Roman emperor from 69AD –79AD. Daniel had prophesied the destruction would be done by the people of the prince (Antichrist ruler) who is to come later in the end time, (Daniel 9:26-27).

Yeshua predicted the times of the Gentiles (Luke 21:20-24). This is the periods of successive reign, power and occupations of Jerusalem and Judea region by the Gentiles. This continued till 1948AD, a total period of almost 1800 years!. The Romans destroyed Jerusalem in 70AD. They continued the destruction and desolation of Judea as they destroyed several villages and towns, killed most of the Jewish population, sold many into slavery and others fled between 132AD – 136AD. Many of the Judean Jews were sold into slavery, or transported as captives, or expelled from Judea and sent to various Roman provinces in the Middle East, Europe and Africa.

After the Romans, the Arabs led by Caliph Umar, took control of Palestine and Jerusalem starting in April 637 AD, and ruled until the late 11th century. After the Arabs came the Crusaders. They ruled until around 1480AD. Then the Turks in Ottoman Empire, ruled from 1486AD until the First World War in 1917. The British took over Palestine and administered it from 1917 and ruled until 1948. And finally the State of Israel was created in 1948. The creation of the State of Israel in 1948AD marked the first time Israel became a sovereign nation since 70AD. It took more than 1,800years, from 70AD to 1948AD, for this to happen. Seventy years (70years) later, Jerusalem was recognized as the capital of Israel. What would be next is the building of the Temple. Then Israel will be firmly established for God.

CHAPTER 38

About The First Disciples First Meeting With Yeshua

Scriptural Verses:

John 1:35-37 (ETB): 35 Again, the next day, John the Baptist was standing with two of his disciples. 36 He looked and saw Yeshua walking by. Then he said, "Look at the Lamb of God!" 37 When the two disciples of John heard this, they went and walked behind Yeshua.

John 1:40(ETB): 40 One of the two people who followed Yeshua, after hearing what John the Baptist said, was Andrew. He was the brother of Simon Peter, [ref John 21:24].

Explanation

John The Baptist had his own disciples. Andrew and one other disciple (called John) were originally among the disciples of John the Baptist. Both Andrew and this other disciple heard when John the Baptist made the remark about Yeshua being the Lamb of God (John 1:29, John 1:35-37). Both of them followed behind Yeshua to know more about Him.

Andrew along with that other disciple of John the Baptist were the first to have a meeting, their first encounter as it were, with Yeshua, (John 1:35-39).

After this, Andrew invited his brother Simon Peter to also meet Yeshua, (John 1:40-42). This meeting of Andrew and Peter happened a day after the baptism of Yeshua by John the Baptist in the Jordan River.

Then the following day after this meeting, Philip and Nathaniel also met Yeshua, (John 1:43-44).

On getting back to the Galilee region, Yeshua being full of the Holy Spirit, which had descended on Him like a dove during His baptism, was led into the wilderness. He went fasting and praying for forty days and nights, (Matthew 3:16-17, Mark 1:9-11, Luke 3:21-22, John 1:32-34,Matthew 4:1-2, Luke 4:1-2).

Subsequently, Yeshua formally started His ministry, after the three major events: His return from the baptism by John the Baptist, the anointing by the Holy Spirit during the baptism, and after the fasting and praying in the wilderness, (Mark 1:9-13, Luke 4:1-2).

Later, Andrew, Peter as well as James and John abandoned their fishing professions in Galilee lake to follow Yeshua as full time disciples, (Matthew 4:18-22, Mark 1:16-20).

Later, others joined as Yeshua's disciples including Matthew (Matthew 9:9, Mark 2:13-14, Luke 5:27-28).

John who became a disciple of Yeshua, was generally believed to be the other disciple of John the Baptist, that went with Andrew to Yeshua, (John 1:35-37).

This John was one of the disciples of The LORD Yeshua. He became Apostle John, one of the twelve Apostles. He wrote the book of John. He also wrote the book of Revelation, and the writer of the first, second and third Epistles of John in the New Testament. He was not writing to report what was told to him by another, but from own person experience from the beginning of the ministry of Yeshua. Apostle John had direct personal experience, and was a witness of what happened during the ministry of The LORD Yeshua, from the early stage to the end. Even among the twelve disciples, John along with Peter were often closer to Yeshua than the others, [ref Matthew 17:1-2, Mark 9:2-3, Luke 9:28-29, Mark 5:36-37, Luke 8:51), Luke 22:7-8).

It was rumored among the disciples that John will not die till The LORD comes back, (John 21:21-23). In the Book of Revelation, John was instructed to eat the little book. He was also informed he would prophesy again before many peoples, nations, tongues, and kings, (Revelation 10:9-11).

CHAPTER 39

About The Only Begotten Son Of God

Scriptural Verses:

John 3:16-17(ETB): *16 For God so loved the whole world that He gave the only begotten (unique, one of a kind born) Son of Himself, so that anyone who believes in Him should not perish but have everlasting life. 17 For God did not send His Son into the world to condemn the world, but rather so that the world can be saved through Him.*

Explanation

There are many references in the Scriptures to angels as sons of God, (Genesis 6:2-4, Job 1:6, Job 2:1, Job 38:7).

There are also many references in the Scriptures to humans as sons of God, (Exodus 4:22-23, 2 Samuel 7:14, 1 Chronicles 17:13, Matthew 5:9, Luke 6:35, Luke 20:34-36, John 1:12-13, Romans 8:14-16, Galatians 3:26, Ephesians 1:5, etc).

Both angels and humans were created. They are not duplicate or born of God Himself. Angels are sons of God, but were created for their purposes. Adam was a son of God, but he was created, not reproduced, born or a duplicate of God. Every believer is a child or

The Only Begotten Son Of God

son of God. But every believer has been adopted as a son, through the begotten Son of God, into His family.

The phrase, "The Only Begotten Son" of God is used only for Yeshua. The "Only Begotten Son" of God means the only unique, one of a kind, born Son of God Himself. Yeshua is unlike other sons of God. He is the exact, unique, one of a kind, the only duplicate of God the Father.

He was not created. For He was with God from the beginning and He is God, (John 1:1-3). He created everything. At the right time, for the purpose of salvation of mankind, He became flesh and live among humans, (John 1:14, Luke 1:35).

No other living being in heaven, on earth or under the earth that has the quality of Yeshua, the begotten Son of God Himself. Even demons refer to Him as The Son of The Most High God, (Matthew 8:29, Mark 5:7, Luke 8:28). And God refers to Him as His beloved Son, in whom He is very pleased, (Matthew 3:17, Matthew 17:5, Mark 9:7, Luke 3:22).

He is of the same seed, the same kind, the same type as God. And though being God, Yeshua did not cling to equality with God when He came. Instead, he humbled himself as a slave would. To accomplish His assignment, He took on the weak human form, was completely obedient to God the Father, and died on a cross to save us. His Name, power and authority is above all others in heaven, on earth or under the earth. Accordingly, every knee bows to Him and every tongue confess He is LORD, to the glory of God The Father, (Philippians 2:6-11).

There are many sons of God. But no other is the begotten Son of God, except Yeshua Himself.

CHAPTER 40

About The Resurrection And Early Appearances Of The LORD

Scriptural Verses:

Matthew 28:1-6 (ETB): 1 Mary Magdalene (of Magdala), and the other Mary (the mother of James and Joseph), came very early in the morning at dawn to see the tomb where the body of Yeshua (Jesus, Iēsous) was kept. This was on the day after the Sabbath, which was (Sunday, Yom Rishon), the first day of the week, [ref Matthew 27:56].

2 And there was a powerful earthquake. For an angel of The LORD (ADONAI) had descended from heaven. He came and rolled back the sealed stone from the entrance to the tomb, where Yeshua was buried. Then the angel sat on the stone. 3 His appearance was like lightning, and his clothing was as white as snow. 4 And the guards shook with fear when they saw him, and became like dead men. 5 But the angel spoke and said to the women, "Do not be afraid, for I know that you are looking for Yeshua who was crucified. 6 He is not here. For He is risen from the dead, just as He said! Come and see the place where His body was lying.

The Resurrection And Early Appearances Of The LORD

Explanation

Death And Resurrection Awaited Since Adam's fall:

As concerning the redemption of all humans, the death and resurrection of the Lamb of God was what God and the angelic host had been looking forward to for centuries since the fall of Adam and Eve. While His death fully paid for the penalty of sin of the fall, His resurrection brings life. The death and the Resurrection of The LORD is therefore the most important thing that happened for all believers. Believers in the LORD would have been without hope and the most miserable if there was no resurrection in The LORD. He is the first fruit of the dead, (1 Corinthians 15:20). His resurrection confirmed there is hope for every believer after this life. For indeed, those that are asleep (physically dead) in Him will rise up again. Then those who are still alive will be caught up together with them in the air to join The LORD, and will be with Him forever, (1 Corinthians 15:20, 1 Thessalonians 4:15-17, 1 Corinthians 15:51-52).

The LORD Yeshua was raised from the dead before dawn on the day after Sabbath, the first day of the week, on Sunday, Yom Rishom. He was raised from the dead by God through the life giving power of the Holy Spirit, (Romans 8:11).

Following His resurrection, there was a powerful earthquake, according to the account of Matthew, (Matthew 28:1-2). This happened when an angel of The LORD (ADONAI) descended from heaven. The angel did not come to resurrect The LORD, for He was already risen by the power of God through the life giving Holy Spirit. The angel did two things. First, he came and rolled back the sealed stone from the entrance to the tomb, where Yeshua was buried. He sat on the stone and waited. Neither did the angel did come to roll away the stone so that the risen LORD Yeshua could come out of the tomb. For The LORD, with His glorified body, could go through any physical barriers of walls, stones, etc. The second purpose of the angel, was for the people of The LORD, His disciples, His followers to see and know that the tomb was empty. Yeshua was no longer there. This was why the angel sat and waited. This was why there was more than one angel, who confirmed to them the resurrection, until The LORD showed Himself!

Here are the events of appearance after the resurrection.

#1 The Women's First Visit And The Empty Tomb:

The women were the first to come to the tomb very early at dawn with burial spices, intending to anoint the body of The LORD in the tomb. They could not do so on the day He died, because it was the Passover preparation day. There was no time by the time Yeshua died and the body released for burial. They had to wait till the third day, the day after the Sabbath. The women who came included Mary Magdalene, also the other Mary (the mother of James and Joseph), Salome (the mother of Zebedee's sons), and other women, (Matthew 28:1, Mark 16:1, Luke 8:1-3). When they arrived at the tomb, they saw the stone used to seal the tomb had been rolled and the tomb was empty. The angel informed and assured them that The LORD Yeshua was risen, (Matthew 28:1-7, Mark 16:1-6).

We do not know how many angels were there. On this great occasion, there may have been a huge company of them, we do not know. Angels can be visible or invisible depending on the purpose of being at a place and instructions they have received from God. Luke reports there were two angels, who spoke to the women about the empty tomb, (Luke 24:3-7). Matthew and Mark report of two, different angels. Matthew reports of one sitting on the stone that had been rolled away, with appearance like lightning, and his clothing was as white as snow, (Matthew 28:2-3). Then, Mark reports of another angel inside the tomb. He looked like a young man clothed in a long white robe sitting on the right side, (Mark 16:5-6).

#2 The Women Leave To Report To The Disciples:

The women were perplexed, fearful and joyful at the same time, being told by the angels The LORD Yeshua was risen from the dead. But they went quickly, to go and tell the disciples of their discovery of an empty tomb, and what the angels told them, (Matthew 28:7-8, Mark 16:7-8, Luke 24:6-9, John 20:1-2). Mary Magdalene in particular, told Peter and the other beloved disciple (John). But their reports were not believed.

#3 Peter And John Go To Investigate:

Peter and the other disciple, (John) ran as quickly as they could to the tomb to see for themselves, (Luke 24:12, John 20:3-10). The other disciple outran Peter. He stooped down, peered into the tomb and confirmed it to be empty. Peter arrived, and did the same. Then Peter went inside. The other disciple followed him inside as well. They saw the linen burial body wrapping cloths and the face cloth neatly folded there. The face cloth that had been wrapped on His head, had been folded together and lying in a separate place by itself. At this time, they saw the empty tomb, the burial clothes, but they did not see any angels or The LORD. Then they left and went away to their places, puzzled about what may have happened, (Luke 24:12, John 20:8-10).

#4 Mary Persists and Was First To The LORD:

Mary Magdalene went in company of other women to the tomb for the anointing of the body. But they met an empty tomb. She went back into the city with the women to report the empty tomb to Peter and John. Then she came back again to the tomb side. Very likely, she did not come back alone, but in company of the other women, (Matthew 27:61, Mark 15:47, Luke 23:55-56, Matthew 28:1, Mark 16:1, John 20:1)

But Mary Magdalene did not quit. She refused to leave the tomb, but wanted to know what had happened to the body of The LORD. She remained standing and weeping by the tomb, (John 20:11). As she stooped down again to look into the tomb, she saw this time, two angels, in white guzzling garments. One was at the head and the other at the feet, where the body of Yeshua had been laid, (John 20:12). While trying to find out from them about the body of The LORD, a third person showed up behind her. She did not know who the person was, but assumed He was the gardener. In fact, He was not the gardener, but the risen Yeshua Himself! (John 20:14-17). Thus Mary was the first among the followers to have seen The LORD. Mark also reported this fact, Mark 16:9-10).

By her actions, Mary Magdalene showed a lot of faith, devotion, determination, tenacity and courage. She left her comfort zone behind. She also ignored the risk posed by the Pharisees, Scribes, chief priests and other leaders of the Jews, who constantly persecuted Him, and finally got Him killed on the cross. And she refused to walk away after Peter and the other disciple did, until she had an answer. No wonder she was rewarded, with being the first to see The LORD after His resurrection.

At this time, The LORD asked Mary Magdalene not to touch Him, because He had not yet ascended to the Father in heaven, (John 20: 17).

We do not know if the other women were there or not at this particular time. However, Matthew reports that The LORD appeared to the women on their way into the city, (Matthew 28:8-10). This time, they did hold unto His feet in joy and worship.

They went (again) and told the disciples, not of the empty tomb, but this time, about seeing The LORD. The disciples still refused to believe their story, (Mark 16:10-11).

THE RESURRECTION AND EARLY APPEARANCES OF THE LORD

#5 Yeshua Appears To Two Disciples Going To Emmaus:

Yeshua appeared to two disciples (His followers) that same day, after resurrection. This was as they had left Jerusalem and on their way to Emmaus, (Mark 16:12-13, Luke 24:13-33). They told some of the other disciples (followers), who did not believe them.But they also went to tell the Apostles.

#6 Yeshua Appeared To Peter:

They other disciples, (followers) did not believe the two disciples from Emmaus when told they had seen The LORD Yeshua, (Mark 16:12-13). Then the two disciples from Emmaus went to tell the Apostles of the appearance of Yeshua to them. As they got there to tell their experience, the Apostles were there. The Apostles and others with them confirmed Yeshua was indeed risen and had also appeared to Peter, (Luke 24:34)

#7 Yeshua First Appearance To The Apostles:

The LORD appeared to the rest of the Apostles, while they were gathered that night in Jerusalem, (John 20:19-25, Luke 24:33-43). They were gathered with the doors lock, and suddenly, The LORD Yeshua showed up in their midst. This was in the evening of that first day, the Sunday of His resurrection. At this time, Thomas was not among them. He decided not to believe until after he sees and touches The LORD for himself.

#7 Yeshua Second Appearance To The Apostles:

After the first appearance to them, the Apostles left Jerusalem and went to Galilee where most of them lived. The angels that the women saw by the empty tomb had told them to tell the disciples to go to Galiee, where The LORD will meet them, (Matthew 28:5-7, Matthew 26:32, Mark 14:28). Yeshua had also instructed them to go to Galilee where He would meet them, (Matthew 28:16-17). He appeared there to them eight days after His first appearance to them. This was also on a Sunday, (John 20:26-29). And this time Thomas was there. He believed after touching His hands and side.

#8 Yeshua's Third Appearance To The Apostles:

Apostle John reported that The LORD Yeshua appeared the third time, after His resurrection to the Apostles, while they went fishing in Galilee, (John 21:1-14).

#9 Yeshua's Final Appearance And Ascension:

In His final appearance, all The Apostles and disciples had moved back to Jerusalem as He instructed them. And He instructed them to remain there until the Holy Spirit arrived, as promised, (Mark 16:19-20, Luke 24:46-53). The LORD Yeshua walked with them to Bethany, where the Mount of Olives was. He ascended to heaven, as He blessed them when they got there. After this, His disciples remained in Jerusalem, and were always going to the Temple, praising and blessing God, (Luke 24:52-53). Then the Holy Spirit came at Pentecost, (Acts 2:1-3).

#10: Other Appearances Of Yeshua:

And there were many other appearances to many other disciples. This included the account of Apostle Paul, of the appearance of The LORD to five hundred brethren at once, (1 Corinthians 15:3-8). Paul had seen Him sometime later, (Acts 9:1-9, Acts 22:6-10, Acts 26:13-18, Acts 22:17-21, Acts 23:11).

The LORD continues to appear from time to time since then as He desires. According to the working of His grace, the one writing this has also seen The LORD Yeshua, a few times (some on His own, some with The Father, and in some appearances with His angels).

He will give eternal life to all believers, who remain faithful to the end. They will be like Him when He suddenly comes to take them away to heaven. His glorified body, the things He could do, going through barriers, appearing and disappearing at will, are few examples of what believers can expect at end time, when they are transformed at rapture.

CHAPTER 41

About Sexual Immorality And Unnatural Relationships

Scriptural Verses:

Romans 1:25-27 (ETB): *25 They have replaced the truth about God with lie. They worshipped and served what has been created (the creature) instead of The Creator, who is blessed forever. Amen.*

26 For this reason God abandoned them to their vile (detestable, abominable) passions. For even their females also exchanged the natural use of their bodies for what is morally against nature (female-female relationship). 27 In the same manner, their males also leave the natural use of (relationship with) the females. Instead, they burned in their lust for one another. Males engage in sexual relationship with males, and committing with their bodies what is shameful. So, they receive in themselves, the penalty which was due for their sin (resulting from their error, delusion).

Explanation

God through the Scriptures has warned against all kinds of sexual immorality, including fornication, adultery, incest, male with male, female with female, human with animal sexual relationships, and all other kinds of unnatural sexual relationships.

SEXUAL IMMORALITY AND UNNATURAL RELATIONSHIPS

We are warned to run away from sexual immorality. Sexual immorality is a sin against one's own body. It is also a sin against God. God is holy and He wants us to be holy unto Him. God cannot inhabit anything unholy. We deprived God of His habitation, for our bodies are the temples of God and the Holy Spirit, (1 Corinthians 3:16-17, 1 Corinthians 6:17-20).

It is also a sin against the natural order of things as created by God. It is an attempt to change or bring it to an end. In the beginning God created them male and female, (Genesis 1:27, Genesis 5:2, Matthew 19:4, Mark 10:6). He created them male and female to provide companionship for each other. And are also to be fruitful, multiply and replenish the earth with their own kind, (Genesis 1:28). God did not make them male and male, female and female, or human and animal. The man became one with the woman in relationship and body.

Any sexual relationship apart from male-female goes against God's purpose. It is naturally impossible for man-man, woman-woman, human-animal sexual relationship to fulfill the command and purpose of God in His creation of the man and the woman.

God also created them in His own image and likeness. His image and likeness are the attributes of God are manifested in fruit of His Spirit. This includes love, joy, peace, gentleness, goodness, godliness, meekness, perseverance and self-control, (Galatians 5:22-23). But because of sin, these attributes and likeness of God in mankind began to degrade over time. As they degrade, so did satisfaction, contentment, quality, and kind of fruit in the natural humans. Then humans began to look for other ways to fulfill that which was missing because of sin.

It started with fornication, adultery and incest, (ref Leviticus 18:6-23). Over time, as sin continued to have its strong hold, sexual immorality has degenerated into even more perverse and abominable kinds, (Romans 1:24-27). Today we have same gender sexual relation, sodomy, homosexuality lesbian, gay, bisexual, transgender, queer, intersex, asexual, lesbigay, bestiality, zoophilia and others. It never used to be at this scale. It is now like cancer spreading rapidly, it is rampart everywhere. The society refuses to acknowledge it is a problem. It has become a vogue. Anyone who dear speaks out otherwise immediately becomes an enemy, a target, and a victim of attacks.

The complete separation of the created from the Creator has consequences. The mind and body have become disorderly, lacking peace within, like being sick and looking for remedy. Sickness came through sin. And sin is a spiritual problem. Yet the society is turning to medical to solve a spiritual problem. Sickness of the body or disorder of the mind is a product of sin and sinful nature which came in through Adam and Eve. It is what came to mankind when the Creator has been pushed out of the created. And it gets worse from generation to generation, unless the Creator is brought back into the life of the created. What used to be unacceptable and abominable because it directly goes against God, is now being promoted as acceptable in the society. The more the creator is pushed out, the more the power of sin increases and the more the societal vices, whether of drugs, sexual issues, etc. Whether drugs or sexual issues, they are human ways of trying to find a cure to a spiritual problem, the cure of peace for the mind and body.

God is Spirit. Mankind is spiritual, with body, soul and spirit. Mankind was not created, designed, to live apart from God, because God created mankind to have a relationship with Him and live together. When God, the Creator and the spiritual part is absent from the body and soul, it brings about chaos, disorder, spiritual sickness in the life of an individual or society.

We know where to take a car or an aircraft when they have issues. They are taken immediately, to the garage or workshop of the manufacturer who repairs them like new. Yet humans created by

God, have failed to acknowledge the existence of the Creator or a close relationship with Him. It is futile.

The restoration of the original relationship with God which brings peace, wholesomeness, to the body, mind and spirit comes through His begotten Son. We must go back to Him, to His workshop and be restored like new. And the workshop is through His Son, (John 3:16-18, 2 Corinthians 5:17). It starts with realizing and acknowledging our error. Then God accepts us back through His Son, His own equivalent of the manufacturer's repair workshop that He has made available for mankind.

But rebellions have consequences, and so it is with God. The present world has the past to learn from. In the days of Noah, the wickedness of mankind had reached epic proportion. They became engaged in unnatural relationships, producing what was not of their kind, (Genesis 6:1-8). So God proceeded to destroy the world through the flood.

In the days of Lot, wickedness had also reached epic proportion. They also were in unnatural sexual relationships. The Scripture says that men were in sexual relationships with each other, (Genesis 19:1-14). The end result was the destruction of Sodom and Gomorrah.

Today, sexual immorality such as same gender sexual relation, sodomy, homosexuality lesbian, gay, bisexual, transgender, queer, intersex, asexual, lesbigay, bestiality, zoophilia and others, are not limited to just a city, state or country. It is now a global practice in every nation and parts of the world. The leaders and governments of nations have made laws to protect, promote, and institutionalize such abominable practices. Wickedness is reaching an epic proportion. The epic proportion of wickedness is a manifestation of the epic level of sin. They go hand in hand. It is a reflection of how far the society has turned away from God. Learning from the past, we know that God will not stay quiet forever. The whole world as it is now is ripe for what happened to people in Noah's time and Lot's time.

CHAPTER 42

About Grace And Being Dead To Sin

Scriptural Verses:

Ephesiand 2:8-9 (ETB): *8 For you have been saved by grace (unmerited merciful kindness of God) through faith. And this is not by the effort of yourselves. Rather, it is the gift of God, [ref Romans 3:24-27, Ephesians 2:8-9].*

9 It is not through your doing any works of righteousness, so that before God no one would be able to boast.

Romans 6:1-2 (ETB): *1 What should we say then? Should we continue to commit sin so that grace (the merciful loving-kindness of God) may increase? 2 Certainly not! How can we who died (and no longer responsive) to the desires of sin, continue to live any more in it?*

Galatians 5:24 (ETB): *24 And those who belong to The Messiah have crucified (nailed, hung) on the cross the sinful carnal passions and desires of the flesh, [ref 2 Corinthians 5:17].*

Explanation

The Scripture says we have been saved by grace, (Ephesians 2:8-9). The salvation and righteousness of every believer are underserved and totally free, through Yeshua The Messiah (Jesus Christ, Iēsous Christos). We become His own and live in Him!

The Scripture further says that those who are in The Messiah are dead to sin, (Romans 6:2-11, Galatians 2:20, Galatians 5:24, Colossians 2:20, Colossians 3:3-5, 1 Peter 2:24).

To be dead to sin is to be totally free from the power, control, inducement, enticement, and desires of sins. Whoever is dead can no longer commit sin, but totally free from the desires of sin, (Romans 6:7)!

A dead body is lifeless and does not respond to anything applied to it. In the same way, to be dead to sin is to be lifeless to sin, but full of life to God. It is to live for God, a completely godly life, free of sin. It is to live for righteousness, (1 Peter 2:24).

To be dead to sin is to be crucified with Yeshua The Messiah. It is for all parts, passions or desires for sin to be dead! (Galatians 2:20). For those who are in The Messiah have crucified the carnal flesh with its passion and desires for sins, (Galatians 5:24, Colossians 3:3). They have put to death what belongs to the sinful carnal earthly nature, including sexual immorality, uncleanness, vile passions, evil desires or cravings, and greed or covetousness. For greed is idolatry, (Colossians 3:5, Matthew 15:18-19, 1 Corinthians 6:9-10, Galatians 5:19-21, Revelation 21:8).

Every true believer has been baptized into the death of Yeshua The Messiah, crucified with Him, (Romans 6:2-4). The believer no longer lives a life of their own, the old self, but of Yeshua The Messiah, (Galatians 2:20). For the old self, the sinful, carnal nature, has been crucified with Him on the cross. The sinful nature of the carnal body has been done away with. It has been rendered inoperative. And as a result, the believer is no more enslaved to sin, (Romans 6:6). The believer is totally immersed, submerged, buried deep into The Messiah Yeshua, and living in Him, (Colossians 3:3).

Being dead to sin, is to live the new life of righteousness in God, with love towards God through The Messiah. To love Him is to obey His commandments, (John 14:15). Being dead to sin is therefore to be free from the desires of a life of disobedience. For disobedience leads to death and not life! For disobedience is sin and sin leads to dead!

Being dead to sin is not to allow any parts of oneself as instruments (weapons) of unrighteousness to serve sin. It is to give oneself completely to God, and to use every part of oneself as instrument (weapon) of righteousness to God, (Romans 6:13).

It is to no longer have the freedom to live a life of sin. It is to no longer be a slave to sin. It is to no longer allow sin to rule over one. Instead, it is to become a slave to righteousness. It is to live under grace, the merciful loving-kindness of God, that comes with righteous living that leads to life. It is to no longer be under the power of sin which leads to condemnation. For living in sin does not lead to life, but condemnation or eternal death!

We have been cleansed from our former life of sin through the blood of Yeshua The Messiah. Through the grace of God, we have now become a new creature in Him (2 Corinthians 2:17). God is now able to live in us as His Temple. Through our fruit of righteous living, we show that we are children of God and He lives in us, (Matthew 7:16-20). Through The Holy Spirit in us, God empowers, energizes us to continue living a godly life that is pleasing to Him. We know what pleases Him through His Law which is now written in our hearts! God does not live in an environment of sin. And neither does The Holy Spirit!. Those who enjoy a lifestyle of sin, will blindly argue The LORD has done all, and the grace is there to cover them. They are those who want to live outside of The LORD, and expect grace to cover them. They are like a branch that wants to live and grow on its own. But a branch that is not in Him is cut off and withers. Then they are gathered and thrown into the fire to be burned, (John 15:6, Matthew 13:41-42, Matthew 13:49-50, Luke 3:17). For if a believer willfully continues to sin after receiving the knowledge of the truth, there is no longer any sacrifice left to cover the sins of such a person. The only expectation from such a person is the certainty of the terrible judgment, and fiery anger which will consume God's enemies, of which such people has become, (Hebrews 10:16-27). For grace is no longer available.

To be dead to sin, is to live within Him. One is either dead to sin by living within Him or dead in sin, living outside of Him. Where God does not abide, sin and death abound. Sin leads to death. A believer cannot continue to live in sin, and expect grace to abound. Such a person becomes an enemy of God. And what abounds from a continued life of sin is death!

God has left the choice to us and it is ours to make: the choice of life or death.

Chapter 43

About Spiritual Warfare And Authority

Scriptural Verses:

2 Corinthians 10:3-6 (ETB): *3 Although we live as human beings in the world, but we do not fight wars as human beings do in the world. 4 For the weapons of our warfare are not like human weapons under the control of carnal flesh. But they are powerful from God. We use them to demolish strongholds, [ref Ephesians 6:12-18, Isaiah 54:17, 2 Kings 6:15-23, Acts 5:1-11, Acts 13:6-12].*

5 We knock down false arguments. We pull down everything that proudly lifts up itself against the knowledge of God. We take captive every opposing thought, and bring it under control in obedience to The Messiah. 6 And after your obedience is total, we always still remain ready to punish any type of disobedience.

Ephesians 6:12-13 (ETB): *12 We are not engaged in combat against human beings with flesh and blood. Rather, we are fighting against principalities, against powers, against the rulers of the dark world, and against a host of wicked spirits in the heavenly realms, [ref 2 Corinthians 10:3-6, Ephesians 6:12-18, Daniel 10:12-13, Ephesians 2:2, Revelation 12:7-9].*

13 For this reason, you should cloth yourself in the entire armor of God. Then you will be able to confront the enemy in the evil day. And after the battle is over, you will still be standing firm

Explanation

Satan, the god of this world has already been defeated and judged. Believers have power over Satan, but it does not include binding him. The time for Satan to be bound is not here yet and believers should not try to bind him. For now, Satan cannot be bound, and will not be bound, until the start of the millennium reign, (Revelation 20:1-3).

During the millennium, he will be kept in hell, a spiritual prison, for one thousand years. And later on, he will be thrown into lake of fire, (Revelation 20:7-10). That is after his job of deception is completed. Until then, Satan still has a job to do. The choice of good and evil, obedience and disobedience to God, both exist to the end. And every human being, from Adam to the end, must be presented with these alternatives and must make a choice between the two. Satan's job is to deceive by presenting the evil alternative alongside the good, for everyone to make a choice.

Until then, the power believers have over Satan is to resist, reject or rebuke him in the Name of The LORD and he will surely flee, (Matthew 4:9, James 4:7, Jude 1:9, Zechariah 3:2). And this power is powerfully effective and works. At a believer's command, Satan cannot hang around, if he is not wanted!

Unlike Satan, however, the demonic spirits, his workers and agents can be bound, (Matthew 10:1, Mark 16:15-18, Luke 10:19-20). Believers have the power to bind them, using the authority of the Name of the Son of God, The Messiah Yeshua of Nazareth.

To do this, a believer must himself be a genuine follower of The Messiah, obedient to God, and unlike the sons of Sceva, (James 4:7, Acts 19:13-17). Each person must totally choose which side he or she belongs. It cannot be one leg in one and another leg in another. It must be either hot or cold, and not lukewarm, in between the two kingdoms. Believers who choose to obey are enabled, empowered by the Holy Spirit to do so.

The spiritual world works by authority. Genuine followers of The Messiah have higher authority over the kingdom of darkness. They derive their powers and authority directly from The LORD himself, (Philippians 2:9-10, Matthew 10:1, Mark 16:15-18, Luke 10:19-20, Matthew 16:19, Matthew 18:18). But the disobedient ones have little or no authority. The devil is their master. They are in fact under the authority of Satan and the demonic spirits. So, how can they control one who is higher than them. Water does not naturally flow uphill, but downhill. Hence the experience of the sons of Sceva.

Satan is always going around, looking to swallow up, looking to incapacitate, looking to tempt believers to fall to his side or to accuse them, (1 Peter 5:8, Job 1:8-10, Job 2:1-5, Zechariah 3:1-5). But believers are protected by the righteousness given to them by God through The Son, (Isaiah 54:17, 1 Corinthians 1:30). Believers have at their disposal, the weapon of the Name of The LORD, the weapon of the Blood of The Lamb, (Revelation 12:10-11), the weapon of The Word of God, which is the Sword of the Spirit, (Ephesians 6:17), and the whole array of weapons of the Armor of God, which are both for defense and for attack against the principalities, powers, rulers of the darkness of this age, and against spiritual hosts of wickedness in the heavenly places, (Ephesians 6:12-18).

What is done in the spiritual realm manifests in the physical. So by taking authority over the Satanic and demonic masters in the spiritual realm, their human agents in the physical also become defeated. That is how it should be done. That is, you focus on destroying the root source, not trying to cut the branches. Just defeating the human agent alone is not enough because the spiritual masters can quickly recruit other human agents. But when the root of power in the spiritual realm is defeated, that power is gone, and cannot operate or recruit other agents in the physical. And also, the battle is really against the spiritual lords and powers, and not against human beings. For God loves souls and wants them to be saved. He sent His begotten son because of His love to save all human beings (John 3:16-17). So, do not focus your power to destroy people, because God is not for that. Rather, focus on destroying the spiritual, the root source, while at the same time, praying for the salvation of the souls of human beings being used by them. God will destroy any human agents, when they are beyond redemption. This was the case with Ananias and Sapphira, (Acts 5:1-10). And to sin out of ignorance or to sin willfully after knowledge are two different things. They knew about God, the Holy Spirit, the people of God and what The Holy Spirit was doing among them. But they willfully went among the believers to deceptively operate to pollute and stop the move of the Holy Spirit. They were blatantly working in sin against the Holy Spirit, and so had no further mercy from God, (Matthew 12:32). God removed His protection over them, since they had willfully and totally rejected His love, and Peter's pronouncement as led by the Holy Spirit took root. This was not the case with Simon the sorcerer who was new, still in ignorance and his life was spared, (Acts 8:18-24). Also, Saul known as Paul had previously acted and blasphemed in ignorance against the move of The LORD and the Holy Spirit. He received God's mercy, (1 Timothy 1:12-14). God is the creator of life, who loves all, knows every heart and has the final say.

[ref 1 Peter 5:8, Job 1:8-10, Job 2:1-5, Zechariah 3:1-5, Isaiah 54:17, 1 Corinthians 1:30, 2 Corinthians 10:4-6, Revelation 12:10-11, Matthew 28:18-20, Matthew 10:1, Mark 16:15-18, Luke 10:19-20, Matthew 16:19, Matthew 18:18, Philippians 2:9-11, Colossians 1:16, Colossians 2:9, Ephesians 6:12-18]

CHAPTER 44

About End Time Apostasy And Troublesome Times

Scriptural Verses:

2 Thessalonians 2:3 (ETB): 3 Do not let anyone deceive you in anyway: For The Day of The LORD will not come until there is first a willful, voluntary or conscious falling away, (also referred to as apostasy, apostasia, defection, departure, revolt, rebellion, turning away), from the truth against God, by some of those who were once believers, (through temptation, deception or persecution), [ref Matthew 24:9-13, 1 Thessalonians 2:3, 1 Timothy 4:1-3].

Also, there will be the revealing, the disclosure of that man of sin, (a human male who has wandered away from the path of uprightness into lawlessness and) who will lead the rebellion against the law of God. He is the son of perdition, (one heading for utter destruction of eternal misery in hell or lake of fire), [ref Daniel 7:25, Revelation 19:20-21].

1 Timothy 4:1 (ETB): Now The Holy Spirit is explicitly saying that in the latter times (end time) some believers will fall away (aphistēmi, depart, withdraw, go away, suffer shipwreck, miss the mark, do not abide, forsake, deny, backslide, turn away) from the faith. They will turn their minds to deceiving spirits and demonic doctrines (teachings), [ref 2 Thessalonians 2:3, 1 Timothy 4:1, Luke 8:11-13, Hebrews 3:12-

14, 1 Timothy 1:19, 2 Timothy 2:18, John 6:66, John 15:6, Matthew 24:15-20, Matthew 24:24].

1 Timothy 3:1-5 (ETB): *1 But you need to know that there will be troublesome (perilous, dangerous) times during the last days or in the end time: 2 People will love only themselves. They will also love money. They will be boastful and proud. They will disrespect and say evil things against God (blaspheme). Children will not obey their parents. People will be unthankful, ungrateful for what they receive (from God or others). They will indulge in unholy lifestyles. 3 People will be hard hearted, unloving to others. They will be unforgiving to those who do wrong to them. They will refuse to be reconciled. They will be slanderous with false accusation of others. They will have no self control. They will be fierce, brutal like savages. They will hate virtues and despise those that are good. 4 They will be traitors and betrayers. They will be headstrong and reckless. They will be haughty, puffed up with pride. They will be lovers of pleasure rather than lovers of God. 5 They will have a form of godliness (religious) but denying its power (that would make them godly). Keep away from people who are like that.*

Explanation

The time ahead of the return of The LORD will be characterized by being lukewarm and low faith in the things of God, (Luke 18:8, Revelation 3:15-17). It will also be characterized by the rise of many false prophets and christs, preaching heresies and performing miracles. It will be such that if it were possible, even the elect (chosen, approved) of God will be deceived, (Matthew 24:21-24). Added to this will be the unprecedented increase in anguish and tribulation. The result is that some believers would willfully, voluntarily or consciously fall away.

This falling away from the truth of God, by some of those who were once believers is what Apostle Paul calls the end time apostasy, (apostasia, defection, departure, revolt, rebellion,) or turning away,

(2 Thessalonians 2:3). It will come through temptation, deception or persecution, (Matthew 24:9-13, 2 Thessalonians 2:3, 1 Timothy 4:1-3).

The spirit of the anti-Messiah (anti-Christ) would be very strong in the world. Then there will be the actual revealing, the disclosure of that man of sin. He will be a human being, a male, who has wandered away from the path of uprightness into lawlessness. Satan will use him to lead the rebellion against the law of God. He is described as the son of perdition, that is one heading for utter destruction of eternal misery in hell or lake of fire, (2 Thessalonians 2:1-12, Daniel 7:25, Revelation 19:20-21).

The Holy Spirit has been restraining that spirit till now and will continue to do so, until the appointed time for his reign, (2 Thessalonians 2:6-7). The man of sin will oppose and also exalt himself haughtily above all that is spoken of God. He will do the same against every object (idols, carved images) that people worship. He will even sit in the Temple of God, claiming that he himself is God, (Daniel 9:27, Matthew 24:15, 2 Thessalonians 2:4, Revelation 13:3-8, Revelation 13:14-17).

The revealing of the man of sin does not mean The Holy Spirit will leave the earth or leave the believers helpless on earth. It just means The Holy Spirit will stop restraining him and will allow him to rise to reign for his appointed time. The Holy Spirit will however continue to convict the world of sin. He will work to strengthen the believers during the great tribulation during the reign of the anti-Christ. He will prepare them for the ultimate day of arrival of The LORD, (1 Thessalonians 4:13-18, Revelation 14:14-16). The lukewarm believers or Church and Israel will first be purified through the persecution they suffer from the anti-Messiah, ant-Christ or man of sin.

The Scripture says that the time will be troublesome, perilous, or dangerous, (2 Timothy 3:1-4). People will become very selfish, loving only themselves. They will also love money. They will be boastful and proud. They will disrespect and say evil things against God (blaspheme). Children will become more disobedient to their parents. People will be unthankful, ungrateful for what they receive from God or others. They will indulge in unholy lifestyles. People will be hard hearted, unloving to others. They will be unforgiving to those who do wrong to them. They will refuse to be reconciled when there is a conflict with others. They will be slanderous with false accusation of others. They will have no self control. They will be fierce, brutal like savages. They will hate virtues and despise those that are good. They will be traitors and betrayers. They will be headstrong and reckless. They will be haughty, puffed up with pride. They will be lovers of pleasure rather than lovers of God.

These will lead to the sudden, unexpected return of The LORD, for the rapture or harvest of the believers. The believers who are prepared and ready will be taken to heaven and it will happen in the twinkling of the eye, (1 Thessalonians 4:13-18, Revelation 14:14-16). Every believer must therefore be ready, watchful and spiritually alert.

More readings: Matthew 24:13, John 11:25, John 14:3, Acts 1:9, 1 Corinthians 15:12-23, 1 Thessalonians 4:13-18, 2 Thessalonians 2:1-12, Matthew 22:23-33, Mark 12:18-27, Luke 20:27-40, Daniel 12:1-2, Matthew 24:36-44, 1 Thessalonians 5:2, Revelation 3:3, Revelation 16:15, Matthew 24:36, Mark 13:32, Matthew 24:44.

CHAPTER 45

About The Two Veils—The Temple Veil And Tabernacle Veil

Scriptural Verses:

Matthew 27:50-51 (ETB): 50 Yeshua cried out again the second time with a loud voice, and released His spirit.51 Then, at that very moment was torn in two, from top to bottom, the Temple Veil. Also the earth quaked, and the rocks were split, [ref Matthew 27:50-51, Mark 15:37-38, Luke 23:45, Ephesians 2:11-18, Hebrews 9:1-14, Hebrews 10:19-23].

2 Thessalonians 2:3 (ETB): 2 There was a Tabernacle with two sections: The first section of the Tabernacle is called the Holy Place or Sanctuary (Tabernacle of Meeting). In this section were the Lampstand, the Table, and the Showbread (sacred loaves of bread) displayed on the Table, [ref Exodus 26:30-37, Exodus 40:22-25].

3 Then there is the second section of the Tabernacle beyond the Holy Place. This second section is called The Most Holy Place (or The Holy of Holies or Inner Sanctuary). And there is the second veil (screen, curtain) separating the Holy Place and the Most Holy Place, (Holy of Holies, Inner Sanctuary), [ref Exodus 26:31-35, Exodus 40:21, Exodus 31:18, Exodus 34:28].

The Two Veils—The Temple Veil And Tabernacle Veil

Explanation

In the old Temple, there were two veils or screens. The first one was the outer veil or screen called the Temple Veil.

It was the veil at the entrance way to the first section of the Tabernacle. The first section of the Tabernacle is called the Holy Place or Sanctuary (Tabernacle of Meeting). The Temple Veil separated the Tabernacle from the main Temple area where the Altar of burn offering was, (Exodus 26:36, Exodus 40:28-30).

The second veil or screen was within the Tabernacle itself. The Tabernacle had two sections, the Holy Place and The Most Holy Place, which were separated by the second veil or Screen, (Exodus 26:31-35, Exodus 40:21).

While The LORD was on the cross, He cried with a loud voice the second time and released His spirit. At that moment, some significant events took place. The Temple Veil was torn from top to bottom. There was also the earth quake and the rocks that were split, (Matthew 27:50-51, Mark 15:37-38, Luke 23:45, Ephesians 2:11-18, Hebrews 9:1-14, Hebrews 10:19-23).

The Temple Veil separated the Tabernacle of Meeting, the Holy Place from the main Temple area. Only the Priests could enter into the Tabernacle of Meeting. But this Tabernacle of Meeting was where The LORD promised to meet with the people, (Exodus 29:42-43).

The tearing of the Temple Veil from top to bottom signifies the removal of that partition. It fulfills this promise of God. It symbolically meant that not only the Levite priest could see or enter the Tabernacle of Meeting, but the people. It means we can fully enter into the priesthood service for our God through The Messiah. And indeed, every believer in The Messiah is a priest of God. For every believer is a chosen generation, a royal priesthood, a holy nation, His own special people, to proclaim the praises of God who called every believer out of darkness into His marvelous light, (1 Peter 2:9). In the Tabernacle of Meeting are the Lampstands, The Table and consecrated showbread, (Hebrews 9:2). As we enter, we should freely feed on the bread of His Word, and our understanding being enlightened with the light from the Lampstand of The Holy Spirit.

There is still the second Veil or Screen separating the Tabernacle of Meeting from the Most Holy Place, the Inner Sanctuary. The Scripture does not mention that this veil was torn. And only The High Priest could go beyond this screen, once a year, into the Most Holy Place. In terms of the earthly Temple, The Most Holy Place is the inner Sanctuary, where God lived. But the earthly Temple and Tabernacle are only a copy of the real, built with human hands. In the heavenly Sanctuary, it is where The Throne of God is. And The Messiah as our The High Priest, has entered into the heavenly Most Holy Place, mediating on our behalf before God, (ref Hebrews 8:1-2, Hebrews 9:1-15). The earthly veil which was not reported torn has been replaced by His body. For His body is the veil in the heavenly Sanctuary. And He is also the High Priest in charge, (Hebrews 10:19-22). As believers, we are sprinkled clean by His blood with no guilt of sin. We enter into the inner Sanctuary through The Messiah. For every believer is in Him and a part of His body. Being in His body takes us right into the inner heavenly Sanctuary where the throne of God is. We must enter with a sincere heart, full of faith and washed with the water of His word, for we are made clean by His word, (John 15:3, Ephesians 5:26). The inner Sanctuary houses the Ark in which are kept the golden pot that has Manna, Aaron's staff that budded, and the two Tablets of the commandments, (Hebrews 9:4).

Those that ate the earthly manna died in the desert. But when we partake of the hidden heavenly Manna we never die again. For The Messiah is the Manna, the bread of life,(John 6:48-51, Revelation 2:17).

The Two Veils—The Temple Veil And Tabernacle Veil

The staff of the High Priest is symbol of authority and The Messiah has given us access to His authority, (Matthew 28:18-20, Revelation 2:26-29).

The Ark of Testimony or Covenant contains God's Law. His law is now written in the tablets of our new hearts, (Jeremiah 3:16, Deuteronomy 30:6, Jeremiah 24:7, Jeremiah 31:31-34, Jeremiah 32:39, Ezekiel 11:19, Ezekiel 18:31, Ezekiel 36:26-27, Hebrews 10:16, 2 Corinthians 5:17). But The tablets were placed in front of the Staff and the Manna. This means, our obedience to God's commands must be in place, be complete, before we can reach and have full access to the authority and eternal life.

Finally, God now lives directly within each believer. For the body of every believer is now a Temple for God and The Holy Spirit to dwell in, (1 Corinthians 3:16, 2 Corinthians 6:16). This has been made possible through the cleansing by the blood of The Messiah.

CHAPTER 46

About The Nicolaitans

Scriptural Verses:

***Revelation 2:6 (ETB)**: 6 But you are doing this well, which is in your favor: It is that you hate the evil works of the Nicolaitans. I too hate their works.*

***Revelation 2:14-16 (ETB)**: 14 But I have a few things to complain about against you. For you have among you those who follow the teachings of Balaam. He taught Balak to put a stumbling block before the children of Israel, to eat things sacrificed to idols, and to commit sexual immorality, [Numbers 31:16, Numbers 25:1-5].*

15 This is how you too came to have among you those who follow the evil doctrine of the Nicolaitans. I hate what they do, [Revelation 2:6, Revelation 2:15].

Explanation

The Nicolatians are a sect who were practicing the error, the evil counsel of Balaam. They put stumbling blocks before the Church of God to make them fall away from their faith. They engaged in ungodly, evil practices that defiled them before God. Idolatry and worship of idols were very common among the Gentile Nations. They encouraged people to eat things sacrificed to idols. They also entice them in committing sexual immorality, (Revelation 2:6, Revelation 2:15, Numbers 31:16, Numbers 25:1-5).

The Scripture clearly warns the holy people of The LORD, the Saints, to keep away from sexual immorality, or not to be associated with things offered to idols, or not to eat anything that still has blood in them. Even now, some believers still go eating the foods or meat offered as sacrifices by others to their gods. Some eat meat with blood in them. The Apostles of The LORD had also warned against these, (Acts 15:20, Acts 15:29, Acts 21:25, Genesis 9:4, Leviticus 17:11-12, Deuteronomy 7:25-26, Leviticus 18:6-23, Genesis 19:1-13, Romans 1:21-27, 1 Timothy 1:9-10, 1 Corinthians 6:9-10, 1 Corinthians 6:17-20, Ephesians 5:5, Galatians 5:19-21, Jude 7, Revelation 22:14-15).

CHAPTER 47

About The Two Witnesses In The End Time

Scriptural Verses:

Revelation 11:3 (ETB)*: 3 "Also, I will give power to My two witnesses. They will be clothed in sackcloth and prophesy for one thousand two hundred and sixty days, (1,260 days or 42-months or three and half years)", [ref Daniel 7:25, Daniel 12:7, Daniel 9:27, Revelation 11:2-3, Revelation 12:14].*

Revelation 11:5-6 (ETB)*: 5 And if anyone wants to harm them, fire proceeds from their mouths and consumes their enemies. Anyone who wants to harm them would be killed in this manner. 6 These two witnesses have the power to shut the sky, so that no rain will fall for the number of days they prophesy (declare). And they also have the power over waters to turn them to blood. They can also strike the earth with all kinds of plagues (pestilences, epidemics). And they can do so as many times as they want, [ref 2 Kings 1:10, Numbers 16:29-35, Exodus 7:17-19, 1 Kings 17:1, Malachi 4:5-6].*

Revelation 11:7 (ETB)*: 7 After the two witnesses had finished their testimony, the Beast (Anti-Messiah, Anti-Christ) that ascends out of the bottomless pit will make war against them. He will defeat them, and* *kill them, [ref Daniel 7:21-27, 2 Thessalonians 2:9, Revelation 13:1-8, Revelation 11:9-10, Revelation 13:13].*

Revelation 11:9-12 (ETB): *9 Then all the peoples, tribes, tongues, and nations all over the earth will see their dead bodies (lying in Jerusalem). This will continue for three and a half days. They will not allow their dead bodies to be buried. 10 And all the people who are on the earth will rejoice over them because of their death. They will celebrate and exchange gifts with one another, because these two prophets tormented those who live on the earth. 11 After the three and a half days, the breath of life from God entered them. Then they stood up on their feet. For this reason, great fear fell on those who saw them. 12 Then the two resurrected prophets heard a loud voice from heaven saying to them, "Come up here." And they ascended to heaven in a cloud, while their enemies watched them going up to haven.*

Explanation

There will be two witnesses or prophets of The LORD in the end time. They will be based in Jerusalem, wearing sackclothes and testifying about God and The LORD, (Revelation 11:3-4). They are described as the two olive trees and the two lampstands, standing in the presence of The LORD of the earth.

They will prophesy for a total of 1,260 days (42-months or three and half years). They will be very powerful, with the power to send fire through pronouncements from their mouths to destroy those they consider as enemies. They will be able to shut the sky not to produce rain, to turn water into blood and strike the earth with different kinds of plagues as they so want, (Revelation 11:3-4). The whole world will be so terrified of them, that the peoples will celebrate when they are killed at the end of their assignment, (Revelation 11:7-10).

In the Old Testament time, Elijah had stopped rain for three and half years. And at the end of the drought, he called on fire from heaven to consume the offering he had prepared before The LORD,

(1 Kings 17:1, 1 Kings 18:36-39, 2 Kings 1:10). He had also sent fire to destroy the soldiers sent by King Ahaziah to arrest him, (2 Kings 1:10-12).

Moses also brought various plagues on Egypt, (Exodus 7:17-19, Exodus 7:14-11:10). And the earth opened and swallowed up Korah, Dathan and Abiram when they rebelled against Moses. Then the fire of God also consumed 250 other men who sided with them (Numbers 16:23-35). Both Elijah and Moses had also appeared with The LORD on the mount of transfiguration, (Matthew 17:1-9, Mark 9:2-10, Luke 9:28-36).

There are two covenants, the old and the new covenants. In the end time, they will come together. They are both for the generation that started from after the flood. And it is the time of this generation that started after the flood that is coming to an end. It makes sense to have two witnesses, one representing the old covenant and the other representing the new covenant as a witness in the end time. Lets look at who those two prophets could be:

From The Old Testament or Covenant: Moses: Why It Would Not Be Him

The Scriptures has not named Moses as coming back in the end time to preach. Also Moses had died (Deuteronomy 34:1-8). And there was even a contention for his body by Satan, until Michael the archangel rebuked Satan, (Jude 1:9). Moses is now in a glorious state of immortality in paradise. So for Moses to come and die a second time, would be farfetched, (Hebrews 9:27-28, Revelation 11:7). For these reasons, Moses is ruled out.

Elijah: Why He Would Be A Witness

The Scriptures clearly mentioned Elijah as a prophet who would come back in end time, (Malachi 4:5-6). Also, Elijah did not die, but was taken away in a chariot of fire (2 Kings 2:11). He was at the transfiguration of heLORD,(ref Matthew 17:1-9, Mark 9:2-10, Luke 9:28-36). Elijah, would be a witness from the Old Testament times, that would testify of The LORD in the end time.

Enoch: Why He May Not Be

Many have speculated that the second prophet would have to be Enoch. He like Elijah, did not die. He was taken away by God, (Genesis 5:21-25). However, Enoch was of the generation before the flood of Noah. He does not belong to this generation that started after the flood. He was not a witness of the Old Covenant from Abraham or from Moses or the Torah that was given to the Israelites. Enoch has nothing to do in the Old Covenant. Elijah already would represent the time of the Old Covenant. And neither does Enoch or Elijah have anything to do in the New Covenant. Enoch was also not at the transfiguration of The LORD. Apart from not knowing the genealogy of Elijah, Enoch and Elijah share similar ministry.

The New Testament Witness:

Lets look at the disciples of The LORD who were witnesses of the New Testament. John along with Peter and James were three disciples who witnessed everything The Messiah The LORD did. These Apostles witnessed the entire New Testament Ministry of The LORD, from the very beginning, to the death on the cross, the resurrection and ascension to heaven, (Matthew 4:21-22, Mark 1:19-20, Matthew 10:2, Mark 3:17, Luke 6:14). They had the power to perform miracles. James was John's brother, and were nicknamed sons of Thunder (or fire) by The LORD, (Mark 3:17). John and James had at one time threatened to call fire from heaven to consume the people of the village who opposed The LORD (Luke 9:54-55). These three, John, along with Peter and James also witnessed the transfiguration of The LORD, just like Moses and Elijah. The LORD prophesied of Peter's death, and Peter himself warned of his impending death when the time came for him to die, (John 21:18-19, 2 Peter 1:12-15). Apostle James also died, killed by Herod (Acts 12:1-2). That leaves John.

Apostle John: Why He Could Be A Witness

Apostle John apart from being an eye witness of the LORD has been a key player in the New Covenant. He also wrote many of the books of the New Testament, (John 1-21, 1 John1-5, 2 John 1, 3 John 1, Revelation 1-22). Elijah fought against the false prophets in the Old Testament. Like Elijah, John also had to fight against the false prophets and heresy in the early Church (1 John 2:18-23, 2 John 1:7-11).

John was later banished to the Island of Patmos, where he received the prophesies in the Book of Revelation,(Revelation 1:9).Before The LORD ascended to heaven, the news had gone round among the disciples that John will not die till The LORD comes back, (John 21:21-23). Furthermore, in the Book of Revelation, John was instructed to eat the little book. He was also furthered informed by the angel that he would prophesy again before many peoples, nations, tongues, and kings, (Revelation 10:8-11). "Again", means later or in addition to what he had or was already doing. And also it would be done before the peoples (of the world). The peoples, nations, tongues and kings will all see him, doing so.

There is no record that John had already done this. Unlike the other Apostles that died, there is no proof or confirmation of Apostle John dying.

Why Remain Alert And Not Speculate

But despite all these, does it really matter who the second prophet would be? Enoch or John? The answer is No! If the knowledge of this is important enough, The LORD would have said it. Therefore, we should not be consumed with much speculations.

There is enough to keep every believer and faithful worker in the Kingdom to be busy. The focus of every believer should be to make their election sure (2 Peter 1:10-11). A lot will happen in the end time and the concern of the true believer should be about winning souls for The LORD and being mindful of the impending sudden appearance of The LORD! Amen!

CHAPTER 48

About The War In Heaven And The Great Persecution

Scriptural Verses:

Revelation 12:7-9 (ETB): *7 Also war broke out in heaven: Michael and his angels fought against the Dragon. The Dragon and his angels fought back, [ref Daniel 10:13, Daniel 12:1-3, Revelation 12:7-9].*

8 But the Dragon and his angels were not strong enough and were defeated. They could no longer stay in any place in heaven. 9 So the large Dragon was thrown out. He is also that Serpent of old, called the Devil (Accuser, Adversary) and Satan, who deceives the entire world. He was thrown down to the earth. Also thrown down with him, were his angels (the fallen stars of heaven), [ref Genesis 3:1-7, Matthew 4:3-11, Luke 4:3-13, Revelation 20:7-8].

Explanation

There will be war in heaven in the end time. It will be between Michael and his angels against Satan and his angels. Though Satan and his angels will be no match for Michael and his angels. So Satan and his angels will be defeated and expelled completely out of every realm of heaven, (Revelation 12:7-9). Presently Satan has access to the lowest realm, and he is the prince of the power of the air. He is also variously referred to as the Dragon, the Serpent of old, the Devil, Accuser, The Deceiver, Adversary and Satan, (ref Genesis 3:1-7, Ephesians 2:2, Revelation 12:9).

This war will take place half-way through the seven years reign of the Anti-Messiah (Anti-Christ) on earth. It would also be half-way through the alliance formed between Israel and the Anti-christ (Daniel 9:27). It would also be when the Anti-christ is fatally wounded and presumed dead, (Revelation 13:2-3).

When Satan is thrown to the earth, he will become very furious against God and anything of God. Satan will go ahead to adopt, as his son the Man of Sin, also known as the Beast. Satan will heal and revive him back to life from his fatal wound. He will also give his power, throne, and great authority to the Man of Sin (Revelation 13:2-4). And because of the full spirit of Satan in him, he would no longer have anything human in him. From that time on, he is more of The Beast, (2 Thessalonians 2:3-9, Revelation 14:1-8). At the end, he will not die the human death on earth, being no longer human. He will be sent straight to the lake of fire, (Revelation 19:20).

One of the first actions after receiving the spirit and power of Satan would be to kill the two prophets who have reached the end of their assignment as witnesses of God in Jerusalem, (Revelation 11:3-7). They would have been prophesying for 1,260 days (42-months or three and half years). Their bodies will be seen from Jerusalem by peoples, tribes, tongues, and nations on earth, (Revelation 11:7-10). Today, in this generation, we are witnesses of the increasing power of technology, knowledge, satellite communications, social media, instant messaging, televisions, and radios all over the world. Many more are being rapidly developed and launched. But twenty centuries or two thousand years ago when John received this prophesy, no one would have believed or understood, except of course those who have absolute faith in The LORD, of His power to make things happen.

The world will marvel at his miraculous come back to life, and the great power he has received from Satan and also at his mighty victory over the two prophets. The Antichrist would also desecrate the Temple, and place in there his image (the abomination of desolation) to be worshipped as the god all over the world. So they will begin to worship him and Satan. Idolatry will become full blown all over the world like never before. He will intensify his blasphemy and pompous words against God, and exalt himself above all else. It is after the abomination of desolation that Israel or the Jews who had formed alliance with him will formally reject him.

And for the second half of his seven years reign, he will go after and intensely persecute the Israelites and the Church (holy people, believers) of God, (Revelation 12:13-17). This will last for a period of 1,260 days (42-months or three and half years). Both woman (Israel) and her offspring (the Church or believers) would be intensely persecuted. For God gave salvation to the world through Yeshua born through the Jews (or Israel). And the Church came from this. And anyone who believes in Him becomes part of the His body or Church, like an offspring. All those who refuse to believe are not His own offspring, Jews and non-Jews alike!

But God will use this time of severe persecution to refine the believers, both Jews and non-Jews alike, (Zechariah 12:10-14, Zechariah 13:8-9, Daniel 9:27, Matthew 24:15, 2 Thessalonians 2:4, Revelation 13:4-8, Revelation 13:14-17). It is at the end of this that the rapture will take place. And many will be saved, (Revelation 7:9-12).

Chapter 49

About The Seal Of God And Number Of The Beast

Scriptural Verses:

Revelation 13:16-18 (ETB): *16 He (Beast) was making everyone, small and great, rich and poor, free and slave, to receive a mark on their right hands or on their foreheads.*

17 And no one was allowed to buy or sell anything unless the person has either the mark of the Beast (imprinted, pricked in, branded or stamped on the body), or the name of the Beast, or the number associated with (of) his name. 18 Wisdom is needed here: Whoever has understanding should calculate (count with pebbles, compute) the number of the Beast. For it is the number of a human being (man): His number is 666 ([from Greek alphabets denoting 600, 60 and 6 computed together as 666, or as in microchip 6-bits in 3 places]). [ref Exodus 12:7-11, Ezekiel 9:3-4, 2 Corinthians 1:21-22, Ephesians 1:13-14, Ephesians 4:30, Revelation 7:2-3, Revelation 9:4, Revelation 13:16-18, Revelation 14:9-11]

Revelation 14:9-10 (ETB): *9 Then a third angel followed them, saying with a loud voice:*

"If anyone worships the Beast and his image (idol, statue), and receives his mark on his forehead or on his hand, 10 That person will also drink

of the wine of the wrath of God, which is poured out in full strength into the cup of His displeasure. The person will be tormented with fire and brimstone in the presence of the holy angels and in the presence of The LAMB. 11 And the smoke of their torment will be rising forever and ever. They will have no rest day or night. This will happen to anyone Who worships the Beast and his image, and anyone who receives the mark of the name of the Beast", [ref Revelation 13:16-18, Revelation 14:9-11].

2 Corinthians 1:21-22 (ETB): *21 It is God who continues to establish us, along with you, in The Messiah. He is the one who has anointed us. 22 And as a guarantee, He has also sealed us and given us The Holy Spirit in our hearts, [ref 2 Corinthians 1:22, Ephesians 1:14].*

Ephesians 1:13 (ETB): *13 And now, you too have trusted in Him, after hearing the word of truth, the gospel of Good News of your salvation. And after believing in Him, you were also sealed with The Holy Spirit that He promised, [ref John 14:16-17, John 14:26, John 15:26, John 16:7-15].*

Ephesians 4:30 (ETB): *30 And do not do anything that will grieve (make sad, sorrowful, offend) The Holy Spirit of God. For you have been sealed (marked down, identified) through Him for the day of redemption (deliverance), [ref 2 Corinthians 1:22, Ephesians 1:14, Galatians 4:30].*

Explanation

The Seal Of God For The Saints

God sets His seal on those who are His, so that they would not be destroyed. The Israelites were told in Egypt on the Passover night to mark their doorposts or lintels with the blood of the lamb, (Exodus 12:7-11). So when the Angel of death saw this mark, he did not enter. But the Egyptians did not have this special mark, and their firstborns were destroyed. Similarly, in a vision, Ezekiel heard God instructing the lead angel clothed in linen to go through the city of Jerusalem and mark the foreheads of those ho grieved and lamented over the abominable (idolatry) things the Israelites and leaders were engaged in. Those without the mark were to all be destroyed, (Ezekiel 9:3-6).

All true believers in The LORD are sealed with The Holy Spirit of God, (2 Corinthians 1:21-22, Ephesians 1:13-14, Ephesians 4:30). Their names are also in the Book of Life of The LAMB, (Revelation 13:8, Revelation 20:11-15). A very strong tempestuous wind of great anguish or tribulation would come all over the earth. Four angels were told to hold it at bay, until the servants or messengers of God had been marked with the seal of God, (Revelation 7:1-3).

The Mark or Seal of AntiChrist On People

Among humans, it was common to mark slaves and soldiers to bear the name or stamp of their master or commander. This was branded or pricked (cut) into their bodies to indicate what master or general they belonged to. Some devotees of certain gods, idols or deities, mark or stamp themselves for the same reason.

In the end time The Anti-Messiah (Anti-Christ) also known as Man of Sin or The Beast will rule over every tribe, tongue, and nation on earth, (Revelation 13:7). He will also have his special identification system for his followers. The Beast will insist that everyone on earth, regardless of their status, bear either his special mark or name or number associated with the Beast. Anyone who does not have any of these will not be able to buy or sell anything, (Revelation 13:16-18). This will be imprinted on either the forehead or on the right hand of each person. His special number has been given in the Scripture as 666, (Revelation 13:18). This comes from the Greek alphabets denoting 600, 60 and 6 and together add up as 666, or as in microchip 6-bits in 3 places. They also signify the evil trinity of the end time kingdom of Satan, consisting of him, the Antichrist and the False Prophet, (Revelation 13:1-12). It is the number of man, human number, given by Satan through the man he will adopt as his son and ruler, to give it to human beings on earth.

Those that are on the side of God or The Messiah will refuse to accept these numbers, anything of the Beast or worship the Beast because they do not belong to the Beast. They are on the side of God. For this reason, they will be severely persecuted, both Jews and non-Jews alike, (Daniel 7:21, Revelation 13:7). And many will be killed as a result, (Revelation 13:10, Revelation 20:4).

Money will still be needed for transactions, but buying and selling such as for foods, clothing, supply of basic utilities (power, water, gas, etc), business or everyday needs will only be possible for those who follow, worship and are loyal to the Beast. And things will become more of a cashless society.

Just like the advances in communications, the stage is well set for that today. The ground work started with credit cards, social security orhealth insurance numbers, etc. Then harmless separation of people in special queues or lines with certain designations or credit card only payment transactions.

And things have advanced more rapidly. The stage is well set for the Beast numbering system. Today, in this generation, the technology, demonstrations, and usage already exists to imprint identification chips with special numbers on people. They carry it around on their bodies. It started with animals, but has moved to human beings putting the special chips on their fingers or foreheads. Some heads of states carry this on their bodies for tracking purposes. Some use it for other purposes. The special chips have the capacity to carry biomedical and health data, travel or passport data, credit card or money for purchases and transactions for individuals. Many countries, hospitals, banks, and other institutions are pushing ahead with this technology, emphasizing the great benefits for them. This will become more global and compulsory in the regime of the Beast.

And anyone who receives the mark of the Beast will not make it to heaven but end up in lake of fire, when it is all over. The Beast will rule for a total of seven years, before The LORD comes to take over the world with His Saints, (Revelation 14:9-11, Revelation 20:4).

CHAPTER 50

About The Eight World Super Kingdoms

Scriptural Verses:

***Revelation 17:9-11 (ETB)**: 9 "This calls for a mind that has wisdom: The seven heads are seven mountains (kingdoms) on which the woman is sitting. 10 There are also seven kings (ruling super world kingdoms on earth). Five of them have fallen. One is presently ruling (the world) as we speak. But the seventh one is yet to come. And when he comes, he must continue to rule over the world for a short time (till the eight kingdom comes). 11 The Beast that was once alive, but is not alive on earth at the present, is himself also the eighth king. But he belongs to the other seven, and is going to perdition, (destruction of eternal misery in hell fire).*

Explanation

Apostle John was told by the Angel, that there are a total of eight kingdoms, (Revelation 17:9-11). The eighth and last one is kingdom of the Beast (AntiChrist), which will come. At the time the angel was talking to Apostle John, the Roman Empire was the kingdom ruling the world. It was the sixth. But before it, there were five other super kingdoms which had already reigned and fallen. The five were the Egyptian, Assyrian, Babylonian, Medo-Persia and Greek kingdoms.

The Eight World Super Kingdoms

Then there would be the seventh superworld kingdom after the Roman Kingdom. And after the seventh kingdom, would come the Antichrist Kingdom, the eight.

Since after the Roman Empire, many kingdoms have tried to rise. Without any doubt, there has been only one recognized economic and military superpower that has dominated the whole world. None other has been able to rule the world over the world affairs, combining economic, military and technology dominance. It is presently ruling the world, though gradually falling from its peak. It will eventually be replaced by the kingdom of the Antichrist.

All the past world superpowers had great influence on Israel:

1) The Egyptian kept the Israelites in slavery for 400years until freed by God through Moses, (Exodus 12:31).
2) The Assyrians took all of the northern ten tribes of Israel into captivity, (2 Kings 17:4-24).
3) The Babylonians took Judah and Benjamin into captivity (2 Kings 25:1-21).
4) The Medo-Persia kingdom under Cyrus freed the Judeans from their captivity in Babylon, (2 Chronicles 36:22-23, Ezra 1:1-4).
5) Under the Greek Empire, the Jews experienced abomination of desolation by the Greek king who took over the Temple and set up his idol in the Temple. He also killed many Jews and sent many into exile as prophesied by Daniel, (Daniel 11:29-35). The eventual defeat of this Little horn, the shadow antichrist, at the end of the Greece Empire, brought about the yearly Celebration of Hanukkah by the Jews since December 14, 164 BCE.
6) The Romans crucified The Messiah (with the help of the Jewish leaders). The Romans later destroyed The Temple and Jerusalem in 70AD just as prophesied by Yeshua The Messiah, (Daniel 9:26, Matthew 24:1-2, Mark 13:1-2, Luke 19:41-44, Luke 21:5-6).

7) Without doubt, the current seventh superworld kingdom will also leave a major mark on Israel before the Antichrist kingdom comes. It will set the final stage for the rise of the Antichrist.
8) The Antichrist Kingdom will first form an alliance with Israel and later take over the Temple (yet to be built) and persecute both the Jews and the followers (The Church) of The Messiah.

And because they are superpowers over the rest of the world, whatever they do affect every other nation or peoples on the earth.

Chapter 51

About The Great City, Babylon The Prostitute

Scriptural Verses:

***Revelation 17:1 (ETB)**: 1 Then one of the seven angels who had the seven bowls came and spoke to me, saying: "Come with me, and I will show you the judgment coming on the Great Prostitute who sits on many waters. 2 The one with which the kings of the earth have been drawn into fornication (of immorality and idolatry). The one with which the people of the earth were made drunk with the wine of her fornication (of immorality and idolatry)." 3 So he took me away in the Spirit into the wilderness (solitary, desolate place). I saw there a woman sitting on a scarlet colored Beast (Anti-Messiah, Anti-Christ) which was full of names of blasphemy. The Beast has seven heads and ten horns, [ref Revelation 13:1-2].*

4 The woman was dressed up in purple and scarlet. She was wearing beautiful gold, precious stones and pearls. She was also holding in her hand a golden cup full of abominations and the filthiness of her fornication of the earth.

5 And on her forehead a name was written:

MYSTERY,
OF BABYLON THE GREAT,
THE MOTHER OF PROSTITUTES
AND OF THE IDOLATRY ABOMINATIONS
OF THE EARTH.
[ref Revelation 14:8, Revelation 16:19, 1
Peter 5:13, Zechariah 5:5-11].

6 I saw the woman. She was drunk with the blood of the Saints and with the blood of the martyrs of Yeshua. And when I saw her, I was greatly surprised, [ref Revelation 16:19].

Revelation 17:18 (ETB): *18 And the woman (called Babylon) whom you saw in the vision represents that Great City which is reigning over the kings of the earth", [ref Revelation 14:8, Revelation 16:19, 1 Peter 5:13, Zechariah 5:5-11, Revelation 17:1-18].*

Explanation

The Angel gave Apostle John the identity of Babylon The Great Prostitute. The Angel told Apostle John that the prostitute woman, called Babylon, represents that Great City which is reigning over the kings of the earth, (Revelation 17:18). The Great City at the time of John was Rome, the capital of the Roman Empire. And its true origin goes back to the Babylon of old and hence the nickname, Babylon (Zechariah 5:5-11, 1 Peter 5:13, Revelation 14:8, Revelation 16:19, Revelation 17:1-18).

Today, Rome no longer rules the world with economic, military, or political power. However, it still continues to greatly influence and rule over kings and people of the world through the power of its religion. For it is described as prostitute full of immorality and idolatry. It has deceived and made the world drunk on its fornication, (Revelation 17:1-2). It is also accused of being drunk with the blood of the Saints and with the blood of the martyrs of Yeshua, it has killed over the centuries, (Revelation 17:6).

Neither it nor its representative leader will be the end time Beast or AntiChrist. The prostitute woman, Babylon will initially take advantage and be riding on the back or power of The Antichrist in the end time (Revelation 17:1-2). As a prostitute spanning many centuries, it has great influence over peoples, nations, kings and languages under its seductive religious power throughout the world. They will initially form an alliance. And indeed, the Beast will also enter into alliance with Israel, other nations and institutions in the world, (Daniel 9:27).

So the Antichrist coming to power in the end time and the prostitute woman, Babylon will seem to be in alliance for the mutual benefit of recognition, power and acceptance. But the relationship will not last. For the Angel also told John, that the ten horns or kings ruling with the AntiChrist in the end time will hate it, (Revelation 17:16-17). They will make her desolate, stripe and expose her naked. They will eat the flesh, that is, take for themselves the riches or wealth of the woman or religion. Then they will completely burn whatever is left of it with fire to destroy. This is according to the purpose and plan of God. For before The LORD God it is a deceiver, a counterfeit with no love for God or for the true things or true people of God and Yeshua The Messiah, *(Jesus Christ, Iēsous Christos)*. And its true origin is in Babylon of old!.

CHAPTER 52

About Trials And Temptations

Scriptural Verses:

James 1:12-13 (ETB): *12 Blessed (joyous, happy) is the person who endures, patiently persevering when going through temptation. When the person has been through, after successfully enduring the temptation, he will receive The Crown of Life which The LORD has promised to those who love Him, [ref John 4:15, John 14:21, 1 Corinthians 10:12-13].*

13 When someone is being tempted, the person should not say, "I am being tempted by God". For God cannot be tempted by what is evil, and He Himself does not tempt anyone (entice anyone to sin), [ref Deuteronomy 8:2, Jeremiah 17:10, Proverbs 17:3].

Job 42:10 (ETB): *10 The LORD restored what Job lost after he had prayed for his friends. Indeed The LORD gave Job double of the possessions he had lost.*

Job 42:16-17 (ETB): *16 After this, Job lived 140 (one hundred and forty) years. He lived long enough to see four generations of his descendants: his children, grandchildren, great-grandchildren and great-great-grandchildren. 17 Then Job died old, and full of days.*

Explanation

God Does Not Tempt But The Devil Tempts

The LORD does not tempt anyone. Temptations are designed to bring about a fall of a person. Temptation is evil and comes from the Devil. Temptation can lead to sin.

God is holy, and nothing sinful originates or is found around Him. Since temptation can lead to sin, temptation does not come from God. When someone is being tempted, the person should not say, "I am being tempted by God". For God cannot be tempted by what is evil. And He Himself does not tempt anyone (entice anyone to sin), (James 1:13, Deuteronomy 8:2, Jeremiah 17:10, Proverbs 17:3). It is because of the potential sinful ending or nature of temptation that Yeshua The Messiah ask us to pray not to fall or succumb to temptation, (Matthew 6:13, Matthew 26:41).

Those who belong to the Devil are already with him and he does not need to do anything more to bring them down to his side. What he does is maintain their imprisoned state.

However, the Devil tempts the children of God.

Why The Devil Tempts

There are two main reasons why the Devil temps:

Firstly, the Devil may tempt because an opportunity has presented itself. This is when he sees a person is being enticed or vulnerable to something in his mind. It is like a low hanging fruit for him to pick.

The Scripture explains this very clearly: That temptation comes when someone allows himself to be drawn away by his own sinful desires (lust). Then the person becomes enticed (entrapped), finding the sinful desire to be pleasurable, (acceptable). When a sinful desire has been conceived (accepted) in the mind, it results in taking a sinful action to satisfy the desire. And when the sinful action has been taken (completed, matured), it results in spiritual death, the separation of the person from God, (James 1:14-15, Genesis 3:6-8).

Secondly, the Devil often initiates temptations of children of God out of pure jealousy. He desires very much to see their down fall like himself. When they sin, they fall into his own sinful state and displease God.

About Trials, Afflictions And Persecutions.

Temptation is about attraction or enticement to the things of the flesh or of the world to bring about sin. Trials and persecutions are like missiles thrown by the Devil to try to break the outer shell(s) of resolve or resistance first. To try to weaken the person to the point of despair or desperation and become more easily tempted to fall or deny God.

So, apart from tempting, the Devil also engages in trials and persecutions. When the Devil does this, he does so purely out of jealousy and hate for the children of God. This was the reason for the persecution of Job by the Devil. The Devil had become jealous of Job because he was so righteous, very pleasing to God and was enjoying God's favor and blessings. The Devil did not like that. So, he went to God to accuse Job, (Job 1:6-12, Job 2:1-7).

Trial and persecutions can lead to or bring about conditions for temptations. So his first objective through trial and persecution is to weaken the resolve of the believer, to the point where the person becomes tempted to deny, sin or fall away from God.

The Devil did not start with tempting Job. Job had consistently proved to fear God, to be righteous, and well. So the initial condition was not right for Job to be tempted to fall. He could not be easily tempted with anything to make him fall. So the Devil resorted first to affliction and persecution. His desire was for Job to be afflicted to the point of despair, when Job may become vulnerable to temptation and so fall into sin. It was at his point of despair for life, that Job's wife was used to tempt him to see if he would curse God, sin and die. But Job refused, (Job 2:9-10).

Although God does not tempt, He does however, examine the content of the heart. The purpose is to show or confirm the brightness or faith of the person in Him. This was also why He allowed Satan to persecute Job.

God's other purpose of examining the content of the heart is not to destroy the person. His desire is to flush out, empty out, every carnal sinful nature or desire of the world from the believer. The person is so to say, refined through fire. In this case, He may allow the Devil to bring out a trial or persecution. God does not go beyond the point of examining or refining. But the Devil does.

Unlike God, the Devil is not interested in refinement but in sin and fall of the person under trail or persecution. So while God may allow the Devil to bring about trial of faith and persecution, the Devil may for his own purpose follow through with temptation. He pushes the trial or persecution beyond the boundary to make the person become vulnerable to temptation. He tries to break the outer shell of resolve resistance first. This is why a person under trail and persecution must remain vigilant through the Holy Spirit. He should resolve through the power and help of the Holy Spirit to remain faithful to God, whether God shows through or not. He must have the spiritual mindset like that of the three Hebrew children. They said to Nebuchadnezzar whether God comes through for them or not, they prefer death to bowing down to the idol or statute of Nebuchadnezzar, (Daniel 3:13-18).

For after a person has been weakened enough to the point that he starts doubting God, the Devil will follow through with temptations, taking advantage of desire. But even when trial transitions into temptation by the Devil, God will not allow us to be tempted beyond our ability, (1 Corinthians 10:12-13).

In the end time, God will refine those who need further refining through fire of trail, (Zechariah 13:9). They will go through severe persecution and trials, or great tribulation to flush out all remaining desires for the things of the world. His purpose is not to destroy, because the Souls are precious to Him. His desire is for them to wholly come to His side, in a pure and holy state, having no desire anymore for the things of the world. It becomes very difficult for them to be tempted by anything of the world the Devil may present to them.

No one looks forward to trials or persecutions in life because they are not enjoyable. Job certainly did not enjoy it and no one out there would naturally enjoy it. However, trials and persecutions are inevitable. But the Scripture says that we should not give up or be saddened when we face trials or persecutions of one type or another. We should remain joyful, by drawing on the strength and joy that comes through the Holy Spirit. The reason is because ultimately, when faith is tested, it leads to the development of patience, endurance or perseverance. When patience is fully developed, it brings about growth and maturity in completeness of approved character, lacking in nothing, (James 1:2-4, Ephesians 5:22-23, Romans 5:3-4, Matthew 4:3-11, Luke 4:3-13, 1 Corinthians 10:12-13, James 1:12-15).

Available Help And Protection From God

God had established his hedge of protection around Job. In the same way, we have God's hedge of protection around us as believers. We are protected by the blood of The Lamb.

Also just as Satan went to accuse Job, he does the same against believers. He accuses them day and night, to see their down fall and condemnation, (Revelation 12:10). But because we have the righteousness of God through The Messiah, no weapon fashion against us will prosper. And every tongue that rises up against us in judgment we will condemn, (Isaiah 54:17, James 4:7). The Scripture also says 'And they overcame the Accuser by the blood of The LAMB, and by the word of their testimony, and they did not love their lives, even when faced with Death', (Revelation 12:11).

Furthermore, we have Yeshua The Messiah who is our Advocate before God. He pleads our case.

He also promised He will never leave us or forsake us, (Deuteronomy 31:6, Matthew 28:20).

When under trial or persecution or temptation, we must also go to God for wisdom, (James 1:5). We should not think we can do it on our own, but through the power of The Holy Spirit. We must also pray and fight back with the sword of the Spirit, which is the Word of God!

Further References And Readings About Trials

More references About trials for the believer: 1 Peter 4:12, 1 Peter 1:6, 2 Peter 2:9, James 1:2-4, Romans 5:3-4, James 1:12-13, 1 Corinthians 10:12-13, Psalm 34:19, Isaiah 41:13, Romans 8:35-39, 1 Thessalonians 3:5, 1 Thessalonians 5:16-18, 1 Peter 5:10, Romans 8:18, Romans 12:12, , 2 Corinthians 1:3-4, 2 Corinthians 4:8-9, 2 Corinthians 11:25-28, Ephesians 6:10-18, Luke 21:36, Revelation 3:10.

More references About God's Protection: Deuteronomy 31:6, Joshua 1:9, Job 1:10, Psalm 5:11, Psalm 46:1, Psalm 91:1-16, Psalm 138:7, 2 Samuel 22;3-4, Psalm 23:1-6, Psalm 121:1-8, Psalm 16:10-11, Zechariah 2:5, Zechariah 2:8, James 4:7, 1 Corinthians 10:13, 1 Thessalonians 5:23-24, 2 Thessalonians 3:3, Hebrews 13:5, Romans 8:35-39, Matthew 28:20, John 17:15, Revelation 12:11.

CHAPTER 53

About The Coming Severe Tribulations In End Time

Scriptural Verses:

Matthew 24:21-22 (ETB): *21 For at that time, there will be great anguish (distress, affliction, tribulation) all over the world. Nothing previously seen from the beginning of the world to that time will compare to it. And never again will there be anything like that forever. 22 Unless the period (days) for the anguish at that time is shortened, no living person would be saved. But because of the chosen (elect) of God, that period will be shortened.*

(Matthew 24:15-22, Mark 13:14-20).

Matthew 24:29 (ETB): *"Immediately after the tribulation at that time: the sun will be darkened. The moon will also not give its light to the earth. The stars will fall from heaven, and the heavenly powers will be shaken, (Isaiah 34:4, Matthew 24:29, Revelation 6:12-13, Revelation 12:7-9).*

30 Then the sign of the Son of Man will appear in the sky. Then all the different tribes or peoples of the earth will mourn (be smitten and in grief). And they will see the Son of Man coming on the clouds of heaven with great power and majesty, (Zachariah 14:1-5, Zachariah 14:12-15, Revelation 19:11-21).

The Coming Severe Testing In The End Time:

In the end time, there will be great tribulation, (Daniel 7:25-26, Matthew 24:21-22, Matthew 24:29, Revelation 13:7, Revelation 13:16-17).

While the unbelievers will be destroyed, God will use the tribulation to refine His children who need further refining through the fire of trail, (Zechariah 13:8-9).

> "Also, this will happen in all the land (earth, nations)," Says The LORD:
> "That two-thirds in it will be cut off and die,
> But one-third will be left in it alive:
> 9 I will bring the one-third through the fire,
> Will refine them as silver is refined,
> And test them as gold is tested.
> They will call on My Name,
> And I will answer them.
> I will say, 'This is My people'.
> And each one will say, 'The LORD is my God' ",
> (Zechariah 13:8-9, ETB).

They will go through severe persecution and trials, or the great tribulation to flush out all remaining desires for the things of the world. The tribulations of believers will be through the antichrist:

> 'The Beast was allowed to make war
> against the Saints (the holy people of God),
> and to defeat them.
> He was given authority to rule over
> every tribe, tongue, and nation on earth',
> (Revelation 13:7, ETB).

> "I was watching, as that same horn was making war

against the saints and winning.
22 That was until the Ancient of Days came.
He declared a judgment in favor of the saints of the Most High,
and the time came for the saints to possess the kingdom.
(Daniel 7:21-22, ETB).

'He was making everyone,
small and great, rich and poor, free and slave,
to receive a mark on their right hands or on their foreheads.
17 And no one was allowed to buy or sell anything
unless the person has either the mark of the Beast
(imprinted, pricked in, branded or stamped on the body),
or the name of the Beast, or the number
associated with (of) his name.
(Revelation 13:16-17, ETB)

Some are now undergoing their fire of refinement, of despair, anguish and self denial, being fully molded ahead as firstfruit of believers from the earth, (Revelation 14:1-5). However, the majority will be refined during the coming end time great tribulations. This is because the Church is presently lukewarm. At that point, it becomes very difficult for them to be tempted by anything of the world that the Devil may present to them.

But they will not be alone. The Holy Spirit will be at hand to help them as in the day or time of Pentecost when He came. And He is still very much around, holding the antichrist at bay. Through these afflictions, many will be saved, Jews and non-Jews alike, from all nations, tribes, peoples, and tongues, who accept The LORD and hold unto Him despite the antichrist:

'Then I observed after these things (to see
what was next). And Look!:
A great multitude, of believers in The LORD,
which no one could count in number.
They were from all nations, tribes, peoples, and tongues!

> They were standing in front of The Throne
> and in front of The LAMB!
> They were clothed with white robes, with
> palm branches in their hands',
> (Revelation 7:9, ETB)

> 'Then one of The Elders spoke to me, saying:
> "Who are these people wearing white robes?
> And where have they come from?"
> 14 And I answered him saying: "Sir (master), you know."
> Then he said to me:
> "These are the ones who came out of the great tribulation.
> They have washed their robes, and have made
> them white in the blood of The LAMB"',
> (Revelation 7:13-14, ETB)

God's purpose is not to destroy. His desire is for them to come wholly to His side, in a pure and holy state, having no desire anymore for the things of the world. By the time He is done, everyone would have lost the desire to resist or to disobey God. Total obedience would be the end result. Then the purpose of God will be fully fulfilled! God will answer them as they call on His Name. He will be their God and they will be His people, forever and ever (Amen).

CHAPTER 54

About Believers Not Made Poor And Unbelievers Rich

God Wants Believers To Be Rich:

It is not a sin to be rich or wealthy. It is the source and attitude to the wealth that could be a sin. Ill-gotten wealth through deception, covetousness, fraud, bribery, embezzlement, exploitation of the poor, etc is a sin. If wealth influences the way we worship God, then it is bad.

Does God want His children be rich? Yes, He does. The example of Job before and after his trial is a confirmation that God wants His children to be rich. As long as their wealth does not take them away from His righteousness, from the worship of Him in Spirit and truth and in building His Kingdom.

God does not want His children, the true believers, to be poor. He is the creator of the heavens and the earth, (Genesis 1:1, Psalm 146:6). The whole earth and the fullness, everything in it belong to Him (Psalm 24:1). The silver and gold belong to Him, (Haggai 2:8). He is the owner of the cattle on a thousand hills, (Psalm 50:10).

God wants His children to be blessed and to enjoy good things on earth. God is not keeping them away to be enjoyed later in heaven but on the earth, while they are here. For heaven's wealth is so much more superior to that of the earth. But the enemy has entered into the midst of the church as a counterfeit and a thief. He has also made some to focus solely on wealth instead of God, who is the source of wealth. Some want to be associated with God as long as there is wealth to be made. They also do not mind the source, if it is ungodly, from the Devil.

The Bible has warned and we have seen that wealth can be a source of temptation. It is a wrong doctrine, if you are poor and believe God wants you to remain poor, or is testing you to remain poor. It is what you have in abundance that can become a source of testing. Job was tried not because he was poor. He was tested because the Devil saw that God had blessed Job with abundance of wealth and yet Job remained righteous before God. The Devil could not understand how or why. The Devil thought Job was faithful to God because of the wealth, (Job 1:1-12). So, God allowed the wealth to be temporarily taken away, so that the Devil can see the steadfastness of Job. To see that wealth or no wealth, Job remained faithful to God. What God wants for us is the ability to handle the abundance He provides along with righteousness before Him.

Before his trial, Job was righteous before God and God blessed him. And God again restored the wealth back to Job at the end of his trial. God blessed Job, with wealth in double measure than he had before, (Job 42:10-12). Both of these confirm that God does not want his children to be poor. Job showed a righteous attitude to God while he was rich before his trial, poor during his trial and rich again after his trial. So it is possible to be poor when under trial, but it is not meant to be permanent. God does restore wealth and blesses.

Increasing wealth is not a measure of one's righteous standing before God. For even unbelievers get rich daily! Also, material poverty is not a measure of the level of God's love for someone. Some dearly beloved of God are poor. It does not mean God does not love them.

The Biblical Ways To Be Rich:

The Scripture gives two godly ways for gaining wealth or riches by believers.

#1: Solomon Type of Wealth Increase: This when there is a sudden increase in wealth from God like He did for Solomon, (1Kings 3:10-14, 2 Chronicles 1:10-12). In this type, there is no sign the person worked hard for it. The person literally does not sweat for it. It comes as commanded by God. Wealth was pouring in to Solomon from everywhere, from all over the world. Under Solomon, silver became as common as stones, not so desirable, in Jerusalem (1 Kings 10:27). Gold was the main thing and all his vessels, and many of his war weapons were made from gold.

This method of wealth as desirable as it may be, is not common. Yet it is the way most believers want to be rich. They pray, pray and pray for God to bless them, for wealth to fall on their laps. They stay as they are and do nothing that will bring in the wealth. So they remain poor all their lives. They either blame God for not hearing their prayers or assume that is how God wants them to be.

#2: The Sowing And Reaping Way To Make Wealth.

This is the sure biblical way for believers to make wealth. It is God's universal principle or secret for wealth increase. It is the one the Church preaches, but also often misunderstood. The Devil also takes advantage of this, and so causes people to miss it.

Wealth increase in Sowing and Reaping has three parts to it.

Part #1: Wealth Through Sowing to reap.

The Scripture says as long as the earth remains, there will be seed sowing time, and harvest reaping time, (Genesis 8:22). The sowing time is the time of hard work to cultivate and plant. It is the time to go and work hard to clear the forest and plant. It is the time to go out, find work and put all your effort into it. It is the time to sweat it out. This is your primary source of income.

It is the time for example to get trained through school or get a professional trade or engage in farming. It is the time to find work or business and start doing it. Then pray to God to bless it. For God says he will bless the works of our hands, (Deuteronomy 28:12). The Scripture tells us that whoever has a lazy hand ends up poor, but the hardworking hand gets rich, (Proverbs 10:4). God does not bless lazy hands. If we have no work that we are doing with our hands, there is nothing in our hands for God to bless. This is why just praying round the clock in the Church or going from crusade to crusade praying for wealth to land on the door step leads to nothing.

Some people are looking for quick rich schemes rather than hard work. Believers must be hard working. Whatever a believer does must be done with all diligence. They should have a primary source of income.

Part#2: Scattering or spreading your seed or bread for secondary increase.

In this, you should not put all your eggs in one basket. Try various godly ventures or investment opportunities, (Psalm 11:24-25). The economists call it diversification. So you can make money from your primary source of income. Your main sowing and reaping. And instead of eating all the profit (or bread) from it, you rather invest some of it elsewhere. This is scattering your bread, for secondary source of income or increase. This has the advantage of providing some cushion for your primary source of income, should something go wrong. It provides income to fall back on, in hard times. Someone whose primary work is farming may not always be able to continue farming when old or when there is a drought for a period. But investing in other sources provides a form of cushion for old age or when the farm is not productive due to drought or lack of rain.

#3: Generously Giving to get increase: The Scripture says that a generous person never lacks, (Proverbs 28:27). Giving can be through a fixed percentage such as ten percent or what the church calls tithing. You should give as you are able, without grudging, but happily. It could start with even five percent, then ten percent or even much more than ten percent.

Most people limit themselves to just tithes. But it should not be. Though Malachi 3:10 is popularly quoted for tithes, but it is actually only a subset of the bigger, more complete picture Yeshua gave in Luke 6:38.

Other biblical ways to give include through regular offering or direct giving to the poor. The believer should always be willing and ready to share with the poor, including the poor in the church and on the street. Whoever gives to the poor is lending unto God, (Proverbs 19:17). And God never owes!

God honors His promises. If you do these three things, God will faithfully increase you to be rich and never lack. You also do not need anyone to lay hands on you, pour bottles of anointing oil on you, or prayer around from church to church for God to bless you beyond measures.

As a believer, keep away from getting your hands defiled through stealing, cheating, deception, fraud, embezzlement, bribery, exploitation of the of the poor or church members, or converting church funds into personal estate. For the wrath of God is stored for the person, and would come on the Day of The LORD.

The Unbeliever or Satanic Way Of Gaining Wealth

We do not need to look very far to see that the unbelievers, the wicked or sinners prosper and get rich. The richest and majority of the millionaires or billionaires of this world are unbelievers.

Believers Not Made Poor And Unbelievers Rich

Why do the unbelievers, despite being not of God, still get rich?

For the unbelievers or the wicked, they do not have to be concerned about the source and means of getting rich. Nothing like 'clean or unclean', 'godly or ungodly' way to get rich. For them the end justifies the means. Anything or source that brings wealth, godly or ungodly, is good enough. It could be through hardwork, or cheating, stealing, deception, fraud, embezzlement, bribery, or exploitation of the poor. The Devil is their father and the god of this world, (John 8:44, John 14:3, 2 Corinthians 4:4, Ephesians 2:2).

Satan, originally called Lucifer was made by God and anointed as a Cherub with all kinds of precious metals, the sardius, topaz, and diamond, Beryl, onyx, and jasper, sapphire, turquoise, and emerald set with gold. He had the music to go with it, for his body was musical, (Ezekiel 28:13). He was made rich.

God blessed Lucifer with gifts power as a Cherub, with gifts of wealth and with gifts of music. And God left them with him, when he fell and became the Devil. God did not take them away from him when he fell, because the gifts of God are without repentance, (Romans 11:29). God does not take back the blessing He has given to someone, for He has more from where He gave that person. Even with the impossibility that He does not have more, He can create more and better!.

Since God does not take away the original gift, some people, pastors or ministers who have backslidden and living in sin or in league with the Devil can continue to demonstrate much power or gifts they originally had and fool others with miracles, speaking in tongues, etc. But they no longer have the fruit of the Holy Spirit because He is gone from them. Gifts and fruit of the spirit are different.

Also the Devil with his power and wealth can in turn anoint anyone he wants to pass that wealth to. The Devil, blesses the unbeliever with wealth, in order to blindfold them. This is so that they have nothing to worry about and continue in their ungodly path, believing they have no need for God.

Satan tried unsuccessfully to tempt Yeshua to bow down to him, and promised he will give Him the riches of all the kingdoms of this world, (Matthew 4:8-9, Luke 4:5-7). Yeshua refused the Devil's offer. Yeshua did not argue with Satan about his ability to bless others. But he rejected the Devil because worship belongs to God Almighty, and true lasting wealth comes from God.

Where the Devil did not succeed with Yeshua, he has succeeded with the rest of the world. He has also succeeded with some unfaithful followers of Yeshua in the church. Many believers, ministers and pastors have gone on to join the Devil and worship him in order to get money and become rich in worldly things. They have joined secret cults or societies of the kingdom of darkness and traded their souls for money and material wealth. And there is still another group in the church, of some unfaithful wicked thieves, parading themselves as ministers, pastors, bishops who have exploited the church to get wealth. They have attracted the resources of the Church members through tithes, offering, firstfruits, thanksgiving, etc and converted into their personal estates. And the wealth they have stolen from the church they show off through their fleets of limousines, planes, mansions, and lifestyle of luxury. They are not of God, of the Devil, like unbelievers in the world. While they preach to their church members that God is their protector, but they themselves have legions of bodyguards on the road and by their pulpits. The Church has become the easy way to become rich. Today, many who would not ordinarily go to church have become pastors. They parade around with the title of Pastors, Bishops, General Overseers, Prophets, etc. They see it as a form of employment or business to make money for themselves. They know one or two verses they quote, or go around preaching wealth and prosperity. But they do not preach how to make heaven, because they themselves are not going there. They do not want to talk about the coming end or the return of Yeshua, because they do not want the end to come. They shy away from these, just like the Devil does not want heaven or the coming of Yeshua to be talked about.

The unbelievers, including the unbeliever false Pastors, Bishops, etc are not of God. They belong to the Devil who is their ruler. What the Devil does is to maintain them in their imprisoned state. He gives them what keeps them under him, and satisfy their lust or cravings for wealth. So, they seem to go on enjoying the things of the world untouched or disturbed. They are boastful, flashy, at ease, prosper with much abundance and increase in riches.

The ungodly way to be rich will include cheating, stealing, deception, fraud, embezzlement, bribery, or exploitation of the poor. They have insatiable appetite and devotion to wealth. They have great love for money or mammon, and pursue wealth and money in every direction. Some are even prepared to kill because of money. And some say they are believers, but separate their way and manner of making money away from their relationship with God or other believers. For them, money is everything and their joy revolves around how much money they have made. Just not to feel very bad, they may throw a little here or there for the poor. But they have no compassion for the poor or who they are dealing with in the process of making the money.

The true believer in The LORD must however never follow, copy or be envious of the unbeliever including the unfaithful pastor. They are on a slippery slope, heading to their destruction with no hope of eternal life with God, (Psalm 73:1-28).

The believers must be careful of how they pursue wealth. The same God who gives wealth also warns of the danger of wealth. The Scripture says what will it profit a man if he gains the whole world, and loses his soul (Mark 8:36). It also says where your treasure is, so will be your heart, (Matthew 6:21, Luke 12:34). No one can serve two masters at that same time. No one can serve God and mammon, (Matthew 6:24, Luke 16:13). Get wealth as God blesses you, but make sure it does not dictate or influence your relationship with people or your worship of God. And remember that godliness with contentment is great gain, (1 Timothy 6:6).

Chapter 55

About The Blood Of The LAMB For Protection

Scriptural Verses:

Exodus 12:13 (ETB): *The blood will be a sign for you marking the houses where you are. And when I see the blood, I will pass over you. Then the plague will NOT come on you to kill you, when I strike the land of Egypt.*

Luke 22:19-20 (ETB): *19 He took some (of the unleaven) bread, gave thanks to God and broke it in pieces. Then He gave it to them, saying: "This is My body which is given (offered, sacrificed) for you. Do this in remembrance of Me."*

20 Also, He took another cup of the drink after supper. Then He said: "This cup is the New Covenant (Brit Chadasha, New Testament) confirmed with My blood, which is poured out for you.

John 14:27 (ETB): *Peace, I leave with you! My Peace, I give you! I do not give to you as the world gives. Do not allow your hearts to be troubled (anxious, worried). And do not be afraid!, [ref Isaiah 9:6-7].*

Explanation
The Earth In Labor or Birth Pangs Phase.

A woman who has been pregnant for eight or nine months, knows there are still two necessary significant events that will take place before the actual final delivery of the baby. The first is the labor or pre birth pangs or pains she goes through. Unlike other pains or discomfort she may have experienced during the pregnancy, the birth pains are different. It is characterized by their repeated occurrence, along with the sharp pains. This period can be short or long. The second landmark event is when the placenta water actually breaks and she enters into the final phase of despair or agony as and then she is delivered of the child.

The world at the moment is in the first phase, the labor or birth pangs. The world formally entered into this phase at the end of 2017. No one knows how short or long it will be. This was revealed and explained in the fourth book, *"Celebrating God's Faithfulness In The End Time"*.

The LORD Yeshua had warned us in the Scriptures to expect this period of birth pangs of the world, (Matthew 24:4-9). It will be characterized by repeated occurrence of deceptions, false christs and false miracle workers with deceptive miracles, promising solutions. There will be wars and threats of wars. Nations will turn against nations. There will be famine or scarcity. And there will be outbreaks of diseases or pestilences or plagues. There will also be other natural events like earthquakes (including volcanoes, violent windstorms like tornadoes, hurricanes, monsoons, mudslides, etc).

The LORD Yeshua warned these things will become frequent occurrence on a global scale. He also said they are not the end but only the beginning of birth or labor pangs for the world, (Matthew 24:8). And He will protect his own.

I revealed and explained in the fourth book, *"Celebrating God's Faithfulness In The End Time"*, that the world formally entered this phase in the last quarter of 2017. This was after The LORD had appeared to me, in another of many visions I received, when I was finishing the third book, *'End Time Count Down Messages'*. This time

He came holding the hand of a baby, and while smiling repeated to me to remember 'Matthew 24:6-8'! This vision was later described in the fourth book. While we now know when the global world birth pangs formally started, but NO ONE knows how long it will last or when The LORD will return, (Matthew 24:36). So we must not allow ourselves to be deceived by false prophets who claim they know when the end will be. They are liars and deceivers.

The second landmark in birth is when the water breaks during the labor pains of a pregnant woman. The woman in this case is the earth, and the people on the earth form the body experiencing it with her. The landmark of water breaking for 'the pregnant earth' is when the Man of sin, the Antichrist is revealed as the Scripture tells us, (2 Thessalonians 2:3-8). The ground is being prepared for this event as we see all kinds of abominations on global, national and governmental scales for both the Antichrist and the False Prophet, who will rule the world in the end time, (Revelation 13:1-17).

During the period of birth pangs, there will be wars or threats of war, and violent natural disasters. There will be pestilences or deadly diseases that will be released. And even as I was finishing this book, a deadly infectious virus called 'Coronavirus or COVID-19', broke out from Wuhan in China. This deadly and highly infectious virus is rapidly spreading to the other nations of the world. As such the whole world is in total darkness and fear about the plague and how to contain or find a cure it. It has economic consequences, as well as social effects, including scarcity of some essentials.

The Believer Will Be Protected By God

Unfortunately for the world, what is happening now, through violent storms, volcanoes, destructive national fires, earthquakes or deadly infectious diseases are only a pre-run, a warm up for what will come as the birth pains continues and the world enters into the events of the end time.

That there will be many more deadly pestilence or diseases and deadly occurrences in the world, has already been stated, (Matthew

The Blood Of The Lamb For Protection

24:4-9). Some will be global. Some will be localized within countries or even communities.

The believer must not be afraid. The LORD has promised protection for all who are His own, who fear Him and call on His Name, pray to Him through Yeshua The Messiah.

The believer needs to know, understand and accept by faith the effective protection that God has provided in place against this and other deadly events that may arise during the birth pangs, before The LORD returns.

Anointing Oil is good and has its place such as for healing. The Scripture says that if anyone among believers is sick, then the person should call for the leaders of the Church (Community, Congregation of The Messiah). They should pray over the person, anointing the person with oil in the Name of The LORD, (Mark 6:13, Mark 16:15-18, John 14:12-14).

However, when it concerns the issue of life and death, the anointing oil may not be enough on its own. It may not turn away death. Only blood can satisfy the demand for blood. For when the angel of death is by the door, something must certainly die. And who dies could be the primary target or subject. It could also be a substitute who is appointed to die in place of the primary subject.

When the Israelites were in Egypt, death through the angel of death had been decreed. But God saved the Israelites, through a substitute, from the dagger of the angel of death. The substitute for the Israelites was a male Lamb of sheep or goat in its first year, without any blemish or defect for every household, (Exodus 12:5). The Lamb was to be killed at dusk or sunset and the blood smeared on the two sides and the top frame of the entrance door of the house, (Exodus 12:6-7).

The blood of the Lamb so smeared on the doors by the Israelites, served as the sign as the angel of death went round, from house to house in Egypt. The blood confirmed to the angel of death, that a substitute had already been killed for that household. The household could no longer suffer another death from the angel of death. Those in the household were covered and protected. So the angel of death would 'Passover' that house and went to the next, (Exodus 12:13).

Through the blood of the substitute that was marked on their door posts, God distinguished the Israelites from the Egyptians when the plague of death was being executed. They were saved.

The Scripture says without the shedding of blood, there is no remission of sin, (Hebrews 9:22). And all through the Old Testament, an animal without blemish was constantly killed, in place of a sinner or sinners, for the forgiveness of sin. The animal died in their place and their sins covered. This gave them life, and the right to remain alive under the protection of God. There will be deadly pestilences, plagues, arrows of death and life situations in the end time.

The Living Powerful Blood Of The LAMB of God:

Under the New Covenant, blood is still a requirement both for the forgiveness of sin and for life. The difference however is that God, through His begotten Son, became The Messiah and The LAMB of God that died as a substitute on our behalf, (John 1:29, John 1:36, John 3:16-17, Lk22v19-20).

The blood of Yeshua The Messiah was shed as the substitute in our place on the cross of Calvary. But unlike the animals, His blood was shed only once, for all time, for everyone, (Romans 6:10, 1 Peter 3:18, Hebrews 7:27). He does not need to die repeatedly. His death covers all the time, for all who place their faith in Him. Nothing compares with His blood which is living and powerful forever. Yeshua The Messiah died so that we do not have to die again. So that we would have life, and have it in abundance.

What The Believer Should Do With It For Protection:

#1 Therefore, the first thing we should do as believers when we are faced with the threat of death, is to call to mind, remind ourselves, that the penalty or demand for our death had already been fulfilled. It was done by the perfect substitute for us, Yeshua The Messiah and Lamb of God. As such we are not to die again, since He has already died in our place.

The enemy comes to steal, kill and destroy, (John 10:10). The LAMB of God was slain even from the foundation of the world, (Revelation 13:8). The LAMB that was slain became manifest in flesh on earth, as The Son of God, who was slain on the cross in Jerusalem. This LAMB, who is also the WORD of God was with God from the beginning, (John 1:1-3). The Scripture tells was the Saints of God overcame the enemy, Satan, by the Blood of The LAMB, and the word of their testimony, (Revelation 12:11). Yeshua is both The LAMB and The WORD of God.

Therefore, as long as we remain believers and followers of Yeshua The Messiah, whatever and whenever there is a new demand or threat of death in our lives, that demand is illegal, and unacceptable. It is null and void. And in the end time, many things will happen that threaten the lives of believers. We must invoke the blood of Yeshua The Messiah all the time. Invoking the blood of The LAMB, Yeshua The Messiah, is laying hold on the horns of the highest of all the Altars, even the Altar of the Most High God for forgives, for mercy, for deliverance and the restoration of life.

Yeshua The Messiah has also commanded us to take the communion as often as we do in remembrance, (Luke 22:19-20). This is so that we would not forget the benefit of what He achieved for us on the cross. Taking the communion is like eating a spiritual meal, which gives energy and vitality. Taking the communion also serves the purpose of reminding us, in case we have forgotten, of what we already have through His death. So taking the communion is good, and we should do this as often as we have the opportunity.

Where a Church, Pastor, or minister is present to lead the communion meal, that is good. But as believers, we are also disciples and royal priests in Yeshus The Messiah, (1 Peter 2:9). We can take the communion meal with our household anytime. The LORD Yeshua who instituted the communion meal did not say we can only have the communion meal when there someone who is a Pastor, Bishop or Priest.

But we should never take the communion in lifestyle of sin. For sin is a major barrier and brings about negative repercussions or even death, (1 Corinthians 11:27-30). We must therefore approach the communion table with a pure heart and clean hands, (Psalm 24:3-5). We should first confess our sins and ask for forgiveness. And God is always faithful and just to forgive our sins, when we confess, (1 John 1:8-10). Then the blood becomes effective to save our lives from either spiritual or physical threat of death. Also the communion elements should have no yeast. As much as possible, use bread or cracker without yeast and non-alcoholic red grape juice. For the Passover is celebrated with bread without yeast. And Yeshua whose blood was shed had no alcohol in His blood. Alcohol has yeast in it. It is defiled by the yeast in it. It is also intoxicating and the Bible warns against it. Be filled with the Spirit and not with alcohol, (Ephesians 5:18). Remember the Scripture warns wine is a mocker, alcoholic drink is a hooligan (bully). And a foolish person is deceived or led astray by it, (Proverbs 20:1, Proverbs 21:17, Proverbs 23:20-21, Proverbs 23:29-35, Proverbs 31:4-7, Isaiah 5:11-12, Isaiah 28:7, 1 Corinthians 3:16, Ephesians 5:18, 1 Corinthians 6:19-20).

Remember it is not only when we take the communion meal that the blood works for us. And it is also not when we are faced with the threat of death, that we should go looking for the communion meal. We may not have such luxury. Some death threats can be sudden. Also in reality, we do not always carry the communion bread and wine with us everywhere we go. We may not have the chance to first go and eat the communion meal before confronting the death threat. For these reasons, what we need to do is to always bear in our minds that we have been set free from death through His own death as a substitute for us. We must constantly remind ourselves of this huge gift of life for us, with or without the communion. As long as we are believers and have faith, it works for us when we simply declare it with our mouths.

#2 The second thing to do as a believer is to pronounce, invoke the blood of Yeshua The Messiah as our covering, of our entire being, consisting of our Spirit, Soul, Mind and Body. We must cover the entry way, to our being, to deny access to the agent of death. This is just like the Israelites by faith smeared the blood of the Lamb on the two sides and top post of the entrance doorway. This blocked and denied entry to the angel of death. Declaring 'The Blood of

The LAMB', or 'The Blood of Yeshua The Messiah', should always be in our minds and on our lips. We should be ready to declare it at anytime, anywhere, with or without the communion. We should always do so by faith.

Therefore, with this knowledge, we must always proclaim, declare to the angel of death in the spiritual realm or to the agent of death in physical realm, that death is no longer appointed for us. The requirement of death has already been fulfilled for us by death of The LAMB of God. We are free.

We should proclaim or declare this by the authority of The Name of The LORD and tell the angel or agent of death to move away, pass over from us.

Now who is the angel or agent of death? Anything that threatens the life of a believer is an agent of death. For example, it may manifest as a disease, infection, pestilence or deadly sickness in the community. It may manifest as physical agents of death sent to attack. It may manifest as an accident or emergency death situation, or in any form.

#3 Thirdly, Yeshua came to die for us, so that by His death, He has released to us not just any life, drained of joy and rejoicing. But He has released to us the abundance of life, the fullness of life, (John 10:10). And whatever we have, whatever that God has blessed us with is part of that abundance. This includes our family, possessions, finances, business, etc. Therefore, we should claim and proclaim the abundance of life on them also, on everything that concerns us or is part of our lives. They are not do die and bring us sorrow. Rather, anyone of them dying, should receive abundance of life because of us. The death or blood of The LAMB of God which we enjoy for your lives, also covers everything that concerns us.

Promises Of God's Protection For His Own

There will be a lot of pestilences, plagues and arrows of death of the enemy in the end time. But it is important to remember God's promises in the Scripture, including in Psalm 91.

Psalm 91 says that whoever remains in the secret place of The Most High, will find rest under the shadow of The Almighty. He will be a shelter and fortress for the person. The Most High God will deliver the person from the trap of the fowler and from deadly diseases. The person will be covered and securely protected under His wings. The faithfulness of God will be the armor and shield.

The person will have no need to be afraid of the danger at night, or of an arrow during the day, or be afraid of sudden outbreak of diseases, or of violent destruction that strikes in the middle of the day. Many others may fall down all around the person, but the person will not be touched. This is because the person has made The LORD, even The Most High, as shelter and home. No disease will come near the person.

In addition, God will assign His angels to protect and watch over the person, wherever the person goes. The person will walk over the lion, the cobra and trample underfoot the young lion and the serpent, (Genesis 3:1, Revelation 20:2, Mark 16:17-18, Luke 10:18-19). These are wicked spiritual powers and principalities, (Ephesians 6:12). For the opponents of a believer are the principalities, against powers, the rulers of the dark world, and a host of wicked spirits in the heavenly realms, (2 Corinthians 10:3-6, Ephesians 6:12-18, Daniel 10:12-13, Ephesians 2:2, Revelation 12:7-9).

The Most High God will always be with and rescue the person in times of trouble, (Psalm 46:1, Psalm 50:15). God will prolong the life of the person, and show His deliverance to the person.

Here is what the Scripture tells us in Psalm 91:

Psalm 91 (ETB)
1 Whoever remains in the secret place
Of The Most High,
Will find rest under the shadow
Of The Almighty.
2 I will say this of The LORD (ADONAI):
"He is my shelter and my fortress.
He is My God, and in Him I will trust."
3 Surely He will deliver you

The Blood Of The Lamb For Protection

From the trap of the fowler
And from deadly diseases.
4 With His feathers, He will cover you.
You will be securely protected
Under His wings.
His faithfulness will be your armor and shield.
5 You will not be afraid of danger at night,
Or of an arrow during the day.
6 You will not be afraid
Of sudden (secret) outbreak of diseases,
Or of violent destruction that strikes at noon.
7 You may see 1,000 (one thousand)
Fall at your side,
Or even 10,000 (ten thousand)
At your right hand.
But it will not touch you.
8 Only with your eyes will you watch,
And see the punishment of the wicked.
9 Since you have made The LORD,
Even The Most High,
Who is my shelter, as your home:
10 Nothing bad (harmful) will happen to you.
Neither will any disease
Come near your home.
11 For He will assign His angels
To protect you.
They will watch over you wherever you go.
12 They will lift you up in their hands,
And you will not hurt your feet
Against a stone.
13 You will walk over the lion and the cobra.
You will trample under your foot the young
lion and the serpent, (dragon),
[ref Genesis 3:1, Revelation 20:2, Mark 16:17-18, Luke 10:18-19].

14 (The LORD says):
"Since he loves Me,
Therefore I will rescue him.
Since he has known (confessed, recognized)
My Name, I will lift him to safety.
15 He will call upon Me,
And I will answer him.
I will be with him in trouble.
I will rescue him and honor him, [ref Psalm 46:1, Psalm 50:15].
16 I will satisfy him with long life,
And show him My salvation."
[ref Job 42:16-17].

Chapter 56

About The Believer, 5G, Coronavirus, Microchip In The End Time

Scriptural Verses:

Daniel 12:4 (ETB): 4 *"But you, Daniel, keep this prophecy a secret. Seal up the book the book until the end time. At that time, many will travel around to places, and knowledge will increase."*

Revelation 13:16-17 (ETB): *16 He was making everyone, small and great, rich and poor, free and slave, to receive a mark on their right hands or on their foreheads. 17 And no one was allowed to buy or sell anything unless the person has either the mark of the Beast (imprinted, pricked in, branded or stamped on the body), or the name of the Beast, or the number associated with (of) his name.*

Revelation 14:9-11 (ETB): *If anyone worships the Beast and his image (idol, statue), and receives his mark on his forehead or on his hand: 10 That person will also drink of the wine of the wrath of God, which is poured out in full strength into the cup of His displeasure. The person will be tormented with fire and brimstone in the presence of the holy angels and in the presence of The LAMB. 11 And the smoke of their torment will be rising forever and ever. They will have no rest day or night. This will happen to anyone who worships the Beast and his image, and anyone who receives the mark of the name of the Beast.*

This book had already gone to the publishers, who were working on it for its final release. At the same time, a deadly infectious virus called 'Coronavirus or COVID-19', had broken out from Wuhan in China. This was just about the same time that the 5G technology had been rolled out in Wuhan and other places. The Coronavirus was rapidly spreading to other nations of the world, in every continent, infecting people and many dying as a result.

As a result, people, including Believers and Ministers of the gospel had become very concerned. They have become confused through the various misleading information about the 5G, Coronavirus, Vaccines, microchip implants, etc.

For this reason, I had to write this Chapter for the publishers to include it in the final version of the book to be released. The purpose is to enlighten the Believers in The LORD about 5G, Coronavirus, microChips and their end time implications. This is as led by The LORD, with His grace upon me, for alerting the world about the coming end time.

Both 5G and Coronavirus are unrelated, except that they both have their purposes in the end time. And they have come at the same time to maximize confusion and fear for the world and the Believers. It is in such an environment that the enemy and agents of the kingdom of darkness thrives. Believer should have the right understand and know what The LORD expect of them.

The 5G Technology And Its End Time Significance.

Being a radio wave, it is harmless on its own. But what becomes possible as a result of it, is what is good on one side and bad on the other, for Believers and the world. Believers should take advantage of the positive side for the Kingdom of God.

The development of 5G is part of the fulfillment of the prophecy by Daniel, that in the end time, there will be increase in knowledge, (Daniel 12:4). In the recent years, this generation has seen very major advancements in other areas including in travels, drones and driverless automobiles, in space, satellite technology, medical, computers and microchips, etc.

The 5G is necessary for the fulfillment of the end time and should be seen by Believers as being according to God's purpose for the end time. His purpose and plan cannot be altered but fulfilled.

But just like the internet or social media have the good and bad sides, so will be the 5G.

The Positive Side of 5G For Believers:

The positive side of 5G for believers relates to the propagation of message of the Kingdom of God. It is God's plan for the gospel of good news of His Kingdom to reach every part of the world before The LORD returns, (Matthew 24:14, Mark 13:10).

The Holy Spirit uses the message of the Gospel that is preached as a means to convict the world of sin, of righteousness and of judgment. Hearing the gospel serves as a witness for the whole world. Through it, some many are saved, being the power of God unto salvation, (Romans 1:16, Romans 10:14-15). And through it, it also serves as a witness against those who hear it and reject God's love He has given the world through His begotten Son, (John 3:16-18).

The 5G technology offers much faster speed, connectivity and data transmission, along with superior audio, video, wifi clarity that what currently exists. It is several orders of magnitude more superior. It will provide a much better way for believers to communicate and spread the gospel much faster and wider to the world. It has the potential to reduce the barrier of distance or the need to travel between places. It can be delivered to even the most remote parts, which would otherwise be difficult to reach due to distance, dangers of perils or natural or political barriers.

Believers can deliver messages in real time, face to face, over several distances, to several peoples, nations, tongues or tribes. They can also be packaged and delivered faster through videos, internet, YouTube, and the likes. Speed and real time delivery of gospel messages around the world becomes possible.

This is what the kingdom of darkness is afraid of, and so decided to create fear and confusion among the Believers, the Church. For the Church will use it to win souls even before the Antichrist takes over.

Believers must therefore remember they have been assigned to preach the gospel. They should therefore take advantage of whatever opportunity that is available to do so, including the 5G. Their focus should not be what the enemy is or will do with it, but on spreading the good news message of the Kingdom of God. For God who has planned it all, will take care of things, including against the enemy.

The Negative Side of 5G For Believers:

There is also the negative side of 5G for Believers in the end time. It is how the Devil will hijack, take advantage of it, and deploy it against the Kingdom of God in the end time. This should not be the concern or focus of the Believers, as it will distract them from their great commission, (Matthew 28:18-20, Mark 16:15-18).

That the Antichrist will come is inevitable, because it is part of the plan of God for the end time. He will be a tool in the hand of God through the great tribulation for the purification of the Church and of the repentance of Israel from its Apostasy.

The end time Antichrist system of one world order, one government, one financial system, one idolatry religious system for the worship of the Antichrist as the god would significantly benefit from the 5G technology and environment.

It is a government of the Antichrist would be evil to the core. It will be worshipped as 'the god'. He will be blasphemous to Most High God, and like never before hateful of anything godly, (Daniel 7:25, Revelation 13:4-8).

It will have unparallel ability to monitor, track, control and manipulate the people in real time. It will be full of deceptive, wicked and ungodly false propaganda, led by the False prophet, (Revelation 13:11-17)

The true Believers, the Saints of The LORD, will refuse the government of the Antichrist, and everything it represents. But two out of every three people on earth will be on the side of the Antichrist in the end time. So the Antichrist and his local agents in every part of the world will detect, passionately hunt down and severely persecute God's people, both Gentile believers and Jews alike. The Scriptures already forewarned that in this war he will wage against the Saints of God, the Antichrist will win or defeat them, (Daniel 7:21, Revelation 13:5-8).

So, while believers take advantage of 5G for the gospel, Satan through the antichrist will take advantage of it for the government of the Antichrist and in its persecution of Believers. The Believers should not be discouraged or focus their attention on the Devil, His Antichrist and False prophet who are on their way. As the Believers focus on doing the will of God, He will faithfully protect them.

Believers must always remain alert, and be watchful as the Antichrist approaches and the end time events unfold.

The wind of the Spirit of the Antichrist and His False prophet is already blowing. But before he formally ascends on his throne, the world must be driven to a point of desperation. This will come through the collapse of the current system, economy, along with the rising environment of divisions, strife, war between peoples and nations, confusion, unrest, scarcity, famine, etc. In the time of the great anguish that is coming on the nations of the world, they will be forced to jointly look for a way out. They will agree to come together for the 'common good' of the people of the earth. The economic and religious systems that are currently dividing the world, will give way. The economies of the nations of the world will also collapse. It is at that point the Antichrist will arise, offering his solution, which will be popularly acceptable to the peoples of the world. The religious bodies will come together as one, with a single world interfaith religious system. This will end up in the worship of the Antichrist.

The Challenge For The Church.

The real challenge lies not outside the Church but within it. On one hand, the Devil is afraid of the potential effectiveness of the propagation of the gospel in the end time to win souls away from him into the Kingdom of God. And the 5G will vastly enable this, even before the Antichrist and his False prophet formally take their positions. So the Devil decided as is consistent with his nature, to spread fear and confusion among the believers, the Church. And there are some within the Church, planted their as agents for the Devil, who willingly magnifies this confusion and fear in their service for the Devil.

On the other hand, there are some in the body of The LORD, the Church, called to be Pastors to shepherd the sheep, but have digressed away from their primary assignment. They have instead become 'leading prophets' in order to get more limelight, praise and rewards for themselves. They have released messages or visions they have heard from themselves or others, and not from God. But no liar will inherit the Kingdom of God. They belong not to God, but belong to the Devil. And the Devil will take advantage and use many of such people in this way, unless they repent and become faithful to God. The Devil will entice and use them once he knows they love accolades, praise and reward from people.

The people, the sheep or followers should not be gullible, lacking in knowledge. They should always pray to check with God, and confirm with His word, the Scriptures. Anything that contradicts what the Scripture says, is very unlikely to be from God.

But such leaders or shepherds focusing on their own glory, which is vain, are doing a disservice to God in His Kingdom, which He is building for the end time. For in a building work, not all are nails, not all are hammers, not all are bricks, not all are plasters, etc.

The Church will be more effective in the end time work if people accept with contentment, where God has assigned them to serve or work in His Kingdom. This is whether as pastors, prophets, evangelists, teachers, administrators, encouragers or even just as mothers bringing up children in the fear of God. None is more important than the other, and only the faithful and obedient get the ticket to heaven when the time comes.

The social media presents a very tempting environment for people to show off and get a few minutes of fame or glory for themselves, and not for God. By the time they are done, they stop being relevant for God because He does not share His glory with any other, (Isaiah 42:8).

Believers should therefore not buy into the fear, confusion, deception and lies of the evil one. But they should take every opportunity both now and in the end time to spread the Gospel, while completely hiding themselves behind God. Let God the sender and His good news message of salvation for everyone who will receive it, be what is seen, be at the forefront. The messenger, should not be at the center stage with ego or the spirit of Gehazi craving for accolades and rewards of all kings, (2 Kings 5:20-27).

The Coronavirus and Its End Time Significance.

The Coronavirus has nothing to do with 5G. It is not a product of 5G. But the timing of the arrival of the Coronavirus and 5G has created much misunderstanding and confusion.

In reality, Coronvirus is of spiritual origin. Here is one of many confirmations of this fact. For no government or nation of the world, irrespective of their power or technologically advancement, have been able to prepare ahead or defeat it. It has made mockery of the power, intelligence and knowledge of nations the world over. It has made mockery of seats of power nations. It has made mockery of all the deadly weapons amassed by nations over the years. They have been unable to see or fire a single shot against the invisible enemy. In so doing, it struck fear and paralyses to their system. And yet it is only a small test run of what is to come on the world as it enters the end time.

The nations of the world will be powerless against what will come, in succession. No nation will be prepared enough to handle it. For the spiritual, which is invisible, more ancient, and more powerful, will always prevail against the physical. No one can see or fight against the spiritual, except by the power of God.

Indeed, the Coronavirus, which is a global pestilence, was a bad breathe, a burp or vomit spilled out by the Dragon himself into the world. Not of the symbolic Chinese dragon, even if China is the first place of contact. For the LORD who does not discriminate loves them, just as He does love all the peoples of the world. And among them will be those who will be saved.

But we are talking about the old serpent, the Devil himself, the prince of the power of the air, who is the real Dragon, (Revelation 20:2, Ephesians 2:2). His breath pollutes the healthy environment of the air. It is very poisonous to the human body, and so brings about pestilence and death. The Dragon aims always to create an atmosphere of fear, confusion, to kill and destroy, (John 10:10, 2 Timothy 1:7). It may do so directly by itself, or through demonic or human agents.

The Coronavirus is the Dragon's part in the formal beginning of the period of birth pains for the world. The LORD has forewarned us about this the birth pains, which include plagues, (Matthew 24:4-8). The birth pains will feature nations going to war against each other, kingdoms rising up in disagreement against each other, famines and scarcities, outbreak of diseases or pestilences, earthquakes in various parts of the world, as well as any other means God may allow including natural disasters, fire, volcanoes, tornadoes, flooding, monsoons, severe storms and weather system, locusts, wild animals, etc (Matthew 24:7, Ezekiel 13:13).

I had already warned that the end time birth pains for the world formally started by the end of 2017. I wrote about this as revealed by The LORD in one of His visits to me in 2017. I sounded this alarm in one of the Chapters in the fourth end time Book, *'Celebrating God's Faithfulness in the end time'*. The birth pains for the world will become more frequent and more painful. Some will be regional, and others will be global.

We must not try to dismiss the Coronavirus in the archives like the Spanish flue, world war I or II and other deadly events that occurred before. The reason is because of Israel. For the end time events are timed around Israel by God. Israel is not the one who starts or brings them about. And it does not mean Israel will not experience the painful end time events. But their occurrence or timing is tied to Israel. Therefore, the end time events, including the birthpains could not have started without Israel. And when those previous events happened, Israel did not exist. For everything is timed around Israel.

In one of the Chapters in the first end time book, *'The Mysteries of End Time Events Revealed'*, I had explained that Israel had been in a sleepy, inactive or dormant state, from 70AD to 1948AD. This was the gap between the sixty-ninth and seventieth week, (Daniel 9:24-27). Israel were rebellious against God against God by rejecting and crucifying The Messiah, (Mark 15:12-19, John 19:12-16, Luke 23:13-24). And as prophesied by The LORD and Daniel, the Temple, along with Jerusalem and Israel as a nation were completely destroyed by the Romans, (Daniel 9:26, Matthew 24:1-2, Mark 13:1-2, Luke 19:41-44, Luke 21:5-6). This happened in 70AD. Israel since then has been in that state of Apostasy against The Messiah of God Most High till now. But the rebellion and Apostasy will come to an end when they will repent, (Zechariah 12:10-14). This will be when the Antichrist commits abomination, with his desecrating idolatry image, which will stand in the Holy Place. It will bring about desolation, or abandonment of the Temple, by the Jews, 'Abomination of Desolation', (Daniel 9:27, Matthew 24:15, 2 Thessalonians 2:4, Revelation 13:4-8, Revelation 13:14-17).

As explained in the first book, Israel spiritually needs the three legs, as a nation, Jerusalem as capital and the Temple for the national worship of God, in order to firmly be up and standing. Since the destruction of Israel by the Romans in 70AD, Israel was not a nation again until 1948. That was when it regained its first of three legs. But like a chair that needs three legs to be firmly standing, there was no way one leg would be enough for Israel to stand and be active. So, although Israel was roused from sleep, but it could not stand on one leg. This was so for another 70years until 2018. For Israel did not regain the second of its tripod legs until 2018. This was when it gained recognition of Jerusalem as its capital. Now with two legs of its tripod legs in place, Israel is in a position to stir itself up to stand. Though still weak, a bit bent, unstable or wobbly and even limping. But nonetheless, it is awake and standing to take its place as regards the start of the end time events.

And remember, I had already revealed The LORD's visit to me end of 2017, to warn or confirm that it was time for the formal commencement of the end time birth pains for the world. And by the following year, 2018, Israel's second leg was restored to it, with Jerusalem as its capital. And no sooner had Israel gotten its second leg in 2018, than the first major global even took started end of 2019.

From now on, the events of the birthpains will begin to unfold, and with more severity. We do not know how long this will be before the third leg is restored for Israel. The restoration will coincide with when the birthpains will transition into the more severely painful end events with the trumpet warnings, when the Antichrist arises. The third and final leg will be firmly in place when the Antichrist enables the building of the Temple in Jerusalem. Then it is going to be severely painful fireworks on earth, with seven parallel trumpet warnings. If the Coronavirus has been painful for the world with the start of the birth pains, then wait till Israel's third leg is restored or the Antichrist comes on stage.

The trumpet warnings on one hand will be unbearable for the world. On another hand, both the Apostate Israel and the lukewarm Church, will experience a period of great tribulation visited on them by the Antichrist. For God will use it to purify them. It is not His desire to destroy them, but to purify them. So God will protect them from destruction by the Antichrist. God will not fail but save His own. It will end in the main rapture of the Believers, Jews and Gentiles together.

God's Unfailing Protection For His Own In End Time

All things, people and good or bad Angels, thrones, principalities, powers, etc were all created by The LORD, and for His purpose, (John 1:3, Colossians 1:16). They are all subject to His Authority. The Angels, good or bad, regardless of their hierarchy are even more aware of this, and never question or disobey His command. They can only do what He desires of them or permit them to do, (Philippians 2:9). The LORD once appeared to me to show or demonstrate this for my understanding, using two columns of very hefty, and powerful Angels, with the good on one side and the bad on the other side. He did not even have to speak, but just an indication of His desire was enough for them to obey. No word spoken and no questions asked. This demonstration for me by The LORD, was when I was writing the fourth book on end time: *"Celebrating God's Faithfulness in The End Time"*. Please refer to it for more details and other revelations.

And am able to confidently write here that neither Satan, nor any Angel good or bad, or the end time AntiChrist or False prophet, can violate the command of The LORD in the end time. They will operate as determined and allowed by The LORD. The Antichrist may try to say pompous and blasphemous words against God, and his false prophets may deceive the people, (Revelation 13:4-8, Revelation 13:11-17). But in the end the Antichrist and his false prophet are sent straight to the lake of fire, having no further use, (Revelation 19:20). For not even the bad angels or their master the Devil, dear to rave and say such pompous and blasphemous words against God. For they know who He is and fear Him greatly.

The purpose of this information above is for every child of God, to know and understand beyond any doubt that nothing can happen without The LORD's permission. And because He dearly loves every believer, He extends His protection around them. And in fact there are Angels assigned for that job for every believer.

But let me also stress that Angels do not answer directly to believers but take their instructions only from The LORD. So it is a waste of time praying to any Angels. For the good Angels, it is sinful. But when we pray to God, the necessary command is given from above to them and they carry it out.

And He is a faithful God, who never fails. So when He says " I will be with you or will never leave or forsake you", He means exactly that, (Matthew 28:20, Deuteronomy 31:6-8, Psalm 37:28, Psalm 94:14, Hebrews 13:5). His faithfulness in protection is well attested to in Psalms (Psalm 91:1-16).

Furthermore, the Believers or Saints, are the harvest of The LORD, in the end time. He is jealously protective over His own, and will not let any of them to be destroyed. But it does not mean they will not be tested or refined through fire of affliction. They will be so, due to lukewarmness, and love for the things of the world.

When God says something is coming, as they will surely come in the end time, to test everyone to the limit, He also provides the help needed. I was so scared with some of the initial visions of the end time The LORD showed me, when He called me to write the first book, "The End of Time Mysteries Unveiled". And I began to wonder how could it be or what He will do for His own.

And to my surprise, He followed through with the second book, *"Finishing Strong In The End Time"*. In it God has provided complete guide on His protection, and the prayers to pray in the end time for every believer to finish strong. For He wants all to finish strong. And we need to pray to get answers in the end time, as He has promised in that second book, and laid out accordingly. It also contains prayers and how to pray effectively to The LORD.

In the end time, not all believers will die before going to heaven or before The LORD returns, (1 Corinthians 15:51-52, 1 Thessalonians 4:15-17). However, it is inevitable that some, a few, may die during the end time birthpains, such as the Coronavirus. Some may also die through persecutions or some other ways. But we need to all understand that it is not because of their sins, for The LORD already took away the sins of those faithful in Him. Rather, it is because their assignments on earth have been finished, with their death coinciding wit the birthpains or persecutions. And everyone dies, when their hour comes.

So no one should be judgmental, thinking they died in the birthpains, such as the Coronavirus, because of their sins and going to hell. No!. It is just because the time of the believer has come. They go to paradise, to rest and to await the resurrection and rapture (1 Thessalonians 4:15-17).

The LORD will put His mark on everyone who is His own, and He knows everyone of them all. That mark is the presence of the Holy Spirit with them.

Then there are those who are unbelievers or lukewarm believers who are at the point of facing death, will repent in their hearts and sincerely call on the Name of The LORD. They will accept The LORD as their savior just before they die. The LORD sees the heart. It reminds us of the two thieves on the cross. One thief on the cross dying chose rail insults at The LORD and refused to repent. But the second thief who was also at the point of death on the cross called on The LORD and went to paradise, (Luke 23:43). So, these too like the repentant thief on the cross, will go to paradise. For God cannot reject any who sincerely calls on Him. His love is too strong to turn a deaf ear to them. His love for mankind is a mystery no one, not even the angels, can fathom. So heaven will be full of surprises, where the last, those not given the chance by humans become the first to get there! This is also why the Scripture warns us not to judge or condemn any one, (Matthew 7:1).

At the point of their death, there may be no one with them to preach or pray for them. But they will remember the message of the good news of the Kingdom of God, which someone probably preached to them in the time past. This is why believers have the great responsibility to keep preaching the gospel of good news, everywhere or time the opportunity arises. It does not matter if those hearing it will accept it at that time or not. For no one can tell at what point someone will repent. And it is The Holy Spirit that does the conversion, not the preacher.

Everyone has an end time on earth. This is whether in the coming end time or much earlier. But the question is this: Is everyone daily ready? For none of us has control of tomorrow, if God does not say so. There are some who may hear the message and never accept it. Or they may hear and postpone or set their time in future when they will be ready to do so, such as after enjoying their lives because of the wealth they have accumulated or because life is so sweet to them. Ot it may even be a believer living in sin and the time of death comes suddenly unexpected, such as in their sleep, or in an accident, or robbers, or riots, or stray projectiles, or heart attack, etc. And for such, the time of salvation is past gone, and there is no more help or heaven available for them.

Finally, since The LORD Himself called me by His grace (which I do not merit) to write and alert the world about the coming end time, I never hesitated to ask Him any question that was too difficult for me. And I told Him I will not write about it unless He completely answered my question with proof. This was towards the end of the 5th book on the end time: *"The Mirror of The Timeline of The End Time"*.

I asked Him to reveal His mind or working to me concerning the death of someone whi had never never heard about the gospel or of Yeshua to accept Him as LORD and savior. I said just saying they know about nature or His creation or doing good (which is filthy rags) is not enough answer for me if He wants to write about it in the book for people to understand and believe.

And He did not only answer me, but demonstrated the proof to me. How God answered and what He does is so wonderful. Since the details are in one of the chapters in the 5th book, *The Mirror of The Time Line of The End Time'*, please refer to it.

Believers and Coronavirus Vaccines In End Time.

Coronavirus is not like any other virus. Its origin is unknown to the world. It has the ability to adapt in a new environment.

As of this writing, the top intelligence and military community of the world have concluded the virus did not originate or manufactured from a lab.

Also the leading Scientific community in their report of the tracking data they have gathered on this and other virus, now believe it did not originate from the city, Wuhan as they originally thought. Rather, it came from a different place outside of Wuhan, and started two to three months earlier than they thought. Their finding also is that the virus cleverly mutates, when it gets to a new place or environment. It mutates from place to place and country to country. And the one in Wuhan was a mutation of the original that came from a different location. The one in Europe is a mutation of the one that came from China. The one in the US are mutations of those that came either from Europe or directly from China. And in a large country, it mutates as it travels round the various regions.

The Coronavirus is a very evil plague, a very poisonous breathe, burp or a vomit coming directly from the Dragon, the Devil himself. It is of Satanic origin, from the Dragon himself. To the physical mind, it may not make sense. But not to the spiritually minded.

Those who understand and accept the plagues in Egypt happened from the spiritual realm through the commands of Moses, will also understand the spiritual can become a devastating reality in the physical. In the days of Moses, the leading minds of Egypt, such as Jannes and Jambres were staunchly skeptical and opposed Moses before Pharaoh and the Egyptians. They continued to try to explain off the initial plagues until they could do no more and concluded it was from the finger of God, (Exodus 7:19). Even today, some will keep trying to refuse to accept, trying to explain it away. But sooner ot later, they will run out of explanations.

The Coronavirus pestilence has its end time significance as explained, (Matthew 24:7). It is of Satanic origin, his first act in the opening salvo in the start of the global period of birthpains. He did this being pleased with his actions to create fear and confusion, and ultimately to choke the breath or life out of people and kill them.

As of now, January 2020, everything written in this book, and submitted for publishing are as received of The Spirit Of The LORD. No vaccine has been developed yet. And how can an effective one be developed, when they are yet to understand the virus. As it is, the virus is living, agile and mutates from place to place. The question is would such a vaccine if developed be clever enough to also automatically mutate from place to place like the virus, to protect against it? Or would a different one be developed for each region where there has been mutation and when will the mutation stop? Or would the recipient take new doses when they travel to a new place. Would there be enough time to demonstrate the effectiveness and safety of what is given to people? There are so many unknowns. But let me not display my ignorance in this field and leave it to the leading experts of the world, some of who are in the Kingdom. Instead, let me focus on the grace God has given me. And this I know: True and wholesome cure or protection

And this I know: True and wholesome cure or protection comes from God. For He is The LORD our Healer, Jehovah Rofecha, (Exodus 15:26). Every true believer must never forget, but always remember The LORD's promise and power to protect, throughout all the events of the end time. For their occurances will continue to originate from the spiritual, even as the angels take turns to blow the warning trumpets of end time and woes. And the physical will not be able to overcome them. For the physical cannot protect against the spiritual enemy. But the LORD knows both, and are under His control.

Vaccines are replicas of the original virus, injected into the human body, for it to overcome it. Past examples include such as for yellow fever, measles, etc. In this regard, humans have tried to liken vaccines to the bronze serpent lifted up by Moses, and as many as looked at it were saved, (Numbers 21:9).

But some vaccines are unlike the bronze serpent that gives life. They are not dead, but very much alive, with its poisonous and dangerous sting. Some cause more damage than the good intended. As for the Coronavirus, the scientists do not even understand it, and so how can they develop a safe and reliable vaccine for it. It is unknown, what the actual effect of the Coronavirus vaccine will be, both in the short or long term.

And this I also know: The LORD, the LAMB of God Himself, who has already been lifted up on the cross, with His bloodshed, is the only true protection. This calls for faith for those who will trust God and walk with Him. For the just shall live by faith and please God through faith, (Hebrews 10v38, Hebrews 12v6).

This I also know: The Israelites of old in Egypt who were told to sprinkle the blood of the lamb on their door posts, were also told to eat with bitter herb, (Exodus 12:7-8).

The Coronavirus plague requires good hygiene practice, and showing love for one's neighbors through what they call 'social distancing' from others, not to infect them. But apart from these, God has also in His mercy, given wisdom of appropriate 'bitter herbs' to eat or drink, for effective remedy against the Coronavirus. This is as demonstrated by those who take the hot bitter herb of lemon, garlic, ginger along with rich sources of vitamin C and Zinc. They recovered and were not affected by the virus. And depending on availability, some others have replaced the lemon, garlic and ginger with the hot bitter herb of bitter leaf, lemon grass, and neem leaves (nimtree, dogonyaro) along with rich sources of vitamin C and Zinc. All these are also very effective cure against various strains of flu, (and so removes the need for a vaccine).

And this I also know: Indeed, some special leaves will have their parts in the end time for healing, (Ezekiel 47:12, Revelation 22:2). For God in His creation of man from the earth, had also created the right foods and leaves as the solution to bring strength and healing to the body. We pray in faith to God, and He in turn shows or provides what our bodies need from the earth for strength and for healing of our bodies. So prayer has its place to receive what is right for our bodies from Him. And when the right foods or leaves God has provided, is mixed with prayer of faith and thanksgiving, it brings great strength or health for the natural body, which must continue to be nourished from the earth. It is the most effective vaccine, along with the blood of The LAMB.

The human introduced the injection of a virus into the body, which has its limits. Nonetheless, if after praying the prayer of faith, and taking the bitter herbs with thanksgiving, but you still feel you need the Coronavirus vaccine, then do what you feel. However, do not be the first guinea pigs in what the humans do not even understand. Exercise some caution, for it may bring about unknown consequences for the body, for the body was not original designed to take in virus for its healing. They are enemies to each other. Also, it may bring about a continuous follow up monitoring for those who took it. This is similar to the yearly flu shots. Those who take it go back for more, year after year. It becomes like an addiction. And if past practices are anything to go by, the manufactures will make sure of that through creating fear and campaigns designed for them to continue to profit from the Coronavirus vaccines, year after year. And if the people don't, they will be in danger of finally succumbing to its fatal claw or pang.

But the plague of Coronavirus that came on the world will not stay like that forever or remain for much longer. This is because there are many other events coming for the end time. It will go just as it came. Its DNA will be wiped out from place to place, even as Believers join in faith to pray to God. They will look for it and not find where it went.

The MicroChip And Mark Of The AntiChrist In End Time

The technology for the end time mark of the Beast or Antichrist is all in place. The world leading minds in biotechnology and microchips technology have perfected it over the last few years, waiting for when the Antichrist arises to take advantage of it. The choice to take it for the Antichrist when he comes will be a voluntary decision each person on earth has to make. But there will be a lot of enticement, campaign, as well as persecutions or tribulations to make it happen, for people, weak believers to switch. But only those who endure to the end will be saved, (Matthew 24:13).

But the technology that will make the imprint possible is already in place. And it is being demonstrated at individual and governmental levels. Some people already carry such microchips in their bodies, and use it for their personal identification and purchases. In this regard, the Scandinavians are ahead on this, being voluntarily injected with the microchip and using it on a large scale.

In Sweden, more than 3,000 people have the microchips, the size of a rice grain, inserted into their bodies. The Swedish passenger train company SJ owned by the government allows people to use microchip implants in lieu of paper train tickets. It has been so since 2017. And the more people see the convenience, the more others opt for it.

Also in 2017, a US company in Wisconsin, developed and rolled out microchip implants with RFID, (Radio Frequency Identification) Chips for its employees. This is so they can make purchases in their office break room shops, open doors, unlock phones, use as ID Cards, store biomedical and health data, perform other office tasks with the wave of their hands. It is similar to the one already widely used in Sweden.

On the government level, the Danish government by their recent action demonstrated how this will be enforced during the Antichrist government. For on March 6, 2020, the Danish parliament hurriedly passed an emergency Coronavirus law which gives the government the legal authority to force citizens to be vaccinated. This is despite that no vaccine had been developed against Coronavirus. The law gives the authorities the powers to force testing, treatment and quarantine with the backing of the police. It also empowers them to prohibit access to public institutions, supermarkets and shops, public and private nursing homes and hospitals, and also to impose restrictions on access to public transport to those who refuse. It is a foretaste of what will happen in the future. For in the end time those who refuse the Antichrist system will not be able to buy things or operate any business to sell services, (Revelation 13:16-17).

Some animals already carry microchips in their bodies. The human Bio-microchip implant in the body is being pushed by various groups for many reasons. It is presently being marketed on medical grounds and for convenience.

For we live in an era of ease and convenience. So the microchip is marketed on the basis that it reduces the time it takes for people to perform some daily routines. It conveniently provides access to their homes, offices, and gyms by simply swiping their hands against a digital reader. It provides easy means to store emergency contacts, social media profiles, house keys/FOBs. It allows those with the implant to make payments in stores and restaurants, and even to buy e-tickets for events and public transportation.

We also live in an era of major medical advances and challenges. So the microchip implants is seen as having the potential to revolutionize medical diagnosis, health monitoring of an individuals' vitals, and allowing both doctors and patients to quickly and accurately access medical data in real-time, from any part of the world.

As things stand today, hospitals and health institutions are lobbying for the adoption and legalization for storage of biomedical data of patients with microchip in their bodies. It may start from as soon as a baby is born. Patients can carry this data on their bodies from place to place, or country to country. It makes it easy for doctors to monitor a patients' medical conditions and to quickly have access to the biomedical history of the patient for treatment. On the remote medical monitoring of patients, the Israelis are very far ahead, although it must be stated that they are not inserting implants into peoples bodies. They do it through Apps and digital devices that capture and record high-quality heart, lungs, ears, throat, skin and temperature readings.

There are no proofs of any kind yet of microchip use with any vaccine. But patients who receive new or dangerous vaccines may need to be monitored for their vital signs. Microchips would make that possible today. The delivery system for both the microchip and vaccines are the same. It is done almost painlessly through the needle. The microchip can be delivered along with a vaccine 'for the good' of the recipient for monitoring and follow up purposes.

Governments are also interested in microchip implants for ease of monitoring, tracking of locations and of control of individuals, anywhere in the world. Some royal and high level government officers already have the microchips on their bodies for security monitoring purposes.

Travel and national border control agencies see microchip implants as a means of easy identification of travelers in place of paper passports.

The financial institutions are pushing microchip implants for ease of transactions and cashless operations. Through it an individual's bank information and financial data can be easily linked or stored. The person goes around anywhere, without the need for physical cash or creditcard to make a purchase.

MicroChip and AntiChrist:

The Scripture describes four characteristics of people associated with the Antichrist that will face the wrath of God in the end time. These are those who worship him and his iamge or idol, those who have the mark of the beast, those who have the name of the beast and those who have the number associated with his name, (Revelation 13:17, Revelation 14:9).

God also has His own seal on those who are His own. But it is not the physical seal. First they are washed with the blood of The LAMB. And He will spiritually mark or seal them through the Holy Spirit living in them, (Ephesians 1:13-14). God does not use a physical human number. For those that serve Him do so in Spirit and in Truth, (John 4:23-24). They accordingly also exhibit the fruit of the Holy Spirit, (Galatians 5:22-23).

However, the Antichrist system is a false system, lead by a human being. So unlike God, the Antichrist does not and cannot offer anything spiritual. So he will use human identification system. The mark of the beast is given as a human number '666' or as in microchip 6-bits in 3 places, (Revelation 14:18). So it will not be a spiritual marking, but human or earthly. The number is imprinted on the right hand or on the forehead of the bearer.

Ultimately, the Antichrist will take advantage of microchip implants technology. This is to identify and reward those who are on its side, similar to party membership cards of some governments.

And two out of three people on earth will choose to be identified on the side of the Beast.

Serving God and remaining faithful for Him to the end is a voluntary decision by each person. So will be the taking of the mark of the Beast. It will be a voluntary decision for each person who takes the mark. So no one will be able to argue the mark was secretly planted on them, without their knowledge. Some may be persecuted to the point they succumb by themselves to take the mark. Only those who endure to the end will be saved, (Matthew 24:13). So every believer on earth at that time has to get to the point of Shadrach, Meshach and Abenego, (Daniel 3:16-18). They told King Nebuchadnezzar who built an idol to be worshipped that they would prefer death rather than worship the image. That will have its end time fulfillment under the Antichrist.

Anyone who hears the Gospel of good news of the Kingdom of God and refuses, automatically chooses to side with the Antichrist. For whoever is not for me, is against me. And whoever does not believe on the Son of God is condemned, (John 3:18, Matthew 12:30).

People will voluntarily choose to go with the beast. They will receive an imprint of his mark or his name, and be identified with him, and worship him as 'god'.

Some will boldly make the choice without any external pressure or force on them. The Antichrist will rule over every tribe, tongue, and nation on earth, (Revelation 13:7). No nation on earth will be exempted. He will have complete control of the religious, political and economic system of the world.

Some people will make the choice to follow the Antichrist through enticements and temptations. This is so they can enjoy the benefits and opportunities the Antichrist offers.

Some others will take his mark due to persecution, refusing to endure on the side of God to the end. For agents everywhere will try to enforce enacted Antichrist laws for persecution of those who do not worship or follow the Antichrist. They will enforce denial of privileges, such as buying groceries or having access to other services, for refusing the Antichrist. They will enforce denial of permits to prevent business people who refuse the Antichrist to continue to operate their businesses. These are all in order to get people to comply and join the Antichrist. The Scripture says anyone who does not have the mark, or name or number of number of the beast imprinted for them, for identification, will not be allowed to buy or sell anything, (Revelation 13:16-17).

The Antichrist And Great Tribulation Before Rapture

The believers have always made the mistake of thinking that the general rapture will occur before the great tribulation. This is not the case. Rapture will follow the great tribulation. The Anticchrist and his false prophet will carry out the great tribulation, which will last for a period of three and half years. God's purpose in this is not to destroy the Believers. But it is for the purification of the Church, Jews and Gentiles alike, to make them fully ripe and ready for His great harvest. So God will protect them from destruction by the Antichrist. A lot has been written about this in the fourth end time book, *"Celebrating God's Faithfulness In The End Time"*.

For before the rapture, two things will happen alongside each other during the reign of the Antichrist. There will be the general different seven trumpet warnings of God for the world, with various plagues on earth designed to get people to repent, (Revelation 6:1-11:19). It will last almost the entire seven years reign of the

Antichrist. Before then will be the beginning of birthpains of the world, (Matthew 24:4-8). The birth pains will feature nations going to war against each other, kingdoms rising up in disagreement against each other, famines and scarcities, outbreak of diseases or pestilences, earthquakes in various parts of the world, as well as any other means God may allow including natural disasters, fire, volcanoes, tornadoes, flooding, monsoons, severe storms and weather system, locusts, wild animals, etc (Matthew 24:7, Ezekiel 13:13).

No one knows how long the various events of the birthpain will last. But at God's own appointed time, the birthpains will transition into the period of end time seven trumpet warnings for the whole world. This is when the Antichrist begins his reign over the earth. It will be a period of major decisions for salvation in God or to follow the Antichrist. The trumpet warnings will then transition into the final seven wraths or woes of God specifically targeted on the followers of the Antichrist. At this point, they are beyond repentance. So the wrath of God with destruction is targeted at them. This will be after rapture. There will still be those who believe in God, in The LORD, but do not make the rapture. They love the LORD but their obedience is not complete for one reason of sin or another such as unforgiveness, pretense, lies, hate, doubt, etc. These will not make rapture. They will not be destroyed, along with the followers of the Antichrist. They will remain on earth.

During the seven trumpet warnings, the believers, Jews and non-Jews, who have made up their minds to follow God will still be on the earth. They will continue to preach to win souls. The power of the Holy Spirit will be mighty in them. While they are doing this, the Antichrist will continue to blaspheme against God. The Antichrist will also continue to visit the great severe tribulation on the Saints for a period of three and half years, (Revelation 13:5-8). During this time, the Antichrist will defeat the Saints. At the end, when the seventh trumpet completes blowing, just before the woes, The LORD will come to rescue the Saints who are fully ripe and ready through the rapture, (1 Thessalonians 4:15-17). Many will be saved, and will celebrate in Heaven in the presence of God, (Revelation 7:9-17).

After the great tribulation and rapture of the Saints, then the followers of the Antichrist, anyone who has been worshipping the Beast and his image, or has received the mark of the name of the Beast, will be subjected to the wrath of God", (Revelation 14:9-11).

As already mentioned earlier, there will still be those who believe in God, in The LORD, but do not make the rapture. They love the LORD but their obedience is not complete for one reason of sin or another such as unforgiveness, pretense, lies, hate, doubt, etc. They do not have the mark of the Beast and are not hateful of God unlike the Antichrist followers. They are just not fully ripe and ready for the harvest. These will still be protected by God on earth. They will not be destroyed, along with the followers of the Antichrist in the wrath of God. They will live and replenish the earth through the Millennium. They will face a second time of testing, after the Millennium, in the second rebellion and deception of the world by Satan. And some of them will follow him. They will follow Gog of Magog, the Antichrist of that time that Satan will use, after the Millennium, (Revelation 20:7-9). They will die and later rise to face judgment of God when the time comes.

The wrath of God will be in two stages. The first one will be immediate, after the rapture. They are the special final seven bowls or woes of wrath that God will pour on earth targeted on the followers of the Antichrist after rapture, (Revelation 16:1-20).

The second wrath of God will come, during the great white throne judgment. This will be for all those whose, from the time of Adam to the time of the Antichrist, whose names are not in the book of life. This second wrath will include any of those who follow Satan in his second deception of the world, after the Millennium. They will all be sent into the eternal lake of fire, after the final judgment, as the final and everlasting wrath of God, (Revelation 20:11-15).

"If anyone worships the Beast and his image (idol, statue), and receives his mark on his forehead or on his hand: 10 That person will also drink of the wine of the wrath of God, which is poured out in full strength into the cup of His displeasure. The person will be tormented with fire and brimstone in the presence of the holy angels and in the presence of The LAMB. 11 And the smoke of their torment will be rising

forever and ever. They will have no rest day or night. This will happen to anyone who worships the Beast and his image, and anyone who receives the mark of the name of the Beast", (Revelation 14:9-11).

And let anyone who has ears listen with careful attention!

CHAPTER 57

About The Future Glory of The Temple In End Time

Scriptural Verses:

Haggai 2:6-9 (ETB): 6 "For this is what The LORD of hosts says:

'It still remains a little while, when I will once more shake heaven and earth, the sea and dry land, [ref Isaiah 13:13, Haggai 2:21-22].

7 I will shake all nations (at that time), and they will bring the Treasures of All Nations. And I will fill this Temple with glory,' says The LORD of hosts, [ref Zechariah 8:20-23, Zechariah 14:9, 14:14, 14:16, Isaiah 60:4-13].

8 'The silver is Mine, and the gold is Mine,' says The LORD of hosts.

9 'The glory that will be of this Temple (in that time) will be greater than the former,' says The LORD of hosts.

'And I will give peace in this place,' says The LORD of hosts", [ref Haggai 2:3, Zechariah 6:12-13].

Solomon's Temple or The First Temple

King Solomon had built a magnificent Temple in Jerusalem for the worship of God, (1 Kings 7:51, 2 Chronicles 5:1-14). This is the Temple referred to as the former one. This first Temple was completely burnt down and destroyed in 587BC by Nebuchadnezzar the king of Babylon when he attacked and conquered Jerusalem. He took away the treasures from the Temple, along with Judeans as captives to Babylon, (2 Kings 24:13-16, 2 Kings 25:8-21).

Zerubbabel's Temple or The Second Temple

The exiles who returned to Jerusalem after seventy years of captivity in Babylon, built a new Temple, in place of the former one in 516BC, (Ezra 6:13-15).

The building of this second Temple was led by Zerubbabel. He was the governor of Judah and leader of the Jews, and descendant of King David. He led the rebuilding of the Temple along with Joshua, the High Priest at that time. (Ezra 1:1-2, Haggai 1:1, Ezra 3:2-3). They faced a series of oppositions, and for many years, the rebuilding work was put on hold, (Ezra 4:1-5, Ezra 4:21). But God used both the prophets Haggai and Zechariah to encourage and support Zerubbabel, Joshua and the people to continue and finish the Temple, (Ezra 5:1-2)

This second Temple was built on a much smaller scale and with fewer resources of materials, gold, bronze, etc compared to the first Temple. This second Temple was not comparable to the magnificent Temple first built by king Solomon, (Haggai 2:3). But, there will be a glorious Temple, whose glory surpasses the first Temple. But it will not be the second Temple built by Zerubabbel and Joshua.

The second Temple built in Jerusalem lasted from 516 BCE to 70 AD. Herod the Great, refurbished this second Temple and expanded on it. This was the Temple during the time of Yeshua, (Jesus) before He was crucified on the cross. Just like the Babylonians, the Romans completely destroyed Jerusalem and the Second Temple in 70 AD. This was just as prophesied by The LORD. He said no stone will be left on another, (Matthew 24:1-2, Mark 13:1-2, Luke 19:41-44, Luke 21:5-6). The second Temple no longer exists and did not ever rise to the same glory as that of Solomon.

The Tribulation Temple or The Third Temple

There would be a third Temple. That this Temple will exist during the time of the Antichrist is confirmed by Daniel (Daniel 9:27), by The LORD (Matthew 24:15), by Apostle Paul (2 Thessalonians 2:4), and by an Angel to Apostle John regarding the two end time prophets (Revelation 11:1-6). They all refer to the Temple in Jerusalem at the time of the Antichrist.

And unlike the first two Temples, this third Temple will not take time to build. It will also not stay long and the Temple will have no glory. The mention of it in the Scripture is mostly in association with the end time tribulation of Israel and the Saints, and rebellion. Satan through the Antichrist will desecrate it as part of the end of his first, and on-going rebellion, since Adam against God. It is in this Temple in which the Antichrist will commit the Abomination of desolation during his seven years reign. He will place an idol, sacrilegious object in it and ask people all over the world to worship it, (Daniel 9:27, Matthew 24:15, 2 Thessalonians 2:4, Revelation 13:4-8, Revelation 13:14-17).

The Branch or Messiah's Most Glorious Temple In End Time

God has promised that a time is coming when He will shake the heavens, the earth and the sea, (Haggai 2:6, Isaiah 13:13). The Messiah in His prophecy also said that Stars will fall from heaven, and the heavenly powers will be shaken, (Matthew 24:29). This will happen in the end time, at the second coming of The Messiah.

It is at this time that there will be a glorious Temple in Jerusalem. For at that time, The Messiah, also referred to as The Branch, will also build a new Temple in Jerusalem. The LORD will be both The King and Priest, (Zechariah 6:12-13). This Temple will be built by

The LORD Himself, with His angels, and not by human hands. It will be the real Temple, and not the copies of Tabernacles that Moses, David, Solomon, Zerubbabel or other humans have tried to build on earth. It is from this Temple The LORD will reign as King and Priest during the 1000 years Millennium when He returns with His Saints to rule the earth.

The glory of this new Temple, will surpass the former one built by king Solomon. This is what the Scripture is saying that the glory of this Temple will be more than the former. And there will be peace, (Haggai 2:9). There will be one LORD and King ruling the world, (Zechariah 14:9).

People from all the nations of the world will go to Jerusalem every year to worship the King, the LORD of hosts, and to keep the Feast of Tabernacles, (Zechariah 8:20-23, Zechariah 14:16). The wealth of the nations will also be taken there, (Zechariah 14:9, 14:14, 14:16, Isaiah 60:4-13). This will be during the 1000 years Millennium reign (Revelation 20:1-10).

No Physical Temple In New Jerusalem

During the 1000 years Millennium reign, the people on earth at that time would have known only peace and good or righteousness. They would have no knowledge of evil. It would be similar to the state of Adam and Eve before their fall in the garden of Eden. These humans on earth during the Millennium will still be mortal like Adam and Eve. This is unlike the Saints that would have been taken in rapture (in the first resurrection) to heaven and then come back with the LORD in glorious bodies with immortality, (1 Thessalonians 4:15-17, Revelation 20:4-5).

But after the 1000 years Millennium reign, The LORD will withdraw, with His angels and Saints who had come to rule with Him. These are the Saints who had been previously taken to heaven in rapture during the first resurrection and have immortality, (1 Thessalonians 4:15-17, Revelation 20:4-5). They are different from the humans on earth with flesh and blood, living like Adam and Eve. These humans on earth would be vulnerable to evil, and would each have to make their choice between good and evil, like Adam did, and all humans do.

After The LORD's physical withdrawal from the earth, then Satan will be released for a short while. Satan will offer the choice of evil to people, the mortal humans on earth, as alternative to the good, righteousness and obedience to God. He will go out on his second rebellion to deceive the people on earth, (Revelation 20:7-9). Many will be deceived. Satan's human leader of the rebellion, the equivalent of the Antichrist of that time, will be known as Gog of Magog. He will gather his army against the Saint's of God in Jerusalem. But God will destroy them, (Ezekiel 38:1-23, Revelation 20:7-9).

Then after this, there will be the final judgment. Satan will be thrown into the lake of fire, (Revelation 20:10). The unrighteous people, who are dead, from the time of Adam to that time, will also be resurrected. Their souls from hell will be united with their unglorious bodies, and all will be judged, (Revelation 20:11-15). This is the final judgment.

After the final Judgment, there will be a new heaven, new earth and new Jerusalem, (Revelation 21:1). At that time, there will be no more any physical Temple. This is because The LORD God Almighty and the LAMB will be the Temple, (Revelation 21:22-27). But the kings of the earth will come into the city with their praise and reverence, (glory and honor), (Revelation 21:24, Isaiah 66:23). This is how it will be forever and ever.

Chapter 58

About The Eight Main Stages Of The End Time

Scriptural Verses:

Daniel 9:24-27 (ETB): 24 *"A combined total of Seventy weeks have been decreed, (a week is a block of seven years). For your people and for your holy city: To finish the rebellion, To put an end to sins, To make reconciliation for iniquity, To usher in everlasting righteousness, To seal up vision and prophecy, And to anoint the Most Holy Place.*

25 "Know therefore and understand, That from the time a command (decree) is issued: To restore and build Jerusalem Until The Messiah The Prince comes, There will be seven weeks and sixty-two weeks, (a week is a block of seven years). The street and walls (of Jerusalem) will be built again (after return from captivity). But it will be done in times of trouble (opposition), [ref 2 Chronicles 36:22-23, Ezra 1:1-4, Ezra 4:7-24, Nehemiah 4:1-23].

26 "And at the end of the block of sixty-two weeks The Messiah (Anointed One) will be killed, looking like he had accomplished nothing for Himself. The people who are of the prince who is to come after them (at a later time) will destroy the city and the Sanctuary (Temple). The end of it will be with a flood (overwhelming misery). Wars and desolation are decreed from that time till the very end, [ref Isaiah 53:3-12, Daniel 9:26, Zechariah 13:7, Matthew 26:31].

27 Then he (prince, ruler) will enter into a covenant popular with many for one week (last block of seven years). But in the middle of the week: He will bring an end to sacrifice and offering. His abominations (idolatry) will get to the peak, and bring about desolation. This will continue till the already decreed complete destruction, Which will be poured out on the desolator, [ref Daniel 9:27, Matthew 24:15, Revelation 13:4-8, Revelation 13:14-17, Revelation 19:19-21].

4 Yeshua replied and said to them:

Matthew 24:4-8 (ETB): "Watch out, be on your guard so that no one deceives you!

5 For many will come in My Name, saying, 'I am The Messiah (HaMashiach, The Anointed One, Christ, Christos),' and they will deceive many people.

6 Also you will hear of wars and rumors (threats) of wars. But do not be frightened (alarmed, worried)! This is because these things must happen. However, it is not yet the end of the world.

7 Nations will go to war against nations, and kingdoms will rise up against kingdoms. Also, there will be famines, outbreak of diseases (pestilences), and earthquakes in various parts of the world.

8 All these things are only the beginning of 'birth-pangs' ('Chevlei Moshiach') before the end.

End Time Not A One Event But Has Stages

What we call the End Time is not a onetime event. The End Time has many stages. The end time events can be grouped into eight(8) stages, through which God will carry out and complete His plans to established His Kingdom on earth. Each stage is like a box or package containing many items or events in it.

Some of the events of the end time may be contained in one package or completed within one stage. But some others may continue and be present in other stages. And when they do, they are even stronger with greater intensity in the new stage.

All The Events Explained In The End Time Books

All of the end time events, God's planned actions and His purpose have been explained in the end time books:

Book#1: "The End of Time Mysteries Unveiled", (2017)
Book#2: "Finishing Strong In The End Time", (2017)
Book#3: "End Time Count Down Messages", (2017)
Book#4: "Celebrating God's Faithfulness In The End Time", (2018)
Book#5: "The Mirror Of The Timeline Of The End Time", (2018)

And this book
Book#6: "Understanding The Bible In The End Time", (2020)

And the Bible
"End Time Bible, ETB".

Get your copies.

These books, when read along with the End Time Bible, ETB provide total understanding about the end time as revealed by God. As they happen, you will not be caught in surprise or unawares. It will be like watching with keen interest in real time and slow motion a movie previously seen.

The Events Before 2017 Did Not Count

None of the events before 2017 counts as part of the end time event. Yes there was the world wars I that happened from 1914 to 1918. Also there was the world war II that took place from 1914 to 1918. Then there were also past major pandemic plagues such as Spanish flu in 1918 and other events that took place in the past before 2017. But they do not count as part of the end time events. The end time event started from the end of 2017. There are two reasons for this:

The first reason is because Israel will be an active participant in the end time events, (Daniel 9:24-27). So the events of the end time cannot start without Israel coming out of its 'dormant or silent period'. Israel wakes up just before or near the beginning of the 70th week. In the first book, "The End of Time Mysteries Unveiled", we noted that Israel requires three legs to stand: These are Israel as a nation, Jerusalem as its capital and the Temple. The Temple, Jerusalem and the nation of Israel were destroyed by the Romans 70AD. Israel only became a nation again in 1948. So Israel was completely dormant for a period of 1,878 years from 70AD to 1948AD. This was the period of the Gentiles with God, in the absence of Israel. And exactly 70years after Israel became a nation in 1948, that, Jerusalem became officially recognized as its capital in 2018. This means the stage has been set for Israel. And it does not require the third leg for things to start. That is for the birth pains to start (Matthew 24:4-9). This is because the Temple will be built with the help of the Antichrist, when he finally comes up and they form alliance together, (Daniel 9:27). This is what happens in stage 2.

The second reason is because The LORD who had called me as His servant, who assigned and gave me revelations and understanding of the end time events to alert the world through the books, had appeared to me and confirmed the start time of end time events. The wind of its arrival, the beginning of birth pains for the world, started blowing by the end of 2017. It was during this time, many parts of the world about the same time were experiencing various kinds of disasters such as hurricanes, monsoons, flooding, earthquakes, volcanoes, fire, etc.

Thirdly, the global outbreak in the end of 2019 of the COVID-19 Coronavirus pandemic, is a further confirmation, at a global level. And the various nations and governments of the world, despite all their knowledge, technology, advancement and postures have all been helpless to understand or stop it. This is so that there is no doubt about it globally. The plague is not a visible enemy that can be shot down with the greatest human weapon. It will only be stopped at God's own timing. For no one will be able to stop or interfere with God's plan for the end time. When the angel of death was visiting the death plague on the Israelites after King David sinned through the census, it took God, to command the angel to stop, withhold the dagger, (2 Samuel 24:15-16).

Also, Apostle John was told in his revelation by the Angel, that there are a total of eight kingdoms of the world, (Revelation 17:9-11). These are super power kingdoms or nations that have controlled the affairs of the rest of the world in their times, using their economic, military and technological advantage. These eight super power kingdoms have already been identified and discussed in this book in 'Chapter 50 About the Eight Superpower Kingdoms of The World'. The sixth one was the Roman Kingdom, and was in power at the time of the Apostles. Before that there were five other super kingdoms which had already reigned and fallen. The seventh world super power has been in power presently in this generation. And after the seventh kingdom, would come the Antichrist Kingdom, the eight and last one before The LORD returns.

Now as is typical with all transitions of power from one kingdom to another system, the existing one must be weakened enough for it to come under and be ruled by the new power. For example, the ruling Babylonian kingdom was defeated and absorbed into the new Medo-Persia Kingdom. And so were others in a similar way. So, before the Antichrist Kingdom takes over, which is the eight and final kingdom of the world, the present seventh ruling power must be weakened enough to submission and come under the eight one. This also will happen fairly rapidly, just as the birth pains are already ongoing. For from the midst of the birth pains, confusion, economic disaster, and kingdoms opposing each other will arise one who is the little horn, the man of sin (Daniel 7:7-8, 2 Thessalonians 2:3-4). He will be a man and not a woman. He will arise to promise solution and a new world order to the people. He will be very smart and persuasive and the people will accept him as the world leader. He will be pompous, proud, and blasphemous towards God. He will oppose and exalt himself above the things of God.

Here are the Stages of the end time and their main events that will occur.

Stage1:

Birthpains, Persecutions, Perilous times, Global Evangelism Etc

Stage1a: Initial Period of Global BirthPains

Characterized by stronger repeated occurrences of events including:

Increased on going deception by false preachers, prophets, messiahs.

There will be Wars and rumors (threats) of wars,

Nations rising against nations, and kingdoms against kingdoms.

There will be Famines and Scarcity of Basic Essentials,

There will be Outbreak of diseases (pestilences, plagues).

There will be Earthquakes in various parts of the world,

As well as other natural occurrences like volcanoes, violent storms, hurricanes, monsoons, mudslides, locusts, etc.

All these things are only the beginning of 'birth-pangs' *('ChevleiMoshiach'*) before the end.

No one knows how long it will be.

[ref Matthew 24:4-9, Mark 13:5-8, Luke 21:8-11, Ezekiel 13:13].

The Eight Main Stages Of The End Time

Stage 1b: Ongoing Persecution Of Believers

Ongoing Persecutions Of Believers, which has been from time of Apostles.

There will be increased hatred for Believers in every nation.

There will be rampart backsliding, or falling away of some Believers from their faith.

There will be betrayal and hatred among Believers, by those falling away.

More false prophets and preachers will arise.

Lawlessness will be on the increase in the world. Love will wane.

[ref Matthew 24:9-13, 2 Thessalonians 2:3, Revelation 13:4-8]

Stage 1c: Global Lack of Care or Love

Increased troublesome or perilous times:

Love of many will grow cold

People will love only themselves.

People will also love money.

People will be boastful and proud.

People will disrespect and say evil things (blaspheme) against God.

Children will not obey their parents.

People will be ungrateful for what they receive (from God or others).

People will indulge in unholy lifestyles.

People will be hard hearted, unloving to others.

People will be unforgiving to those who do wrong to them.

People will be slanderous with false accusation of others.

People will have no self control.

People will be fierce, brutal like savages (including terrorism).

People will be traitors and betrayers.

People will be headstrong and reckless.

People will have a form of godliness (religions) but denying its power.

[ref Matthew 24:12, 2 Timothy 3:1-6].

Stage1d: Global/worldwide Evangelism

The gospel of good news of The Kingdom of God will reach all the world.

God will sample His harvest on earth by taking away His firstfruit from earth.

Not everyone will be part of this.

They are only those who are fully ripe and ready for Him at that time.

This event would be a complete surprise.

This event will causes the sleepy Church and Apostate Israel to wake up.

Both the Church and Jews, who will later be harvest through the main rapture will be made ready through great tribulations in the end time.

The power of the Holy Spirit will be released in great measure. Many will repent and be saved. Many will be empowered through the great tribulation to endure to the end and be saved.

[ref Matthew24:14, Revelation14:1-5, Exodus 23:15-19, Zechariah12:10-14, Joel 2:28-32, Luke 12:42-48].

Because the firstfruit are already faithful, fully ripe and ready for The LORD, they will not have to go through further refinement through the great tribulations of the Antichrist. The exact timing of their being taken is not known. It may be just before the start or anytime during first 3 ½ years of the government of the man-of-sin.

Stage2:

The AntiChrist Kingdom

Stage 2a: The Rise of The AntiChrist

The Man-of-sin, the Antichrist will arise. His government will rule the world for 7 years.

The Antichrist will form alliances with various bodies, and nations of the world, including Israel.

This will enable the Temple to be built in Jerusalem within a short time.

Two End Time Prophets in Jerusalem will arise as witnesses for God. They will do this in Jerusalem for 42-months (3 ½ years). At the end of their assignment for God, they will be killed by the Antichrist and their bodies displayed on the street of Jerusalem. Then after three days, they will be resurrected and go to heaven. This may also be around when the firstfruits are taken away.

The breaking of the seven seals and the warning trumpet judgments will continue on earth.

[ref Daniel 9:27, Matthew 24:15-22, Mark 13:14-20, 2 Thessalonians 2:4, Revelation 6-9, Revelation 11:1-13, Revelation 13:4-8, Revelation 13:14-17]

Stage 2b: Abomination of Desolation & Great Tribulation

There will be war in lower Heavens between Michael and his angels, against Satan and his angels. Satan will be defeated and cast down to the earth, never to return back to any level of heaven.

Satan will give full power to Antichrist or Beast. It is with this power he will be able to kill the two prophets, and fight against the Saints of God.

The Antichrist will passionately hate anything of God, the Believers, the Jews and whatever is Holy.

The Antichrist will overpower the Saints.

Antichrist will desecrate the Temple with his abominable Idol Image to be worshipped.

The Jews will abandon, make desolate the Temple

The Jews will repent and accept Yeshua as LORD and savior.

The Antichrist will severely persecutes the Gentile Believers, and the Jews.

There will be great brutality towards women, pregnant women and nursing mothers.

There will be great anguish (distress) never seen before all over the world.

The breaking of the seven seals and the warning trumpet judgments will continue on earth.

[ref Matthew 24:29, Revelation 6:12-13, Revelation 12:7-9, Zechariah 12:10-14, Daniel 7:21, Revelation 13:7, Zechariah 14:2, Matthew 24:19]

Stage 2c: Great Miracles By False Prophet & Followers

The Antichrist and false prophet will reign on earth.

Many more false prophets will arise for Antichrist.

The false prophet will perform many great false miracles and wonders to deceive many people.

The elect will not be deceived.

There will be global idolatry and worship Of Antichrist.

There will be global adoption and use of the mark of the Beast (666).

There will be more severe persecution of Believers.

Believers will be refined through fire of tribulation.

[ref Matthew 24:23-28, Mark 13:21-23, Revelation 13:1-8, Revelation 13:11-17, Zechariah 13:8-9].

Stage 3:

Main Rapture Of Believers

There will occur the main harvest (or rapture) of believers from earth to heaven.

These are Believers who would have been refined through the great tribulations of the last 3 ½ years of the Antichrist.

The event will be a surprise.

They will be many, both gentiles and Jews together.

[ref Matthew 24:29-31, Mark 13:24-27, Matthew 24:36-44, Mark 13:32-37, Luke 21:34-36, Isaiah 26:19, 1 Thessalonians 4:15-17, 1 Corinthians 15:51-52, Revelation 7:9-16, Revelation 14:14-16].

Marriage Super In Heaven

Marriage supper of The Lamb in Heaven with the Saints. God and the angels will also be in attendance.

[ref Matthew 26:29, Revelation 19:5-9].

Stage 4:

Punishment Of Antichrist And Babylon The Great

God will unleash severe punishments and woes on Antichrist and his followers on earth.

God will also punish Babylon The Great, the great prostitute and has deceived the world with her fornication (of immorality and idolatry

The Great Babylon becomes a desolate place, inhabited by demons.

[ref Revelation 16:1-21, Revelation 17 & 18, Revelation 18:2].

Stage 5:

War Of Armageddon

The Second coming of The LORD to the Earth with His Angels and Saints.

There will be the war of Armageddon

The Antichrist and False Prophet will be captured and thrown into Lake of Fire.

The vast army of the Antichrist will be killed. They will resurrect later to face the judgment.

[ref Revelation 19:11-21, Zechariah 6:12-13].

The Millennium Reign of The LORD

Satan will be bound and thrown into Prison of Hell for 1000 years.

The LORD will build the Millennium Temple, where He, The Branch, reigns as King & Priest for 1000 years.

At that time, things on Earth will be like the time before Adam and Eve fell

There will benoo Sickness, war or death during the 1,000 years

[ref Zechariah 6:12-13, Revelation 20:1-3].

Stage 6:

Second Rebellion After The Millennium

The LORD will withdraw from the earth.

Satan will be released from prison for a period.

Satan's will embark on his Second Deception of the world.

Gog Magog will lead Satan's army of rebellion.

God will intervene to end the rebellion

[ref Revelation 20:7-9, Ezekiel 38:1-23].

Stage 7:

The Great White Throne Final Judgment

Satan will be judged and thrown into lake of fire.

There will be the Resurrection of All the unrighteous who had been dead.

Hell and Death will be Cast Into Lake of Fire

Anyone whose Name is Not found in Book Of Life will be sent into the lake of fire.

Names are continually added or deleted based on activities of each person. Backsliders names are removed when they backslide.

[ref Revelation 20:10-15]

Stage 8:

Fresh New Start

There will be a New Heaven, new Earth and new Jerusalem

God will finally establish His Kingdom on Earth.

God will live among His people on new earth.

[ref Revelation 21:1, Revelation21-22]

And to God Almighty,
The creator of all, the faithful Father,
Be all the glory, through Yeshua The Messiah,
In The Power Of The Holy Spirit,
(Amen).

About the Author

The writer is simply a messenger, not the author. He has no message of his own, being simply assigned to echo what God, the Speaker and true Author, is saying to this generation. He initiated nothing, receiving the visions, revelations, understanding, interpretation and direction as given him by God. He lives in the suburb of Houston, USA with his wife and children. Had also lived in Africa and Europe, and travelled to many countries in Asia, Central and South America, and the Middle East.

www.ingramcontent.com/pod-product-compliance
Lightning Source LLC
Chambersburg PA
CBHW071426070526
44578CB00001B/19